"Mike McManus has written one of the best researched and most lucid accounts of the plague of marriage breakdown in America to appear so far. He explodes the myth of 'trial marriages,' showing how live-in relationships before marriage make divorce more likely, rather than less. He also illustrates some remarkably successful programs of relationship restoration that have drastically cut down divorce rates in several churches and communities across the country."

David Aikman
Senior Correspondent
TIME magazine

Mike McManus is right to suggest that the church contributes to divorce by preparing people not for lifelong marriages but for weddings and does little afterward to hold couples together. What's encouraging is that *Marriage Savers* points to many ways in which some churches are pioneering with answers, such as training mentor couples to be "Marriage Savers." And Mike has planted "Community Marriage Policies" in a dozen cities, demonstrating that Catholic priests and pastors of mainline and evangelical Protestant churches can cooperate to slash divorce rates on a community-wide basis.

Gary Bauer
President, Family Research Council
Former White House Director of Domestic Policy

MARRIAGE SAVERS

MARRIAGE SAVERS

SAVERS

Helping Your Friends and Family
Stay Married

Michael J. McManus
Foreword by George Gallup, Jr.

ZondervanPublishingHouse
Grand Rapids, Michigan

A Division of HarperCollins*Publishers*

Marriage Savers
Helping Your Family and Friends Stay Married
Copyright © 1993 by Michael J. McManus

Requests for information should be addressed to:
Zondervan Publishing House
Grand Rapids, Michigan 49530

Library of Congress Cataloging-in-Publication Data

McManus, Michael J.
    Marriage savers : helping your family and friends stay married / Michael J. McManus.
    p. cm.
    ISBN 0-310-48241-0 (pbk.)
    ISBN 0-310-48240-2 (hardcover)
    1. Family—United States—Moral and ethical aspects. 2. Divorce—Religious aspects—Christianity. 3. Divorce—United States. 4. Marriage—Religious aspects—Christianity. 5. Marriage—United States. I. Title.
HQ734.M443   1993
646.7'8–dc20
                                                                                    92-39968
                                                                                         CIP

Edited by Mary McCormick
Cover design by Barfuss Creative Services
Cover illustration by Roger Timermanis

Page 283 is hereby made part of this copyright page.

Printed in the United States of America

93 94 95 96 97 98 / ❖ DH / 10 9 8 7 6 5 4 3 2 1

This edition is printed on acid-free paper and meets the American National Standards Institute Z39.48 standard.

For Harriet
With whom I've joyously shared twenty-seven years of marriage,
Who was the first to suggest, then urge that I write this book,
Who also was its first and last editor,
And the mother of three treasured sons,
Adam, John, and Timothy,
To whom this book is affectionately dedicated,
With the prayer that they also will
Create lifelong marriages.

Contents

Foreword   9

Acknowledgments   13

1. America's Churches: Part of America's Divorce Problem   15

2. The Splintered American Family   27

3. The Church: Missing in Action!   47

4. Helping Keep Your Teenager Chaste   59

5. Getting Serious—Help for the Seriously Dating Couple   85

6. A Crucial Need: Weigh Your Relationship's Strengths and Weaknesses   105

7. Marriage Prep—Help for the Engaged Couple   121

8. Newlyweds: The Honeymoon Is Over   145

9. Marriage Encounter: The Best Marriage Saver   171

10. Saving Troubled Marriages: Marriage Ministry, Retrouvaille, Solution-Oriented Therapy   197

11. No-Fault Divorce: The Need for Legal Reform   229

12. Community Marriage Policy: How to Cut Your Town's Divorce Rate   253

Appendix   279

Foreword

by George Gallup, Jr.

If a disease were to afflict the majority of a populace, spreading pain and dysfunction throughout all age groups, we would be frantically searching for reasons and solutions. Yet this particular scourge has become so endemic that it is virtually ignored.

The scourge is *divorce*, an oddly neglected topic in a nation that has the worst record of broken marriages in the entire world. Divorce is a "root problem" in our country and is the cause of any number of other social ills.

Mike McManus makes us take notice of the problem in *Marriage Savers*, a clearly-written book that promises to have a significant healing effect upon a society torn apart by disrupted and unhappy marriages. Mike bases his steps toward healing upon programs that have already proven effective, both in guiding people away from unworkable marriages and in saving threatened ones. In providing advice to the reader, Mike points to specific, proven strategies that he has reported upon in his nationally syndicated newspaper column, "Ethics & Religion."

Noting, on the one hand, that unrestrained American individualism is at the heart of many broken marriages, he states boldly and forthrightly that marriages should rest firmly on biblical principles. He reports that thousands of churches themselves have, lamentably, contributed to divorce. Though three-quarters of all marriages are blessed by America's churches, he charges that most have become "blessing machines" that fail to offer practical help so that engaged couples will bond together for life. Mike asserts that if America's churches were doing their job, America could slash its 60% marriage dissolution rate.

On the other hand, *Marriage Savers* puts a spotlight on marital pioneering by many churches that are models of saving marriages:

— To 80,000 engaged couples a year, churches administer a premarital test called PREPARE that can predict with 80% accuracy who will divorce.

—Some 1.5 million married couples have gone on a retreat called "Marriage Encounter" that prompts nine out of ten couples to fall back in love with each other!

—In one church seven couples, whose marriages were once on the rocks but have healed, have worked with thirty-three couples whose marriages seemed hopeless. In five years of this "Marriage Ministry" in Jacksonville's St. David's Episcopal Church, none of those couples have divorced.

The author calls for new and stronger laws—a reform of so-called no-fault divorce—to encourage couples to save their marriage rather than to bail out. Mike also urges cities and towns to follow the example of pastors in a dozen cities who have signed "Community Marriage Policies" in which they cooperate in offering the best-known programs to better prepare people for marriage as well as nurture and sustain existing marriages. In fact, Mike came up with the Community Marriage Policy idea and personally persuaded the clergy to sign the covenant in such diverse cities as Modesto, California; Fairbanks, Alaska; and Peoria, Illinois. Couples who want a church wedding in any of eighteen denominations in Peoria, for example, must take four months of marriage preparation, a premarital inventory like PREPARE, six counseling sessions (two of which are in the first year of marriage), meet with an older mentor couple with a solid marriage, and attend a retreat for engaged couples, such as Engaged Encounter. Why? As Peoria's pastors put it eloquently in their Community Marriage Policy:

> Our concern as ministers of the Gospel is to foster lasting marital unions under God and to establish successful spiritual families. Almost 75% of all marriages are performed by pastors, and we are troubled by the more than 50% divorce rate. Our hope is to radically reduce the divorce rate among those married in area churches.

> It is the responsibility of pastors to set minimal requirements to raise the quality of commitment in those we marry. We believe that couples who seriously participate in premarital testing and counseling will have a better understanding of what the marriage commitment involves. As agents of God, acting on his behalf, we feel it is our responsibility to encourage couples to set aside time for marriage preparation instead of concentrating only on wedding plans. We acknowledge that a wedding is but a day; a marriage is for a lifetime.

The priests, pastors, and rabbis of every community should consider signing a similar covenant. It should mean more to get married with God's blessing than by a Justice of the Peace. The Peoria *Journal Star* praised this initiative as a "bold and necessary step." In an editorial published October 16, 1991, the paper said:

Our best reason for supporting this policy is that we are committed to children. After endorsing an array of ideas in education, day care and environment, to name a few that address the legacy we want for our children, how could we not support something as fundamental as sound marriages and families?

The stakes are too high to continue to do nothing. Society pays dearly—for welfare, for schools, for nonproductivity—when half of its children are from broken homes. A severed engagement is far less crippling and much less costly than a broken marriage.

I might add that Peoria's Community Marriage Policy puts an equal emphasis on helping existing marriages make it. For example, the churches are urging *every* married couple to go on a Marriage Encounter or Marriage Enrichment weekend. They have also set a goal of creating a "Marriage Ministry" like that of St. David's in Jacksonville, in which mentor couples work with couples in the most troubled marriages to save them.

America's churches and synagogues have a central responsibility to help bond couples together for life, to help them live up to the vows promised in millions of wedding ceremonies: "to have and to hold from this day forward, for better or for worse, in sickness and in health, to love and to cherish until we are parted by death; as God is my witness, I give you my promise."

Acknowledgments

Although I have been a journalist for three decades, I have never attempted a book before. During the year I've struggled to write *Marriage Savers*, I have felt like I was under water, with seemingly endless chapters to write, rewrite, or edit. Writing my newspaper column will seem easy after this experience! This book is more than one person's vision and effort. I would never have even started *Marriage Savers* if it weren't for my wife, Harriet. She's given my life so much joy that I wanted to share something of what we have learned in twenty-seven years of marriage. Five years ago, Harriet was also the first to suggest that I write the book, and the regular encourager and prodder. She was the one who first convinced me, albeit slowly, that I had more to say about how to save marriages than I was able to put into "Ethics & Religion," my syndicated newspaper column. As I wrote chapter after chapter, Harriet read my copy and handed it back, often with helpful comments. I'd look at her suggestions for change and adopt almost all of them.

I am also particularly grateful to three people at Zondervan Publishing House—first to the man who caught the vision of this book and made a commitment to it: Lyn Cryderman, Senior Acquisitions Editor. It was Lyn who came up with the zippy book title, *Marriage Savers*. I also want to thank Scott Bolinder, Zondervan's publisher, whose advance for this book made it possible for me to turn my full attention to writing for the Lord. Interestingly, his brother, Reverend Garth Bolinder, was on the original committee of Modesto, California, pastors who drafted the nation's first "Community Marriage Policy" described in Chapter 12. Finally, I want to express my affection and respect for Mary McCormick, the working editor of *Marriage Savers* who took my original 500+ pages and pruned them to what you now see. She once said, "Are you aware that to produce one gallon of maple syrup—*forty gallons* of maple sap *must be boiled down*?" And she was always encouraging.

Finally, I want to thank the people who were kind enough to read early drafts of various chapters and pencil in hundreds of suggestions for improvements: my unmarried sons John and Tim, who constantly reprimanded me for writing for other fifty-year-olds, suggesting how to make the book more interesting for their younger generation; Ann and Bill Latimer, long-time friends and sharp-eyed editors; Susan Grigsby, whose life insights were as valuable as her editing; and various experts who are quoted in *Marriage Savers*: Dr. Jim A. Talley, one of America's foremost Marriage Savers, whose success with seriously dating couples is reported in Chapter 5 and who after hearing me propose it in a speech drafted America's first "Community Marriage Policy"; Dr. David Olson, creator of the PREPARE/ENRICH inventories that gave Harriet and me our first experience as a mentor couple with young couples; Dr. Larry Bumpass of the University of Wisconsin, whose *National Survey of Family and Households* provides a startling picture of America's dying marriages; George Gallup, Jr., who graciously encouraged me by offering to write a Preface for a book I had not started and generously made available polling data on the causes of marital breakup (cited in Chapter 7); and Stan Weed, President and CEO of The Institute for Research and Evaluation, which put a spotlight on the handful of sex education programs that actually slash teen pregnancy in half, as reported in Chapter 4.

I also want to thank the editors of more than 100 newspapers who publish my nationally syndicated column, "Ethics & Religion," which gave me the opportunity to research many of the examples of Marriage Savers reported in this book. I'm grateful to Fourth Presbyterian Church in Bethesda, Maryland, for giving Harriet and me the deeply rewarding opportunity to be a mentor couple with young couples in our church, reported in Chapters 5–8. Finally, I owe a deep debt of gratitude to some people who must remain nameless to protect their privacy but who shared their lives with searing honesty and complete trust that their often-painful stories might help others. Some were simply seriously dating, while others were engaged, recently married, or in a deeply troubled or strong marriage. Still others were victims of divorce—suffering the trauma of losing a mate, or innocent children who lost a parent. All were vulnerable, open, and candid and quite willing to read their chapters and correct my mistakes.

Of course, I take full responsibility for the accuracy of the data and the judgments made about why marriage in American is dying and what can be done to bring it to restored vitality.

And thank *you* for buying *Marriage Savers*. If you are married, I hope you find ideas for strengthening that marriage and are motivated to reach out and be a Marriage Saver with others. If you are unmarried, my prayer is the book will help you avoid a bad marriage and make a lifelong bond with whomever you do marry.

Michael J. McManus
November 7, 1992

ONE
America's Churches: Part of the Divorce Problem

What God has joined together, let man not separate.

—Matthew 19:6

This nation has the highest divorce rate in the world.

—National Commission on Children, 1991

Our marriage was under great stress by 1976. My work in Connecticut had ended, and I found myself commuting from Stamford, Connecticut, to a temporary job in Washington, D.C. I would get on the train at 2:00 A.M. on Monday and try to sleep as it lurched towards the nation's capital, pulling in at 8:30 A.M. I worked all week, staying at my in-laws' and came home Friday night, rolling into Stamford at about 10:30 P.M. Harriet put up with this for months. She'd have a lovely candlelight dinner awaiting me. I was too tired, however, to pay much attention. I buried myself in paperwork on Saturday, stumbled to church on Sunday, and then consumed the newspaper until I got back on the train again late that night. Another week's cycle of work and travel began. . . .

At a church we had just started attending, several people came up to me, saying, "Why don't you and Harriet go on a Marriage Encounter weekend?"

I asked, "What is it?"

They were rather mysterious about it. We heard few details, but any couple who had gone on such a retreat would say, "It is a great weekend—a good way to strengthen your marriage."

Somewhat miffed, I retorted, "I already *have* a good marriage."

"But Marriage Encounter is designed to make a good marriage better!" they would say. It seemed to me like a good idea, but when I mentioned it to Harriet, she was very cold: "I don't want to go."

"Why not?" I responded. "We need to take some time off together."

"We can't afford it," she said. She had a point.

So when another couple came up and suggested that we go to Marriage Encounter, I shook my head: "We can't afford it."

"—But your way is already paid for! People you have never met love you enough to have made it possible for you to go!" I was impressed. I told Harriet about it and said, "We hardly know any of these people, but they believe in this ministry and love us enough to pay our way to go! And someone has volunteered to take the kids!" Harriet had run out of excuses and nodded her assent.

On a Friday night we drove about seventy miles to a motel and arrived in time for dinner. Our first shock was that *every* couple at church who had urged us to go on Marriage Encounter was there. To beat us to the motel, they had taken off early from work so that they could decorate the place with balloons, fix the meal for two dozen couples, serve it, and go home! "We told you that we love you!" they said. We were overwhelmed!

After dinner we heard presentations by three married couples who were searingly honest about the most intimate problems of their marriages and how they tackled them. Their most important message was that "Emotions must be *ex*pressed—not *re*pressed. One's feelings are neither right nor wrong. They simply are. However, we can't expect our spouse to know those feelings unless we express them."

We were then given an assignment, the first of many over the weekend: to go back to our motel room for a "10-and-10" (ten minutes of writing a "love letter" to our spouse, and ten minutes of sharing privately). The first letter was easy—to describe what we liked most in our mate. Suddenly, I was enormously grateful that I had come. Harriet and I needed to spend time alone with one another, away from our children.

But the task became more challenging later in the weekend. In one "10-and-10" we were asked to share something that "I have wanted to share with you that I either couldn't or didn't share." I was shocked by Harriet's letter. She wrote that she felt "bruised" by my work in Washington. "You left me for a year and a half . . . quite voluntarily . . . I felt deserted."

In our conversation she shattered me by adding, "*This is no marriage!* I never see you during the week. You moved me to Connecticut where I did not know anyone. All week long I have only the children to talk to. You come home Friday night and I fix a nice dinner—but you fall asleep. Then you work all the time on the weekend and don't even have time for a swim with the boys. This is not why I married you! You are a workaholic. You love your career more than me and the children!"

I broke down and cried. I was so absorbed in the difficulty of my life that I had not realized its impact on Harriet! I asked her forgiveness and resolved to change my work. In the eleven years that we had been married, I thought that we communicated well. Neither of us had ever considered a divorce, but I learned at Marriage Encounter that Harriet had been holding this burning feeling within her.

That weekend we learned the absolute importance of taking time out *every day* for unstructured talk, Scripture reading, and prayer. We learned how to put Christ at the center of our relationship. For years now, we have been taking time in the morning over coffee—sometimes an hour a day. That keeps us open to one another and to the Lord. We would never have learned the importance of this step had not friends at church persuaded us to go. Though we could not afford it, at our Marriage Encounter we prepaid *two* other unknown couples' way, to grant them the blessing that others had given us.

In fact, 1.5 million couples have gone on Marriage Encounter. And in October 1991, pastors of churches of all major denominations in three Illinois cities—Moline, Peoria, and Quincy—signed a covenant that they will encourage "all married couples to attend a couples' retreat such as Marriage Encounter or Marriage Enrichment." (To learn more about Marriage Encounter and other retreats for married couples, read chapter 9.)

There are many ways to save marriages.

First, married readers can learn ways to strengthen their own marriage. That is an essential first step before you can help your friends, relatives, or loved ones avoid divorce. When the joy of your own life overflows, you can be persuasive with others. Why did our church acquaintances keep urging us to go to Marriage Encounter—until we went? Because their own marriages had been transformed, and they wanted us to discover the same joy. We did. We came away feeling as though we were on a second honeymoon. More important, that radiance has not faded. Why? We learned how *to renew and refresh our relationship daily*. Our joy has only grown richer with the passing years. That's one reason I wrote this book.

"MARRIAGE IS FOR A LIFETIME"

That's what parents used to tell their children. Now marriage is a gamble . . . a losing gamble. More than half of U.S. marriages fail. Six of ten new ones will end in divorce or separation, according to the *National Survey on Families and Households* by the University of Wisconsin.

Nevertheless, marriage can once again be for a lifetime.

That expectation can be restored. In fact, I think that it is possible for any church to nurture a congregation of *marriage savers*, couples with solid marriages who are trained to reach out and help engaged couples, newlyweds, and even those with deeply troubled marriages—discover the "joy that passes all understanding." A church that cultivates "marriage savers" can save nine out of ten marriages. What's more, almost all couples can find new happiness.

THE CHURCH IS PART OF AMERICA'S DIVORCE PROBLEM

How could there ever be such a monumental change? How can we ever assure ourselves, our loved ones, and friends that God has, indeed, "joined together" those of us who exchange marriage vows "until death us do part?"

How can millions of marriages heading for the divorce courts be saved?

First, we must see that *the church, itself, is part of America's divorce problem*. Ironically, the United States is the most religious of modern nations: Two-thirds of Americans are members of a church, and a surprisingly large 42% of the nation attended religious services in any week of 1991, according to the Gallup Poll.

What's more, three-fourths of all American marriages are blessed by pastors, priests, and rabbis of America's churches and synagogues.

Clearly, organized religion is involved in most marriages, but it is often simply a "blessing machine" that has no more impact on the couple getting married than does a Justice of the Peace. Too many churches have allowed their role to deteriorate to being little more than that of a "wedding factory" with a rented chapel, a hired pastor, and an organist.

Be that as it may, the church's very access to most American marriages is also a source of great hope. We all want to save marriages.

What if you, as a church member, had a clear vision about how your congregation could do a far more rigorous job to prepare couples for marriage? What if you could say, "In our church, only five or six percent of engaged couples ever get divorced, because we teach the fundamentals of 'divorce insurance' "? Wouldn't you feel better about urging your own son or daughter to attend your premarital classes? Or, if you are engaged and have heard about a church premarital program that lowers the odds of divorce, wouldn't you sign up—even if it required months of work? Probably, you'd advise engaged friends who don't even go to church—to check it out!

Equally important, what if your church offered a sure-fire way to strengthen existing marriages, such as a weekend retreat that almost guarantees that long-married couples will fall back in love? Honestly, wouldn't you and your spouse be the first to sign up? Who would not like to add more zest and joy—and yes, even better sex—to their own marriage?

Of course, we'd all like to be marriage savers, especially of our own!

In fact, a 1991 survey by America's family physicians reveals that two-thirds of couples with children, suffering from marital stress, "will talk separately with family and friends about their marital problems." People in trouble *seek out* advice from others.

Now think about friends' or loved ones' marriages that are in deep trouble. Even if you are lucky enough to have a solid, rewarding marriage, do you feel helpless when you see others heading for the divorce courts? Do you tell yourself, "Who can know the complexity of the problems between two people?" You remain silent, thinking it presumptuous to give such a couple suggestions on how to heal their relationship. And, to be honest, even if you had the courage to speak up, would you know what to say? The ways to save marriages are not obvious.

Yet there is hope, and believe it or not, that hope often comes from America's churches.

AS A COLUMNIST, I HAVE LOOKED FOR ANSWERS AND FOUND THEM

Over the past decade, as the writer of "Ethics & Religion," a nationally syndicated column published by 100 newspapers, I have come across many creative strategies to save marriages. I have reported dozens of them in my column. However, it is published in only about a tenth of the nation's newspapers. Therefore, I have longed to put these stories down in one book that can proclaim the good news that:

- *Bad marriages can be avoided before they begin.*
- *Almost all marriages can be improved.*
- *Even the most ailing marriages can be saved and restored to health.*

We all see marriages in trouble—if not our own, those of family or friends. And many of us see single people headed toward marriages that we fear will be disastrous. However, most people feel helpless, not knowing what to say or do that could save those marriages. Our churches have not given *us* divorce insurance—let alone equipped us to save other marriages.

Marriage Savers suggests answers. It will enable you as a spouse, a parent, or a friend to know how *you* can be a Marriage Saver.

Of course, the marriage you save may be your own. For example, if you feel bored, or ignored, or frustrated in your marriage, consider going on a "Marriage Encounter" weekend. The experience that Harriet and I had was not unique. Thirty academic studies, involving interviews of couples before they went and after they returned, conclude that 80% to 90% of those who make a Marriage Encounter weekend, fall back in love with their spouse—and at a much deeper level. (Read chapter 9.) If the problems in your marriage are much deeper and seemingly hopeless, take the stronger medicine suggested in chapter 10 of going on a "Retrouvaille" (Rediscovery) weekend. Half or more of those who attend are *already* separated, yet eight out of ten marriages are saved.

In fact, each chapter of *Marriage Savers* examines the best answers I have seen for a different age group or marital status. In addition to chapters 9 and 10, which suggest ways to strengthen existing marriages, I offer answers to questions like these:

— How can parents increase the odds that their teenagers will develop the discipline needed for a lifelong marriage? See chapter 4.

— What steps can seriously dating couples take to be sure they have made the right choice of a mate, and to improve their odds of avoiding divorce? See chapter 5.

— Half of newlyweds are horrified by the problems that arise after they say "I do." What can they do to straighten things out? See chapter 8 of *Marriage Savers*.

— How can the law be changed to make divorce more fair to the single parent and children who are often forced into poverty? See chapter 11.

— How can your community *as a whole* slash its divorce rate in half by putting all of the best-known strategies to work in all local churches? See chapter 12 of *Marriage Savers*.

At the heart of most of the answers suggested by *Marriage Savers* is a new kind of church that invests energy into bonding young couples into relationships that can go the distance—and a church that is determined to strengthen the marriage of every couple in its pews.

Certainly, the bishop who married Harriet and me had no such vision. He did not even talk about God, much less about our relationship with Him. In our one "premarital counseling" session of fifteen minutes, we only remember his asking us two questions. To Harriet, he said, "How are your parents?" A social chat followed; then he asked me: "What kind of work do you do?" It was not until a decade later at Marriage Encounter that we learned that God can be the strong third partner of our marriage.

INDIVIDUAL FREEDOM: THE ENEMY OF LIFELONG MARRIAGE

Today's marriages are built on a slippery slope of changing feelings and circumstances—not on a rock of *commitment*. Many easily find excuses to walk away from marriage vows, spouses, and children. According to polls by George Gallup, what sparked three-fifths of divorces was simply poor communication. What a shallow reason to abandon one's spouse!

We live in a fast-paced culture that honors only one constant value: individual freedom. For example, the so-called no-fault divorce laws that swept the nation in the 1970s stipulated that no grounds are needed to obtain a divorce; neither spouse has to prove fault or guilt; either the husband or wife can unilaterally get a divorce without the consent of the other spouse. Today, America is such a throw-away culture that hardly anyone criticizes a man or woman who discards a spouse or children.

Regrettably, the church has not stood up to such trends, which trash the biblical concept of marriage. Not even the Roman Catholic Church, which does not believe in divorce, testified against the first no-fault law passed in California in 1970! For a generation, religious leaders have been sleepwalking. At no national convention—whether Catholic, mainline Protestant, or evangelical—are marriage and divorce even discussed.

That's how the world's most religious nation finds itself destroying its families faster than does any other country.

Not only are most marriages failing, but fewer people are getting married at all. The percentage of men in their thirties who have *never* married has nearly tripled just since 1970! Why? Cohabitation has soared fivefold just since 1970. For millions, "living together" has replaced marriage.

Americans call it "doing your own thing." I call it *irresponsibility.*

WHO PAYS THE PRICE FOR PARENTAL SELFISHNESS? THEIR CHILDREN!

No one suffers more from parental selfishness than children do. A million kids a year have their lives shattered by the divorce of their parents. *Half* of them will not see the parent who leaves in the first year after divorce. And another million children a year are born to parents who are not married. That's two million innocent victims every year!

The tragic results are well-known. By age eighteen, six children out of ten will live in a single-parent family, and half of those absent parents are *not required* even to provide child support (according to the Census Bureau). Of those to whom payments are due, only half get full payment. Another quarter gives only partial support. Therefore, a third of kids with absent fathers live in poverty. Many do poorly in school, are vulnerable to substance abuse, get pregnant as teens, or make others pregnant. The dreary cycle is perpetuated.

And what has been the church's response?

Silence. Scandalous, sinful silence.

Have you *ever* heard a sermon on "living together?" Moreover, how many years has it been since you heard one on divorce—let alone one on marriage, or the love of husband and wife? We hear a lot about the love of Christ and how we are to love our neighbor, but pastors avoid sermons on how we are to love our spouse, or to prepare our children for a lifelong marriage.

Churches are ignoring their central pastoral duty: to bond people together in families so that they can withstand the swirling cyclones of a secular world that tear people up and scatter them across a landscape of broken marriages, long-forgotten vows, or the loneliness of broken relationships with never-made vows.

Yet couples still want to get married in church. Why? Because they want to learn how to put Christ at the center of their marriage so that it is built on a rock that will endure? Hardly. They want a "beautiful wedding." The church, however, has leverage to transform that wedding into a solid and

21

lasting marriage by teaching relationship skills that can greatly increase a couple's odds of success. Does it happen? Rarely.

IS YOUR CHURCH UNWITTINGLY DISINTEGRATING FAMILIES?

Most churches only help couples prepare for elaborate weddings, not for lasting marriages. Many couples go through something called "premarital counseling," which rarely is rigorous enough to result in broken engagements. Thus, most of America's churches are only "blessing machines" mouthing pious words at wedding after wedding: "I now pronounce you man/husband and wife."

Put the scenario on fast forward. Half of all newlyweds will divorce. Another tenth will permanently separate. That's a sickening 60% dissolution rate. *And organized religion is intimately involved.*

Its guilt is invisible. Its steeples are still lovely against the sky. Its stained windows sparkle. And its words still resonate within our souls: "Dearly beloved, we are gathered today. . . ." But the church is unwittingly a partner in the disintegration of the American family. Here are two snapshots of America's wedding factories:

- In 1960, when four-fifths of all first marriages were blessed by the church, there were only 393,000 divorces.
- In 1990, when three-quarters of all first marriages were *still* being blessed by the church, breakups tripled to 1,185,000 divorces.

Thus, divorces *tripled* despite the regular access of pastors to more than three-fourths of all marriages. Organized religion did not cause soaring divorce rates, but it was impotent and blind to its own complicity.

Yet there is hope. Paradoxically, that hope is growing out of what I call "marital pioneering" in scattered American churches.

For example, Catholics do a much better job of preparing engaged couples for marriage than does any other denomination. Couples are required to undergo six months of marriage preparation during which they meet with older, solidly married couples who volunteer their time as mentors. Wouldn't that make sense for engaged Protestant couples as well? Similarly, a Baptist pastor who has designed a course called "Reconciliation Instruction" for separated or divorced couples, has had the joy of remarrying ten couples who had been apart for five or six years! Why don't Catholic and Methodist churches plant his approach in their congregations?

Let me illustrate two strategies that *Marriage Savers* covers in detail, in which *you* can save marriages:

1. Couples Who Live Together Can Expect Failure.

First, are you living with someone? Or do you have an unmarried friend or a child living with someone of the opposite sex? That's quite possible—millions of couples are cohabiting. Have you had a premonition that tragedy lies ahead for that person, yet you fear to say what is on your heart?

Your premonition was valid!

A 1985 Columbia University study cited in *New Woman* magazine found that "only 26% of women surveyed and a scant 19% of the men—married the person with whom they were cohabiting." The more comprehensive *National Survey of Families and Households,* based on interviews with 13,000 people, concluded, "About 40% of cohabiting unions in the U.S. break up without the couple getting married. . . . And marriages that are preceded by living together have 50% higher disruption (divorce or separation) rates than marriages without premarital cohabitation"!

So instead of a 50% divorce rate for cohabiting couples, it is 75%.

Let's simplify those numbers, using the more conservative *National Survey* data. Of one hundred couples who begin living together, forty will break up before marriage. And of the sixty who marry, at least forty-five will divorce. That leaves only fifteen intact marriages out of the original one hundred couples! Conventional wisdom is that, "It's better to try on the shoe before you wear it," but you now have the data to prove that this does not work when applied to marriage. You have *secular* evidence that St. Paul was right when he wrote to the Corinthians, "Flee from sexual immorality" (v. 6:18 KJV).

You don't have to be tongue-tied when you see your friend. Tell him or her these statistics to prove that almost certain disaster lies ahead—either a broken relationship now or a broken marriage later. The odds are 4 to 1 *against* any cohabitation evolving into a lasting marriage.

If you reach out with that data, you could be a Marriage Saver. It is like telling a teenager who is smoking, "Have you heard that people who smoke —die— eighteen years earlier than nonsmokers?" It is embarrassing, of course, to speak up, but it's *life insurance* to the teen.

2. A Test That Predicts Who Will Divorce

A second form of divorce insurance is to help equip the engaged for life-long marriage. Are you considering marrying someone? Or do you have a child or a friend who is engaged? Would you like to give the engaged a gift that will either strengthen the relationship—or help you or them discover that they have chosen the wrong person to marry?

There is such a "gift" that I will give to my three sons, who are now in their twenties—when they are engaged. I will pay the twenty-five dollar cost of a premarital inventory that exposes relationship strengths and weak-nesses. PREPARE's 125 questions almost give a pastor, counselor, or mentor couple an X-ray of any engaged couple's relationship. The areas of health or of needed growth are revealed by how the man and woman react to 125 state-ments like these:

- "Time will resolve most of the problems that we have as a couple."
- "There are times when I am bothered by my partner's jealousy."
- "When we are having a problem, my partner often gives me the silent treatment."

Since 1978, 500,000 couples have taken PREPARE, had their answers compared by computer, and discussed the results with their pastor or coun-selor. This "premarital instrument" has an astonishing track record: Three studies show that PREPARE can predict with more than *86% accuracy* which couples will ultimately divorce! When I mentioned those results of the PREPARE test to a small group of engaged couples that my wife and I are mentoring at church, four couples *wanted* to take the test. And why not? With a 60% marriage-failure rate, any couple would be foolish to avoid the oppor-tunity that PREPARE offers. A couple who discovers that their scores indicate that they have only one chance in five of success has received a stern fore-warning. A wise couple would work very hard to resolve conflicts that PREPARE dredges up. If that fails, the wedding should be postponed, or the engagement broken altogether. Actually, a tenth of those who take PREPARE *do* break their engagements.

Surely, a broken engagement is better than a broken marriage! (To learn more, read chapter 6.)

A CHURCH STRATEGY FOR LONG-TERM MARRIAGES

Even if you are not married, you can help *save* marriages.

One key arena for action is your church. Is your church a "blessing machine" that grinds out weddings with no attempt to keep track of how many of them end up in the divorce courts? Or is your congregation a place where young people learn skills and attitudes to build a lifelong marriage?

Really, this is not something that can be learned well in the few weeks before a wedding. Ideally, it begins with teenagers. Some questions come to mind:

1. Does your church teach them *why* sexual abstinence makes sense—and *how* to achieve it? If not, why not? Discipline learned as a teenager makes it easier for that person as an adult to be faithful in marriage. True, teens are sexually active at earlier and earlier ages with more and more partners, and there are a million teenage pregnancies, but as only half of teens are sexually active, and as chapter 4 makes clear, this trend can be reversed. There are even two public school curricula that slash in half the percentage of sexually-

active kids! Surely your church could do a better job than a public school, which can't cite Scripture. There is a superb videotape series called "Why Wait?" that *60,000 churches* have already found to be very effective.

2. What does your congregation do to help seriously dating couples to learn how to put Christ at the center of their relationships? What is your church doing to counter conventional wisdom about living together? There is a course that your church could offer to seriously dating couples that can cut the divorce rate of those who marry to less than five percent!

It is called "Relationship Instruction" (See chapter 5 of *Marriage Savers*.)

3. What does your church do with engaged couples? Does it offer the PREPARE test that can predict with 86% accuracy who will divorce? Does it urge couples to attend "Engaged Encounter," which is patterned on "Marriage Encounter" and is so successful that a tenth of the participants decide *not* to get married? Most Catholic churches now require six months of marriage preparation and have trained older couples with solid marriages to be counselors. Does your church have a minimum preparation period, or can one get married in a month? Do the engaged work with older married couples (like Harriet and me) as mentors? What is the divorce rate of those married in your church? *Hard questions need to be asked and answered if your church's marriages are to last.*

STRENGTHENING EXISTING MARRIAGES

What does your church do with newlyweds? Does it require counseling sessions *after* the wedding? That step is very rare today, alas. My church has a Bible study for "newly marrieds" so that they can learn not only Scripture that is related to marriage but also meet other couples trying to keep God as a third partner of their marriage. My congregation also has a similar class for "mid-marrieds"—those married five to thirty years. Does yours?

How does your church handle deeply troubled marriages? Do you have any options besides counseling?

CAN EVERY MARRIAGE BE SAVED? NO—BUT 90% CAN BE!

Am I saying that every marriage can be saved? No. Where there is repeated physical abuse, incest, or other forms of heinous behavior, divorce may be the best answer, but according to the Gallup Poll, such cases can be found in only about a tenth of today's marriages.

I am convinced that *most marriages can be saved*. Your church may be able to push its divorce rate down to 10%—a tiny fraction of the 60% marriage dissolution rate. Some churches claim an even lower rate.

Also there's secular evidence of hope for marriage, seen in *TIME* magazine's February 19, 1990, headline: "America's New Fad: Fidelity." A poll by Gallup for *Psychology Today* found that 90% of married men and women say that they have never had an affair, 60% describe their marriage as very happy, and two-thirds are still married to their first spouse! "The sexual revolution is overrated." That's grounds for long-term hope.

What's more, I think any community could slash its divorce rate in half within a decade if its churches cooperated in a conscious plan to save marriages. The divorce rate of Europe is about half that of the United States, yet average church attendance in Great Britain, Germany, France, or Scandinavia is only 10% or less. That's only a fraction of the 42% of Americans attending church services in any week of 1991, says George Gallup, Jr. Surely, if our churches really concentrated on saving marriages, any community could achieve Europe's low marital-breakup rate.

The fact is that nearly a dozen cities have adopted a "Community Marriage Policy," signed by pastors from every major denomination. The first was in Modesto, California, in January 1986, when ninety-five pastors signed a covenant to require four months of marriage preparation for anyone getting married in an area church; a minimum number of counseling sessions, some of which are conducted by mature mentor couples; the taking of a premarital test; and encouragement for the couple to attend an engagement seminar. Why?

What the Peoria pastors said in their Community Marriage Policy bears repeating: "Our hope is to radically reduce the divorce rate in area churches. . . . We believe that couples who seriously participate in premarital testing and counseling will have a better understanding of what the marriage commitment involves. As agents of God, acting on his behalf, we feel that it is our responsibility to encourage couples to set aside time for marriage preparation instead of concentrating only on wedding plans. We acknowledge that a wedding is but a day; a marriage is for a lifetime."

For a generation, America has operated on the opposite assumption—that most divorces are understandable, necessary, and even beneficial. Few children of divorced parents would agree. In any case, my thesis is not only that most marriages can be saved, but that *you* can save them.

First, however, you need to know more about why America's families are splintering and what the *consequences* are. For too long, the issue has been seen as a private matter. Chapter 2 shows that the destruction of the American family is having a calamitous impact on society as a whole.

TWO
The Splintered American Family

There is a way that seems right to a man, but in the end it leads to death.

—Proverbs 14:12

The American family is splintering.

The breakup of the family is the central domestic problem of our time, yet the issue has hardly been recognized. We are living through a massive, galloping tragedy that our country has not fully grasped, the scale of which almost defies comprehension.

1. *Six out of ten new marriages are failing.* Divorces have tripled since 1960. And before they are eighteen, three-fifths of children will see their parents divorce.
2. *Cohabitation has soared sixfold since 1970.* The *majority* of all marriages in America are preceded by cohabitation. And those who cohabit before marriage increase their odds of divorce by 50%.
3. *Fewer young people are getting married at all.* In 1991 there were 41 million adults who had never married—twice the number in 1970 (21 million). The percentage of men aged 30–34 who have never married has *tripled* from 9% to 25%.
4. *Only 55% of adults are married today—the lowest figure ever.*
5. *Who gets hurt the most? The innocent—the children.*

Each year a million kids are born to unmarried parents. Another million annually see their parents divorce. Some 15.8 million children, nearly triple the number in 1960, are now living with a single parent. In fact, the *majority* of American kids in the 1990s will *not* live with their natural father and mother until age eighteen. Growing up in a broken home with a single parent—or no parent—is sadly the majority U. S. experience!

Compared to an American child, a Japanese child is *four times* more likely to be reared by both parents, according to the U.S. Census Bureau. The stability of Japanese families and the chaos of American families is a major reason that Japanese students are so much more successful in school than are American children—and a major reason for the success of the Japanese economy. *People with stable family lives will be more successful.*

Actually, although *only 38.6%* of children are in single-parent homes as a result of divorce, according to the Census Bureau report, "Marital Status and Living Arrangements: March 1990," nearly as many (30%) live with 4.8 million *never* married parents!

Since 1972, about twenty-three million kids have lost a parent to divorce. And out-of-wedlock births shot up from 224,000 in 1960 to one million in 1990—a fourfold growth of illegitimacy. Who are the other single parents? A staggering number—1.9 million parents are still married but separated from the absent parent.

A century ago, only 7% of Americans got divorced. The divorce rate has increased steadily ever since—though there have been plateaus followed by spurts of marital breakdown. As recently as 1960, there were only 393,000 divorces. By 1980, only twenty years later, the figure *tripled* to 1,189,000 divorces. That figure has held remarkably constant through 1991 when there were 1,187,000 divorces. Since the population has increased, the current plateau has made the divorce rate edge down slightly.

The number of marriages from that same 1960–1991 period did increase modestly from 1,523,000 to 2,371,000. But most of those added marriages are remarriages. As one pastor put it, "Most divorces end in marriage!" More than three-fourths, in fact, remarry. Nearly half of today's weddings (45%) involve one or more divorced people.

It is often said that half the marriages end in divorce. However, this figure does not include separations that dissolved 2.9 million marriages.

For this reason, the *National Survey of Families and Households* measures a "a marital dissolution rate," which includes both divorce and separation. By that measure, *60% of new marriages are failing*, according to the Survey's director, Professor Larry Bumpass of the University of Wisconsin. The Survey's conclusions are based on 100-minute interviews with 13,000 people—more than ten times the number normally interviewed by the Gallup Poll. Therefore, its findings are very credible.

"The exact level of marital instability is less important than the simple fact that *it is a majority experience among both children and adults*," writes Bumpass. "Marriage has become a most uncertain lifetime guarantee for either parental stability for children or economic security for women and children."

Do those who enter a second marriage "live happily ever after?" Their odds are no better than first marriages. "Second marriages are just as likely to fail as first marriages," says Barbara Foley Wilson, a senior demographer with the National Center for Health Statistics. And second marriages that break apart do so more quickly—about six years for a second divorce, after an initial median marriage of eight years.

About 40% of children will see their parents divorce by age eight, and half will see a second pair of parents divorce by age eighteen!

Undoubtedly, there are lessons to be learned from the experience of a bad marriage about how to make a marriage work, but those lessons are *not* being learned. *Experience alone is not an adequate teacher.*

IMPACT OF DIVORCE ON ADULTS

These statistics seem so dry and bloodless. What does it mean to see one's dreams as a bride or groom shatter? I think of a family friend whom I'll call Joan, now age 51, who is still grieving over her marriage that broke apart eight years ago. Unlike 85% of women who divorce, she receives alimony as well as child support. Financially, her situation is much better than most.

Yet she told me, "Divorce is like suffering death without a funeral. The pain never ends. It is a living death, and our society does not let us grieve. A normal death with a funeral is acceptable. But there is something wrong if one is divorced. You are tainted. Somebody is at fault.

"I know of twins, one of whom was widowed, and the other was divorced about the same time. The widow mourned with her friends who cried with her, brought her dinner, and fixed her up with dates. My friend who was divorced was a pariah. Nobody brought her food. Her friends took sides rather than understand that both people are in pain."

Joan's experience is typical. How do we know? Dr. Judith Wallerstein interviewed sixty families when they were getting divorced—both parents and children. She reinterviewed them five years later, and again, *ten years* after the divorce. In fact, she saw many of them *fifteen years* later! This is an unprecedented longitudinal study. She published the results in a book that I recommend to anyone who has experienced divorce: *Second Chances: Men, Women, and Children a Decade After Divorce.*[1] Written with Sandra Blakeslee, the book is also must reading for anyone who is considering divorce. As the authors put it, "Few adults anticipate accurately what lies ahead when they decide to divorce. Life is almost always more arduous and more complicated than they expect. It is often more depleting and more lonely for at least one member of the marriage."

However, when Dr. Wallerstein began her research in 1971, she assumed (as did most social scientists and lay people) that "divorce was a brief crisis that would soon resolve itself" in the lives it touched. Like many, she saw divorce as a "second chance" to build a new life and find a new mate. But five years after the divorce, she was shocked to find most families "were still in turmoil. Their wounds were wide open. . . . Many adults still felt angry, humiliated, and rejected and most had not gotten their lives back

---

[1]Judith Wallerstein and Sandra Blakeslee, *Second Chances: Men, Women, and Children a Decade After Divorce.* Ticknor & Fields, New York, 1989.

together. An unexpectedly large number of children were on a downward course. Their symptoms were worse than before. Their behavior at school was worse. Their peer relationships were worse," she writes.

Second Chances is a secular book, but as I read it, I kept thinking of Proverbs 14:12: "There is a way that seems right to a man, but in the end it leads to death." Divorce seems right to many couples. But Joan described her divorce as "death without a funeral." Paul wrote to the Corinthians, "A wife must not separate from her husband. . . . And a husband must not divorce his wife." That's the rule. If one violates it, a price must be paid. Sadly, however, the greater pain is often suffered by the one who wanted to maintain the marriage, not the one who departs. But many times, all suffer, especially children. *Second Chances* spotlights the pain:

1. "In two-thirds of the former couples, one person is much happier after divorce . . . relatively free from anxiety and depression . . . The other partners in these couples have not succeeded in improving the overall quality of life ten years after divorce. They feel unhappy much of the time, often suffer from loneliness, anxiety, or depression, and may be preoccupied with financial concerns as a regular pattern of daily life.

2. "In only 10% of couples do *both* husband and wife reconstruct happier, fuller lives by the decade mark. For the remaining quarter, neither the man nor the woman is better off.

3. "Many hope for a better life within a happy second marriage. Here, too, the odds are less favorable. Most of the time, only one of the former partners found a stable second marriage, while the other tried and failed or never remarried.

4. "Nearly one-third of the children were party to intense bitterness between the parents. True, some couples were no longer standing in the same kitchen screaming at one another; they were on the telephone instead. Or they fought face-to-face while dropping off or picking up children. *The illusion we had held—that divorce brings an end to marital conflict—was shattered.*" (Emphasis added.)

THE IMPACT OF DIVORCE ON HEALTH

Divorce has become so commonplace in the United States that many assume that its pain and consequences are limited to anguish.

Not so, says Dr. David Larson, a research psychiatrist for a dozen years with the federal government and now research director of the National Institute of Healthcare Research. "In light of current research, the Surgeon General might consider warning married couples about the potential health and behavioral risks of divorce," he wrote in an article, "Divorce: A Hazard to Your Health?" in *Physician* magazine, coauthored with his wife, Susan.

"Research studies show that divorce and the process of marital breakup puts people at much higher risk for both psychiatric and physical disease—even cancer . . . Being divorced and a nonsmoker is only slightly less dangerous than smoking a pack or more of cigarettes a day and staying married. Every type of terminal cancer strikes divorced individuals of either sex, both white and non-white, more frequently than it does married people," the Larsons write.

They cite the research of J. J. Lynch, author of *The Broken Heart: the Medical Consequences of Loneliness,* which reveals that divorced men are twice as likely to die from heart disease, stroke, hypertension, and cancer as married men in any given year! And death for the divorced is four times more likely via auto accidents and suicide; seven times higher by cirrhosis of the liver and pneumonia; eightfold greater by murder, and psychiatric illness is ten times more likely!

Similarly, the Larsons cite a study of 20,000 white women between the ages of eighteen and fifty-five, which found that married women are far less prone to physical illness than are single women who suffer more chronic conditions and spent more days in bed than did married women. For example, divorced women's odds of dying in a given year from cancer of the mouth, digestive organs, lungs, and breast, in a given year are two to three times that of married women.

Therefore, the Larsons utterly reject the idea that divorce is an *answer* to marital problems. A book they coauthored for medical students puts it plainly: "It is wiser to improve a marriage rather than dissolve it, and physicians should encourage marital therapy for troubled marriages. In a five-year longitudinal study by Cookerly (1980), more than 50% of couples who had experienced conflict and obtained marital therapy were still married after five years."

CHILDREN OF DIVORCE

What happens to children of divorce?

It was not long ago that marriages held together "for the sake of the children." No longer. Seventy percent of all households in 1960 were made up of married couples. By 1990 the proportion had slid down to 55%. Nearly ten million children, as a result of divorce or separation, live in a single-parent family. Every year since 1972 a million children a year have seen their parents divorce. Nearly as many see their parents separate.

Even though three-fourths of divorced people will remarry, that is no guarantee of stability for kids. Why? Half of children who have seen one parent leave them will "experience a *second* divorce before they leave high school," says Commissioner Wade Horn of the Administration of Children, Youth and Families of the U.S. Department of Health and Human Services.

And even when there is no second divorce, there is almost always intense friction between children and a stepparent.

Finally, despite all the remarriages, a child is four times as likely to be living with a divorced single parent in the '90s as in 1960.

One impact of divorce on kids is economic. "Children whose father would leave saw their mean monthly family income fall from $2,435 four months before he left to $1,543 four months after he left—a 37% drop," according to a March 1991 Census study of the period from 1983 to 1986. And these figures *include* child support. However only 44% of the families with children in this Survey of Income and Program Participation received *any* child support. This result is slightly different from that reported above because it focuses on children of divorce or separation—excluding children of never-married parents. Nevertheless, its results are quite similar: Most children of divorce (like most children of never-married parents) get *no* financial support from the absent parent.

Paradoxically, one effect of mothers and children suffering from a decline in their standard of living is that the departing fathers typically see a ten to fifteen percent increase in *their* standard of living after a divorce, according to the Panel Study of Income Dynamics at the University of Michigan's Survey Research Center. Since they aren't supporting their families as they once did, the dads have more money to spend on themselves.

EMOTIONAL AND BEHAVIORAL IMPACT OF DIVORCE

The impact of divorce on children is far more fundamental than economic. Karl Zinsmeister summarized a widely held thesis of the experts in an article for *The American Enterprise* in March/April 1990:

> There is a mountain of scientific evidence showing that when families disintegrate, children often end up with intellectual, physical, and emotional scars that persist for life. . . . We talk about the drug crisis, the education crisis, and the problems of teen pregnancy and juvenile crime. But all of these ills trace back predominantly to one source—broken families.

What compounds the difficulty that children of divorce have in bonding to someone of the opposite sex in adulthood is that divorce robs children of *both* parents, says Seattle psychotherapist Diane Zerbe. "Both parents are so devastated by it that their parenting abilities are interfered with. So that really the kids are struggling not just with the divorce but with the fact they've lost both parents' emotional availability."

Another point of view on this issue comes from Ann Latimer, a mother of three boys and three girls ranging in age from eleven to thirty, who, with her husband, Bill, has counseled engaged couples. After reading a draft of this chapter, she wrote me as a mother with years of experience. Says Mrs. Latimer:

The child is a composite, a whole created by the coming together of his two parts, his parents. He is a whole distinct being only by virtue of being one part his father and one part his mother. It takes time, though, for the halves to fuse, to grow to *be* a whole, a little in the way the parts of a grafted tree will fuse and become one strong, mature tree.

If one parent, one-half the child's self, is prematurely lost to divorce, before the two immature parts become a mature whole, it is as if the growing child himself is *ripped apart*, violently torn in two. An injured tree will usually live but will grow scars, as will a child. This tree may grow sickly, more susceptible to pollutants, disease, further injury, and so may the child. If the tree matures, it will likely in some way be deformed; it will certainly be changed—never be the same tree it was created to be. And so the child.

HOW DIVORCE AFFECTED SCOTT AND DIANA

Scott is the nineteen-year-old son of Joan, quoted earlier, who is still grieving over her divorce. He remembers that when he was in the sixth grade, his father moved into the basement. He heard his dad using the phone to court a colleague at work, a female attorney, as if the father were eighteen. Up until that time, Scott had good grades. Then he recalls, "I stopped trying. I stopped doing my work. My mother said, 'You are angry with your father. That's why you are doing badly in school.'" She sent him to a psychologist. Scott disagrees: "I don't see it as a direct—divorce equals bad grades. I've plenty of friends whose parents got divorced, who got good grades." However, Scott continued to do poorly through high school and barely graduated two years late, though he was sent to a private boarding school that gave him very individualized instruction.

Now he hangs out at his mother's house or his father's, or New York, and is not working *or* going to college, which he is bright enough to handle. He did yard work for a while but quit. He worked as an apprentice to a guitar maker but quit. He currently lacks both the drive and discipline to succeed. Why? As often happens in more affluent divorced homes, the guilty father lavishes his children with fat allowances, clothes, car, and makes no demands of them. Why work if you get money without working? The pattern is absolutely destructive.

Scott's hell has been kept alive by his father's continuing affair with his paramour of a decade ago, who now lives with him, unmarried. Dad takes the woman and his children on vacations together! "That's a downer," says Scott. "You want to go out to dinner with him, not him and his girlfriend. She is a b---- who feels very threatened by my sister and me. We compete for his time against her."

His older sister, Diana, 22, has been negatively impacted too. She used to pick up the phone, when her father lived in the basement, and hear his "secret conversations" with the girlfriend. Her mother confided in Diana, from an early age, which was quite a burden on her. Diana has now cohabited with two somewhat older men while attending college far from home. Each affair lasted about a year. This is a common reaction for a daughter of divorce—a desperate search for love, an inability to form permanent relationships with men, and cohabitation as an alternative.

"HE HAD TO LEAVE FOR A WHILE"

Phil was not destroyed by his parents' divorce as was Scott. He graduated from college in 1992 with a nearly straight-A (3.7) average and was president of his fraternity. Even so, the divorce was shattering.

"I remember spending a lot of time with him," Phil recalls. "My friends were jealous because we spent so much time together. He took me and my friends to Yankee and Met games. I was in soccer, hockey, and tennis—three different sports that he encouraged. We had a real good relationship. But one day, my dad said that he had to leave for a while and go to Europe. I did not question it, since he ran an airline office. He never gave me a reason why he left." His mother later told Phil that his dad felt "trapped. He got tired of marriage and wanted out."

"It was very painful. A lot of nights my mom, sister, and I cried a lot . . . Some years later, I talked to him about it. He began crying and said, 'I made a big mistake.' But he remarried four years ago."

One deeply negative impact was financial. Phil's father provided $600 a month child support until Phil turned eighteen and went off to college. Phil got *no* help from his father to go to college. Indeed, his $300 share of child support stopped. Phil's mother sold her Long Island house to help finance his college education and moved to a townhouse in Virginia. He joined the ROTC to help, not because he wants a military career. Now he is a military officer who is helping his younger sister go to college.

Phil has had to shoulder the responsibility of a parent. But this sacrifice was unnecessary. As his father says, "I made a big mistake."

THE DEVASTATING LOSS OF FAMILY STRUCTURE

How typical are the stories of Phil and Scott, two young men that I happen to know? Quite commonplace, I'd judge from reading Judith Wallerstein's book, *Second Chances*. She gives evidence that divorce "is almost always more devastating for children than for parents . . . Conditions in the post-divorce family were more stressful and less supportive to the child that the conditions in a failing marriage . . . Half saw their mother or father get a second divorce in the ten-year period after the first divorce. Half grew up in families that stayed angry at each other."

I urge any children of divorce to read *Second Chances* to gain an understanding of the divorce's impact on their lives. Some added excerpts:

1. "Divorce is a different experience for children and adults because the children lose something that is fundamental to their development—the family structure. The family comprises the scaffolding upon which, children mount successive development stages, from infancy into adolescence. It supports their psychological, physical, and emotional ascent into maturity. When that structure collapses, the children's world is temporarily without support . . .

2. "Children of all ages feel intensely rejected when their parents divorce. When one parent leaves the other, the children interpret the act as including them. 'He left Mom. He doesn't care about me.'

3. "Children get angry at their parents for violating the unwritten rules of parenthood—parents are supposed to make sacrifices for children, not the other way around . . . They were also intensely angry at their parents for giving priority to adult needs rather than to their needs. Few children were truly sympathetic or really understood why their parents divorced even when their parents thought it obvious.

4. "I was surprised to discover that the severity of a child's reaction at the time of the parents' divorce does not predict how that child will fare five, ten, and even fifteen years later . . . Girls seem to fare much better psychologically immediately after divorce than boys. [But a] 'sleeper effect' in females surfaced of 'troubles they are experiencing now at entry into young adulthood [which] came as a complete surprise. Girls who have never been betrayed or abandoned by a lover fear betrayal and abandonment . . . Many find maladaptive ways to cope. Some take many lovers at one time. Others seek out older men who are less likely to betray a younger woman.

5. "Ten years after divorce, close to one-half of the boys who are now between the ages of nineteen and twenty-nine, are unhappy and lonely and have had few, if any, lasting relationships with young women . . . One out of three young men and one in ten of young women between ages 19 and 23 at the ten-year mark are delinquent, meaning they act out their anger in a range of illegal activities including assault, burglary, arson, drug dealing, theft, drunk driving, and prostitution."[2]

COHABITATION: ANOTHER SPLINTER OF THE FAMILY

The most rapidly growing splinter of the American family is cohabitation among unmarried couples. According to the Census Bureau's "Current Population Survey," there were only 523,000 couples living together as recently as 1970. Within a decade, by 1980, that figure had *tripled* to 1,589,000

---

[2]*Second Chances*, op. cit., excerpts taken from pp. 10–70.

couples. And the number redoubled over the following eleven years to three million cohabiting couples in 1991.

The *National Survey of Families and Households* conducted by the University of Wisconsin, estimates that at any given moment, a sixth of never-married couples plus a third of divorced or separated people under age thirty-five, are cohabiting, according to *Survey* directors, Larry Bumpass and James Sweet.

And these estimates understate the pervasiveness of the pattern. They give only a snapshot, based on interview samples at a moment of time, of cohabiting couples. Census data does not suggest how many currently married couples might have shared the same household before their wedding, or how many presently single people might have lived in "trial marriages."

Fortunately, the *National Survey of Families and Households* probed for answers in its interviews of 6,881 married couples and 682 cohabitants (an oversample of that group). "The proportion of first marriages that were preceded by cohabitation, increased from 8% in the late 1960s to 49% among those in 1985–1986," said Bumpass.

That's the same sixfold growth in a generation identified by Census.

In fact, "more than half of recent marriages were preceded by cohabitation," said Bumpass in his 1990 presidential speech to the Population Association of America. The numbers are even higher when a *re-marriage* is involved (with one or both parties who have been divorced): "Two-thirds of recent remarriages were preceded by cohabitation."

This is a profound change. What was morally reprehensible for centuries until as recently as 1970—is now the norm. Being unmarried is no longer synonymous with being single, due to cohabitation. This widespread pattern of living together is thus redefining what it means when a man and woman decide to create a union. No longer is marriage the time when most men and women undertake one of life's major transitions from being single to being a couple, with a shared household, sexual intimacy, and children.

What's behind this trend? Bumpass points to two factors: "The first is the erosion of normative expectations." That's a $100 phrase for an erosion of moral standards. The sexual revolution weakened support for chastity before marriage and increased an acceptance of what used to called "shacking up." Only a sixth of young adults "explicitly disapproved of cohabitation under any circumstances," Bumpass notes.

The *National Survey* points to another factor—the belief by 51% of male cohabitors and 56% of female cohabitors that living together helps couples to "be sure they are compatible before marriage. As the fragility of marital relationships is increasingly recognized, couples may sense a need to 'try out' marriage by living together before making a long-term commitment," said Bumpass. In 90% of cohabitations, at least one partner wants to marry. Wallerstein also found that many children of divorce, in order to avoid the mistakes of their parents, want to "live with the person they love before getting married."

CONSEQUENCES OF WIDESPREAD COHABITATION

What are the consequences of widespread cohabitation?

They are largely negative. This is not surprising, since cohabitation begins with a minimal commitment of the man and woman to each other. The result is greater unhappiness—more conflict and even violence, more illness, a new phenomenon called "premarital divorce," and a much higher divorce rate among those who do get married. The data is overwhelming:

About 40% of cohabitations break up with no marriage, according to the *National Survey.* Average duration: 1.3 years. After a year of living together *as if* they are husband and wife, separating can be as painful as divorce—especially for the woman. They suffer from what James Sweet calls "premarital divorce." Further, millions of people are going through one affair after another—without finding a marriage partner. This is a major reason that the number of men aged 35–39 who have never married has soared *fivefold* from 557,000 in 1970 to 2.86 million in 1991. Similarly, there were only 713,000 unmarried women in their late thirties who had never married in 1970—but a big 2.6 million in 1991.[3] Bumpass and Sweet estimate that half of the decline in marriage rates is due to cohabitation.

Cohabitation is thus *a cancer eating away at the front end of the institution of marriage.*

It is also *a cancer eating away at the center of marriage in America.* "Marriages that are preceded by living together *have 50% higher disruption rates,* than marriages without premarital cohabitation," according to the *National Survey of Families and Households.* Thus, the couples who think that cohabitation is a trial of marriage are profoundly mistaken. It is a training for divorce!

Soaring cohabitation and divorce rates have slashed the percentage of American adults who are living as married couples down to 55%. That's the lowest figure in history, down from 64% a generation ago.

It is not surprising that conventional wisdom on cohabitation is wrong. "All a man's ways seem right to him" (Proverbs 21:2). But where has the church been on this issue?

Invisible. Unheard. Silent.

In 1992, I asked dozens of editors of Southern Baptist newspapers a simple question: "Have you ever heard a sermon on living together?" I saw one hand tentatively rise, part-way up.

Why do those who cohabit have 50% higher odds of divorce? Larry Bumpass says that those who live together outside of marriage are inherently less committed to marriage and therefore more likely to divorce. As evidence,

---

[3]*Marital Status and Living Arrangements*, Census Bureau, March 1991.

he notes that only 55% of cohabitants agree with the statement that "Marriage is a lifetime relationship and should never be ended except under extreme circumstances." On the other hand, 71% of married people felt that way. I don't find this analysis persuasive. First, the commitment to marriage by the already married would be expected to be higher than that of cohabitants. Second, in the late 1960s, when only 8% cohabited, were the other 92%—those who did not cohabit before marriage—more committed to marriage as a lifetime relationship? Hardly. The number of divorces nearly doubled in the 1960s (soaring from 393,000 to 708,000).

No, the evidence is that cohabitation *produces* marital instability. The *National Survey* found that unmarried couples living together are twice as likely to be unhappy in their relationships as married people. Judith Krantz, writing in *Cosmopolitan* in 1976, explained why: "When a woman lives with a man without the couple's making mutual and whole-hearted investment of themselves implicitly in what is now so scornfully called 'a little piece of paper'—i.e., a marriage certificate—she immediately loses the following things: her independence, her freedom to make choices, her privacy, all of her mystery, any practical bargaining position in the power struggle of love . . . the prospect of having a child other than an illegitimate one, and the protection of the law." In interviews with many women, she found "NONE . . . happily married today. Each settled for less than she hoped for."

Indeed, the result is often violence! *TIME* magazine reported September 5, 1988, that "In almost two dozen recent studies, experts across the country estimate that an average of 30% of all unmarried individuals, whether dating or living together, have been involved in physical aggression with the opposite sex. *Couples who live together may be the most violent of all.*"

A 1922 U. S. Justice Department study, "Female Victims of Violent Crime," found that 56,900 wives reported violence by husbands in an average year of the 1980s. But cohabiting women reported 198,000 cases. That's four times as many from a population of three million cohabiting women compared to fifty-three million married women. With population taken into account, a cohabiting woman is *seventy-six times* more likely to be assaulted by a live-in boyfriend than by a husband. Husbands respect wives. Boyfriends do not.

SECULAR EVIDENCE OF BIBLICAL WISDOM

Surely, this is secular evidence of the wisdom of Scripture:

> For this reason a man will leave his father and mother and be united to his wife, and they will become one flesh. The man and woman were both naked and they felt no shame.

> Genesis 2:24–25

The biblical sequence is summarized in three steps:

1. A man leaves his father and mother.
2. He is "united to his wife."
3. *Then* they "become one flesh" and feel no shame in being naked.

By reversing the sequence, of becoming "one flesh" before marriage and agreeing to live together without marriage, people *do* feel shame and a lack of commitment that continues even if the couple later marries.

CHILDREN OF NEVER-MARRIED PARENTS

The final splinter of America's shattered families is the most forgotten person of all: the child of never-married parents. In the past, to our shame, they were called "bastards," or "illegitimate." Today, they are more euphemistically called "out-of-wedlock" children. By whatever name, these children have many more strikes against them than do children of divorce—*economically, academically,* and *sociologically,* because most have never even known their father, let alone had financial and emotional support from him. Is not a broken parental relationship better than one that never existed?

Sadly, there is no faster-growing group of children in America.

In 1960 only 4% of U.S. children were living with a never-married parent. By 1990 the figure had soared to 31%—nearly an eightfold growth. The actual numbers *have skyrocketed twentyfold,* from only 243,000 such children in 1960–to 5,568,000 youngsters living with a never-married single parent in 1991!

The issue is parental irresponsibility and its grim consequences, on a scale vastly larger than most people imagine. Get a pencil and answer this question by circling one of the options:

How many unmarried couples have children living with them?
a. 200,000; b. 500,000; c. 750,000; d. 1 million?

Did you guess that there are nearly a million cohabiting couples with children—mothers and fathers with their own children at home, who refuse to accept their partner as husband or wife, or their children as a mutual responsibility? To be exact, the figure was 962,000 in 1991 and rising about 50,000 a year, which would put it at one million in 1992. That is *five times* the 197,000 never-married couples with children in 1960.

Now to test your knowledge of children born out of wedlock and their parents, what percentage of their parents are black?
a. 70%; b. 60%; c. 50%; d. 40%.

Did you circle an answer before reading on?

I'm betting that most readers would circle 60% or 70%, but the actual number is about 40%. Most mothers of out-of-wedlock children are white. In 1990, of the 913,000 unmarried women between ages fifteen and forty-five who had at least one child, 543,000 were white and 349,000 were black, according to the Census Report, "Fertility of American Women: June 1990."[4]

During the week that Martin Luther King's birthday was celebrated nationally for the first time (in January 1991), the National Center for Health Statistics reported that 63.5% (nearly two-thirds) of all black American babies are born out of wedlock. Because blacks are only a tenth of the nation's population, their share of the total illegitimacy pool is still smaller than births to unmarried white women.

A March 29, 1992, *New York Times* story added a new horror to this picture of the disintegration of the inner-city family, reporting that in Frick Junior High School in Oakland, California, "more than half the 750 youngsters live with *neither a mother or father!*" This is a new norm in the ghetto, where both parents are often "lost to crack or locked in jail" and the kids "are living with grandma, auntie, or a stranger." The result? "Many of them are routinely out of control: fighting with classmates and shoving or cursing teachers. . . . Scarred by years of abuse and neglect, many of these children are angry and disruptive even after they settle in loving foster homes."

How many "zero parent families" and "new orphans" are there? According to the "Kids Count Data Book," an annual profile of American children by the Annie E. Casey Foundation and the Center for the Study of Social Policy, "nearly one of every ten American children lives in a household headed by someone other than a parent," said the *Times*.

What is often ignored by the media (dominated, of course, by whites) is that *white* illegitimacy has soared even faster than black—though from a lower base. When Martin Luther King began his ministry in 1950, only 18% of black babies were born to unmarried women. The percentage doubled by the time of his death in 1968 and is now 63.5%—3.5 times the 1950 level. In the same years, white illegitimacy soared *tenfold*! It was only 1.7% in 1950 but hit 17.8% by 1988. Overall, out-of-wedlock births quadrupled from 224,000 in 1960 to one million in 1990.

SOME PARENTHETICAL THOUGHTS ABOUT ADOPTION

Parenthetically, it must be added that as illegitimacy crescendoed, the percentage of children being adopted fell *nearly 90%*! In 1970 there were 89,000 adoptions of U.S. children unrelated to the parents, about 75,000 of whom were babies. That was about a fifth of 400,000 babies born out of wedlock in 1970 being adopted by stable, two-parent families. Now only about

---

[4]Census data is based on estimates from the Current Population Survey that interviewed 57,400 households. However, some residents refused to talk, or could not be found. A more accurate figure of the number of births out of wedlock is not 917,000 but 1,005,000, according to the National Center for Health Statistics, whose data is from actual births recorded in hospitals.

25,000 of 1990s' one million out-of-wedlock babies were adopted. That's a pathetic 2.5%![5] Can anyone argue that a half million teens who gave birth are better off by keeping the baby? Half of today's welfare rolls are women whose first baby was born while she was a teenager, a child herself. A mother who makes the tough choice to give the baby a better future by adoption is 50% more likely to get married.

Why are so few babies being adopted? Surely, it is not because of a lack of willing parents. The National Committee for Adoption estimates that a million parents would like to adopt a child if they could. Since 1985, more than 10,000 children a year have been brought in from Korea, Peru, Romania, and other countries by desperate, childless couples. But why should Americans have to go to Korea to find a baby when a million are born out of wedlock right here in the U.S.?

The supply of American babies for adoption has dried up. And the pro-life movement has to bear some responsibility. The pro-life forces are so intent on convincing a pregnant woman not to abort her baby that they focus their energy on convincing her that "You can keep your baby. We will help you." The "adoption option" may be mentioned, but what matters is results. The adoption rate of the crisis pregnancy centers affiliated with the Christian Action Council is terrible. It persuaded only three to four percent of 200,000 women seen in 1991 to relinquish a child to adoption, according to CAC Director Tom Glessner. And only 1% of Birthright's 400,000 counselees permitted adoption—which is less than the 2% average of the 500,000 seen by Planned Parenthood. A study by Dr. Edward Mech of the University of Illinois, however, shows that *if a counselor* is persuaded that adoption makes sense, 40% of unwed mothers will do so.

In his acceptance speech for the 1988 Republican presidential nomination, President Bush said, "We must change from abortion to adoption," but his administration did virtually nothing about it. What *could* it do? The federal government grants 150 million dollars to Planned Parenthood's centers. Why not ask the federally funded counselors of a half million women to take a course on the "adoption option," meet parents who want to adopt, introduce pregnant women to adults who grew up as adopted children and are grateful for the opportunity that adoption gave them? Why not have a White House Conference on Adoption to educate the media and the nation? Neither step would cost much and could save hundreds of thousands of lives and strengthen as many marriages with the blessing of children.

---

[5]*Adoption Factbook, United States Data, Issues, Regulations and Resources,* National Committee for Adoption, *June 1989.*

FEWER PREGNANT WOMEN MARRY
THE FATHER OF THEIR CHILD

One reason for soaring illegitimacy cited by the Census Report is that vastly fewer women who become pregnant with their first child—marry the father. Thirty years ago, 52.2% of women who conceived a baby out of wedlock married before the child was born. That figure has plunged to 26.6%. (Among black women, about one-third of unmarried pregnant mothers married the child's father before its birth in 1960–64. Now only 10% do so. "The propensity to marry before childbirth also fell off a cliff among white women, from 61% in 1960–1964 to 34% in 1985–1989," said the Census Report.)

The author of the Census Report, Ms. Amara Bachu, said that the explanation for the sharp decline of premaritally conceived births being legitimized before the child's birth "may reflect the opinion of some women that they may be better off in the long run by relying more on the support of their parents and relatives for financial aid and emotional assistance than by entering a potentially unstable marriage undertaken solely to prevent an out-of-wedlock birth."

They may *think* they'll be better off but are grievously wrong because:

1. Marriage sparked by a pregnancy will be more shaky than one begun without a pregnancy. But marriage is vastly more stable and hopeful for the mother and child than for her to depend on her parents, or the future commitment of a father unwilling to marry the future mother.

2. Women who have been married and divorced are three times as likely to be awarded child support as those who have never been married (72% versus 24%), says Census. This is simple common sense. A man with a legal commitment is more likely to fulfill some level of his commitment.

3. Being awarded child support is not the same as getting it. "Two-thirds of the birth certificates of the babies born to unwed teens contain no information about the father, and only 14% of fathers of children born out of wedlock provide any regular support to these children," according to Isabel Sawhill of the Urban Institute. "Where are the fathers?" she asks. "At the same time that women are provided a means of going it alone (welfare), men are relieved of any liability for their behavior." She's right. According to the Census Bureau, 16.3 billion dollars in child support payments should have been paid in 1989, the last year with data. Of that sum, only 11.2 billion was paid. In other words, *fathers stole five billion dollars from their own children.* That money is unlikely ever to be collected. And 42% of women had *no* child support orders. If they had, and the awards were the same as those who do have them ($1,400 per child per year), another twenty to twenty-five billion would be collected, according to Ron Haskins of the House Ways and Means Committee staff! That would be enough to move millions of women and children out of poverty, *if* all fathers were forced to support their children.

4. Divorced women received nearly twice as much child support in 1989 ($3,268) than did never-married women ($1,888)—if they were lucky enough to get any support at all.

5. The U.S. Civil Rights Commission found that while only 6% of never-married white women have one or more children, 44% of never-married black women have at least one child. That's a major reason why so many blacks are poor—not because of race but because of marital status. The Commission said that married black women have an income that is nearly three-fourths that of married white women, while the unmarried black woman has less than two-thirds of what unmarried white women earn.

Why? Comparatively few white unmarried women have babies to care for.

6. To put it more simply, 44% of families with children headed by women were in poverty since 1970 versus only 6% or 7% for married couple families.

7. Those who "follow the rules" (graduating from high school and getting married) are very unlikely ever to be in poverty. For white females who followed the rules, only 3% were poor at age twenty-five in contrast with 13% for black females. In fact, married black males with a high school degree had less than a 5% chance of living below the poverty line, versus 1% for similar white males.

8. Now consider those who break the rules. Among white females who dropped out of school and gave birth as a teenager, 22% were in poverty in 1985, as were 48% of blacks. In 1969, black men aged 25–34 without a high school degree earned $14,000. In 1984 they earned $6,500, said Republican Members of Congress in a report, "Moving Ahead." Even those with a high school diploma saw their earnings drop in real terms from $16,000 to $10,800—25% less than for black males *without* a diploma in 1969. "The point: Black women have tightly constrained economic choices in looking for husbands," notes "Moving Ahead." That is a major reason that few black women are getting married.

Thus far, I've only outlined the economic price of being born out of wedlock. But the most devastating impact is *personal*, not economic. "On almost every outcome study so far—including delinquency and crime, school achievement, and college attendance, to name a few—children raised without fathers are worse off than children raised by both parents," said the Republican members of the House Wednesday Group.

Education: Thirty percent of children who live with never-married mothers have repeated a grade, compared to only 12% of those living with both biological parents and 22% of those living with a formerly married or a remarried mother, according to the National Center for Child Health Statistics. In big cities, as many as half of the students drop out of school. They are not only marginally literate and virtually unemployable, but "dropouts are

3.5 times as likely as high school graduates to be arrested, and six times as likely to become unmarried parents," said the report of the National Commission on Children.

Children from single-parent homes are twice as likely to have behavior disorders as children from two-parent homes, according to Dr. David and Susan Larson. "Psychiatric disorders were also found to be almost twice as common in children from single-parent families."

Children Having Children: "Each year, approximately 1 million teenage girls become pregnant; nearly half of them give birth. Approximately half of these births are to young women who have not yet reached their 18th birthday," said the Commission.

Half of those now on welfare had their first child out of wedlock as a teenager. The children of teenage mothers often repeat the cycle.

Crime rates among juveniles are more "associated with family structure than with either poverty or race," according to a study by D. A. Smith and G. R. Jarjoura, reported in the "Journal of Research in Crime and Delinquency." They note that many studies that find a significant association between race and crime fail to take into account differences in family structure. Neighborhoods with high percentages of single-parent households have high rates of violent crime and burglary.

Half of the inmates of state prisons grew up without two parents. Some 36% were in a single-parent household, compared with 17% of the general population, and 17% lived with grandparents or other relatives, according to the Larsons.

Child Abuse. One of the most frightening studies I've read is "Child Abuse by Mothers' Boyfriends" by Leslie Margolin of the University of Iowa, who notes that most single mothers become involved with boyfriends through dating or cohabitation. Those men—who are not genetically related to her children, and who are often perceived by the kids as having an "Illicit, indefinite, and extra-legal" relationship with the mother—are sometimes given child-care responsibility. Violence often is the result. Of 339 cases of physical abuse reported to Iowa's Department of Human Services by nonparents, such as teachers or counselors, 290 were caused by boyfriends. Although mothers' boyfriends performed only 1.7% of nonparental child care, they were responsible for *half* the child abuse by nonparents.

In a number of cases, violence was preceded by children's making explicit references to the boyfriend's illegitimacy. Responding to a boyfriend's order, a four-year-old said that he does not have to listen to him "because you're not my real dad." Even more cases involved children's siding with their mother in an argument with her boyfriend. And in a dozen instances out of 105 studies, a boyfriend became violent toward the children because the kids were perceived to be on the mother's side. For example, one boyfriend turned away from his girlfriend after a disagreement, approached her nine-month-old infant, slapped the infant across the face, walked back to his girlfriend, and said, 'That's for you, b----.' "

Suicide vs. Murder: Both children of divorce and out-of-wedlock kids can be very violent—but in very different directions. Kids of divorce may be self-destructive, more likely to commit suicide, while illegitimate youth are more likely to turn their anger on others in violent crime.

Suicide has tripled among adolescents, from 3.6 deaths per 100,000 in 1960 to 10.2 deaths by 1986—in the time that divorces also *tripled*. "Suicide is now the second leading cause of death among adolescents, after accidents," said the National Commission on Children. A study of state and county data over forty-seven years found that "those regions with the highest divorce rates also had the highest suicide rates," report the Larsons. (In contrast, suicide rates were lowest in those areas with the highest rates of church membership.) "Unlike homicide, it is more common among white teens than black teens," said the National Commission on Children. "Abusive families with high levels of stress seem to put their children at greater risk of self-destructive behavior, and rates of suicide seem to be higher among those who have lost both their parents through death or family breakdown."

Younger and younger inner-city children are committing more serious and more violent crimes. The drug business and the widespread availability of guns—coupled with the lack of parental control—has produced chaos in most inner cities. Much of the escalating murder rate comes from out-of-wedlock kids' being brought up in the streets rather than in homes.

On February 3, 1992, *The Washington Post* published a major story, "A Crazed Fascination with Guns." To understand why Washington has become the murder capital of the United States, the *Post* interviewed a number of young black men in prison. Richard Paul Vernon, twenty, got his first gun in the sixth grade when he was eleven. Why? "It was just the thought of having a gun. I was just happy to have a . . . gun," he told the *Post*. Who was supervising him at that stage of his life? Only his mother. "I'm just a gun freak," says the young inmate convicted on drug charges, who is known for having stylish semi-automatic weapons. "When I had an Uzi, I was just waiting for somebody to mess with me."

Of 114 older inmates interviewed, 95% said that when they were growing up, "it was more important that a man be handy with his fists" than to have a gun. But now 84% say that it is more important "that a man have a gun." Two-thirds had fired a gun at someone, and 55% said that they had injured a person. Some 17% admitted having killed someone.

Ricky Wages, twenty-four, who was brought up only by his father, claims that he "can't remember all the people I shot." He says that the first person he shot, he killed. He watched an account of the crime on TV one night and said, "I had no remorse. I didn't lose no sleep. I don't think about it now. He was after me." Nevertheless, he was not convicted of any of his murders but for assault and will probably be back on the street in 1994.

"My favorite gun was the 9-millimeter," he told the *Post*. "It would never lock on me. The Uzi would lock on me."

Today, more teenagers in America die from gunshot wounds than from all natural causes combined. "Between 1984 and 1988, gunshot deaths increased by over 40%. . . . Black teenage boys are eleven times as likely as white teenage boys to be shot to death," said the National Commission on Children. "Among these delinquent youth there is often a history of abuse or family violence as well as failure in school. . . ."

If Ricky Wages and Richard Paul Vernon had been reared in suburbia by two-parent families, would they be gun-wielding thugs? It is highly unlikely. The father of Ricky Wages was not around as he grew up, nor was the mother of Richard Paul Vernon. And their irresponsibility has foisted a horror on the community: killers of innocent people.

The irresponsibility of their parents has foisted a horror on us all.

THREE

The Church:
Missing in Action!

Couples who are religiously committed are protected against divorce.

—Dr. David Larson,
Research Psychiatrist,
National Institute of Mental Health

The LORD is slow to anger, abounding in love and forgiving sin and rebellion. Yet he does not leave the guilty unpunished; he punishes the children for the sin of the fathers to the third and fourth generation.

—Numbers 14:18

FIRST, PREACH SCRIPTURAL TRUTH

Can God be so angry with the sins of the mothers and fathers of one generation that he punishes their children? Can anyone doubt it in looking at the lives of Richard Paul Vernon and Ricky Wages, the two killers whose stories were summarized at the end of chapter 2? Neither set of parents of these young men remained committed to each other. In today's culture that's a minor sin (if any think it a sin at all), but examine the ghastly consequences of a few moments of long-forgotten sex: hard-bitten criminals, one of whom can't remember how many people he has shot.

If the parents of these young men had realized what their sin would produce, would they have been so irresponsible? Perhaps not. But were they taught the possible negative consequences of having sex out-of-wedlock?

Did the mothers of both young men attend church? I don't know, but the odds are, yes. According to Gallup Polls, three-fourths of black people are members of a church, and half attend religious services in any given week— *higher* attendance rates than for whites. If those two mothers did attend church, did they hear a case for remaining chaste till marriage? Probably not. With 63.5% of black children born out-of-wedlock, I place some blame for this pathology on the black church's failure to teach morality.

The data suggest that *either black churches ignore sexual moral issues, or they are totally ineffectual.* The *same* charge can be leveled at white churches that have stood by, silently watching white illegitimacy soar tenfold, from

47

1.7% to 17.8% by 1988. *Either they ignore the sexual moral issues, or they are totally ineffectual.*

Briefly consider the sin of divorce and its consequences for children. The National Commission on Children concluded that divorce devastates children: "Depression, trouble getting along with parents and peers, misbehavior stemming from anger and declining school performance are common" and "continue or worsen" as they get older.

There's God punishing "the children for the sin of the fathers," some might think.

As the Commission put it, "When parents divorce or fail to marry, children are often the victims. Children who live with only one parent, usually their mothers, are six times as likely to be poor as those living with both parents. . . . Children do best when they have the personal involvement and material support of a father and mother . . . living and working together in a stable marriage."

No church would disagree, but have you ever heard a sermon on the evils of divorce? Probably not. The issue is delicately sidestepped. Why? Too many divorced people whose feathers might get ruffled are sitting in the pews!

Those of you who grew up in divorced homes—did your church reach out to you and show any sympathy or any help for your loss of a parent? Was there a Sunday school class for children of divorce to help them cope? Or Sunday school to help the divorced themselves rebuild their lives?

Probably not, even though twelve million marriages shatter each decade, and a million children a year see their parents divorce. How can pastors not know your pain?

INTERNATIONAL COMPARISONS OF CHURCH ATTENDANCE AND SINGLE PARENTHOOD

Is it fair to hold the churches of America responsible for the acts of individuals? Not if no one attends church. (The Christian church in Japan is less than half of one percent of the population.)

According to George Gallup, Jr., *two-thirds* of Americans are members of churches, and 42% attended church in any given week of 1991. And 73% of first marriages are blessed by the church, according to the Census. Clearly, the American church—300,000 local congregations—has *access*—a latent power to influence most people. This is in sharp contrast with the church's access in Europe, where church attendance is 4% in Finland, 12% in France, and 14% in Great Britain according to a 1986 Gallup Poll.

Yet look at the table on page 49. Japan, with almost no Christians, has one quarter as many single parents as America, and every European country and Canada do twice as well as the United States in holding two-parent families together. This is partly explained by cultural differences such as high U.S. mobility.

Japan: 5.9% of homes headed by a single parent
U.S.: 22.9% of homes headed by a single parent
United Kingdom: 12.7% of homes headed by a single parent
France: 10.9% of homes headed by a single parent
West Germany: 17.5% of homes headed by a single parent
Canada: 14.8% of homes headed by a single parent

(*Source: Bureau of the Census report, "Children's Well-Being: An International Comparison," Bureau of the Census, 1992.

Clearly, the nation with the deepest church penetration has the *least* impact on central moral issues involving the rearing of children.

What is the role of the church? Surely, its first task is to speak clearly from a biblical perspective, denounce the sin, and warn of consequences. Second, the church must suggest *life-giving* alternatives.

OPPOSE THE PHARAOH

To popular black TV-host Arsenio Hall it's a joke that Wilt Chamberlain had sex with 20,000 women. How many of them got pregnant and had babies who grew up fatherless, angry, and criminal? If only five percent of his copulations produced illegitimate children, that would be 1000 fatherless children! Geraldo Rivera wrote a book, *Exposing Myself*, telling salacious details of his sexual exploits. It landed him on talk shows where all laughed at his irresponsibility. What about the pain that must have been inflicted on his first two wives and their children, both at the time he lived with them and then all over again when he bragged in print about his conquests?

Some of the heroes of youth today pay a price for promiscuity: Magic Johnson and Mike Tyson come to mind. But the media's message is the opposite—the characters in the TV series, *L.A. Law,* never get pregnant, or acquire a sexually transmitted disease from their promiscuity.

The church must take a stand. "The role of the church is to oppose Pharaoh, not to accommodate him," said Don Wildmon. "We Christians should not be timid and fearful in the face of popular sin. We serve neither our Lord nor our fellow humans when we are fearful and timid. There is a thing called righteous indignation, holy anger. Jesus expressed this: 'Then Jesus went into the temple of God and drove out all those who bought and sold in the temple, and overturned the tables of the money changers. . .'" (Matthew 21:12)

"We are often told that because Jesus loved people, He did not rebuke them," said Wildmon.[1] "But He did ... 'Woe to you scribes and Pharisees, hypocrites! For you are like white-washed tombs which indeed appear beautiful outwardly, but inside are full of dead men's bones and all uncleanness. . . . Serpents, brood of vipers! How can you escape the condemnation of hell?' " (Matthew 23:27, 33 NKJV).

SCRIPTURE ON DIVORCE

If the sins of the fathers are borne by their children, there is a double reason for pastors to be clear in preaching from the pulpit on the consequences of sexual immorality and divorce. At least two generations are affected by the sin: those sitting in the pew, and their children.

Still, the primary reason is that Scripture itself is starkly clear. On divorce, for example, inspect the last book of the Old Testament, Malachi, which contains some of the sternest rebukes in all Scripture for pastors or priests. And what was their sin? Failing to teach what they know about God's plan for men and women in marriage!

> "And now this admonition is for you, O priests. If you do not listen, and if you do not set your heart to honor my name," says the LORD Almighty, "I will send a curse upon you, and I will curse your blessings. Yes, I have already cursed them, because you have not set your heart to honor me. . . . For the lips of a priest ought to preserve knowledge, and from his mouth men should seek instruction—because he is the messenger of the LORD Almighty (Malachi 2:1–2, 7).

And how have the people stumbled, due to the failure of priests and pastors to teach God's Word? A few verses further down, we read what happens to people who ignore the Scriptural mandate on marriage and divorce:

> . . . You flood the LORD's altar with tears. You weep and wail because he no longer pays attention to your offerings or accepts them with pleasure from your hands. You ask, "Why?" It is because the LORD is acting as the witness between you and the wife of your youth, because you have broken faith with her, though she is your partner, the wife of your marriage covenant.
>
> Has not the LORD made them one? In flesh and spirit, they are his. And why one? Because he was seeking godly offspring. So guard yourself in your spirit, and do not break faith with the wife of your youth.
>
> "I hate divorce," says the LORD God of Israel (Malachi 2:13–15).

---

[1]Don Wildmon, president of the American Family Association in his *AFA Journal*, January 1991.

Does the New Testament soften any of this on the divorce issue? Not at all. In fact, Jesus is quoted on it in three of the Gospels. He was very clear (Matthew 19:3–6, 9).

Some Pharisees came to him to test him. They asked, "Is it lawful for a man to divorce his wife for any and every reason?"

"Haven't you read," he replied, "that in the beginning the Creator made them male and female? For this reason a man will leave his father and mother and be united to his wife, and the two will become one flesh. So they are no longer two, but one. Therefore what God has joined together, let not man separate.

"I tell you that anyone who divorces his wife, except for marital unfaithfulness, and marries another woman commits adultery.

"The disciples said to him, 'If this is the situation between a husband and a wife, it is better not to marry.'

"Jesus replied, 'Not everyone can accept this word, but only those to whom it is given.'"

Clearly, the disciples were shocked by what Jesus said. He ruled out all divorce. True, in Matthew 5:32 he offered one slender exception that was not repeated in any other Gospel:

"But I tell you that anyone who divorces his wife, except for unfaithfulness, causes her to become an adulteress, and anyone who marries the divorced woman commits adultery."

Yet have you heard a sermon stating that divorce is wrong in all other circumstances? It is doubtful. According to the Gallup Poll, only 17% of marriages break up because of adultery. But 47% end because of "incompatibility." Most Japanese marriages must be approved by the couple's parents, and the Japanese divorce rate is *one-quarter* of that of the U.S. Clearly, both Japanese men and women have concluded they must *work* to be compatible because they believe that a stable marriage and family is more important than untrammelled individuality, which separates man and woman. I'm not saying that Japanese marriages are happier but that the Japanese work harder at them.

Without knowing 1 Corinthians 13, the Japanese seem to know that the Americans are wrong in thinking that love is a *feeling*.

Scripturally, *love is a decision*. As Paul wrote:

Love is patient, love is kind. It does not envy, it does not boast, it is not proud. . . . It always protects, always trusts, always hopes, always perseveres.

Is anyone naturally patient? Certainly not this writer! Even after a quarter of a century of marriage, I am still not patient enough with my wife. I have to consciously curb my quick retort. Loving takes self-discipline. But when have we heard such a sermon? For decades I have gone to strong preaching churches and have never heard such a sermon about the essential need for selflessness in marriage. Of course, that is the absolute opposite of TV marriages like those in the "soaps," and I'll wager that you never heard your pastor preach that *the children will be punished for the sin of divorce by the father and mother.*

Why not?

That makes God sound too harsh. But instead of questioning God's wisdom, look at the evidence of what happens to children of divorce reported earlier. Reread chapter 2. Isn't it time to start preaching what Scripture says and what secular evidence proves? The very silence of the church on what is destroying 60% of marriages is itself a sin. Thus, the church bears part of the responsibility for America's splintering of the family.

Too often in an acceptance of divorce, the church mirrors the culture. Why? Maybe the rising divorce rate of pastors themselves prompts caution.

More likely, the strategies to save marriages are not obvious.

THE CHURCH NEEDS NEW MODELS OF SUCCESS

Churches can cite *secular proof* that those who are active in their faith are *twice* as likely to stay married as the nonreligious! But the churches must find ways to help people at many stages of the life cycle discover how to find a marriage partner for life and to strengthen all marriages. We all need to see visible examples of success to give everyone hope of making it. With so much failure on all sides of us, it is not enough to simply crack a biblical whip.

On this issue, Jesus may not seem to be a role model, yet he is our best example of how we might love our spouse. Jesus was celibate. He did not "date," or become engaged, or marry, or become a father.

In a far deeper sense, however, Jesus demonstrates what love is and promises to help any of us to love others. He is a unique resource for any husband and wife who turn to him. The Gospel message read in Episcopal wedding services is from St. John: "This is my command: Love each other" (15:12).

What does that mean in practical terms? In a recent wedding, the Reverend Henry Stuart Irvin, Rector of All Saints' Church, Chevy Chase, Maryland, said:

> The wonderful thing about God's commandment is that when He asks us to follow Him . . . God supplies the strength to do what He asks!. . . . No life and no marriage is without times of testing, and no marriage achieves emotional and spiritual depth and inner strength if the couple fails to work through those down times or seasons of anger and disappointment. And what a difference it makes when we discover that God in Christ is there to walk with us through the stress times. . . . He gives of Himself to the bride and groom so that their "joy may be full." But, ultimately, it is up to the bride and groom—husband and wife—to decide how much

they will allow God to truly bless the marriage by allowing Him to reign and rule in the relationship.

GOOD NEWS: VALUES REALLY CAN BE TAUGHT AT HOME

There is independent evidence, however, that *any family can develop the values that hold marriages together.* Peter, in his first epistle, wrote that believers "like living stones, are being built into a spiritual house, to be a holy priest-hood" (1 Peter 2:5). A husband and wife can be the priests of their home, reflecting the holiness of God, speaking for God in the home, and to God, on behalf of the family.

The Massachusetts Mutual Insurance Company conducted the first "American Family Values Study" in 1989 and another in 1991 and found a great deal of agreement that the most important "core family values" identi-fied by small groups and a survey of 1,200 people included:

— Being responsible for one's actions
— Respect for others (especially one's children and parents)
— The desire to form emotionally supportive relationships
— Having a happy marriage
— Leaving to the next generation the world in better shape than we found it
— Having faith in God
— Following a strict moral code
— Being married to the same person for life

The commitment of people to these values grew stronger between 1989 and 1991. For example, the percentage of those who felt that "one of the most important" values is that one should respect one's children, increased from 33% to 43% in those two years, says Massachusetts Mutual. The desire to leave "the world to the next generation in better shape than we found it" grew by 9%, as did "respecting one's parents." Those who felt that it is most important to follow a "strict moral code" grew by 6%, and those who felt that having faith in God is most important grew from 40% to 45%.

By contrast, the percentage who felt that "having nice things" is most important fell from a very low 8% to 6%—despite the recession. Materialistic values have declined, ironically, in the middle of a recession, when most fam-ilies felt quite pinched financially.

However, while two-thirds of Americans found their own family life "very satisfying" or "extremely satisfying," 57% believe that the quality of American family life in the broader society is only "fair" or "poor." And there is a widespread consensus that "the American family and American family values are in decline."

How can both perceptions be correct? "In essence, Americans were say-ing, "I'm okay, but you're not."

One of those interviewed by Massachusetts Mutual said, "You talk about the morals and the values declining in America. We see this every day in people stepping on each other to reach the top to succeed. . . . Things are declining. I really believe it." He wanted things to turn around and for people to go "back to the old traditional values of teaching their kids to pray before meals, going to church regularly, honesty, and dependability."

What's important about this study is that it shows people feel they can, in fact, control the quality of their lives and those closest to them, regardless of external circumstances. As noted above, this sense of the importance of key family values has *grown* as the recession began and deepened between 1989 and 1991.

In that context it is quite encouraging that a striking "97% of survey respondents agree with the statement that 'family is the place where most basic values are instilled.'. . . More than three-quarters say they learned each of the core family values in their family: responsibility, respect for others, and the value of emotional connection in their family." And 71% acquired the value of "following a strict moral code" at home (versus only 4% who learned it in church!).

And what's the most important influence in saving marriages? *Not the church but the home.* Some 69% said that their value of "having a happy marriage," and 67% "having faith in God," was learned *at home!* By contrast, only 22% learned the importance of having faith in God at church, as did a mere 17% of those who valued having a strict moral code.

What makes this particularly heartening is that two-thirds of those same people say that "American family values have gotten weaker recently."

So even if you go to a weak church, remember that Jesus said "Where two or three come together in my name, there I am with them" (Matthew 18:20). Your home can be a place that worships God and nurtures values that will save marriages. Often, of course, that is not the case. In fact, Massachusetts Mutual found two influences on kids that are more powerful than parents:

— TV and movies: the mass media
— Other young people: peer pressure

This is because many parents *don't try* to influence their kids on such issues as chastity. Chapter 4 proves that parents, if they make a reasoned case, can be more influential than the media or peers.

MAKE YOUR HOME A SMALL CHURCH THAT WORSHIPS GOD

Therefore, the first major suggestion of *Marriage Savers* is that every couple—especially you parents—should see yourselves as priests of your own home. Look upon it as a small church centered on Christ, studying the

Word of God, worshiping him, and praying for each other. This begins with a husband and wife themselves. They need time alone together to nurture their love.

My wife, Harriet, and I take time each morning in our home to read Scripture, a page or two of commentary, and pray for each other, our sons, and for their future spouses (whoever they may be). To be honest, most of our time is spent talking about hopes and worries, but it is the Scripture, commentary and prayer that gives our time together a depth and Christ-centeredness.

Recently, we have taken an hour every morning, generally from 8:00 A.M. to 9:00 A.M. My office is in my home, so it doesn't matter too much when I get started. This time is very precious to me—a time to begin my day, grow closer to God and to Harriet. Three years ago, when Harriet had to be at work at 8:30 A.M., the whole schedule shifted back to 7:15 A.M. or so. In fact, she used to get up at 5:45 A.M. to get one son off to a bus, and another at 6:15 A.M.. She'd then fix coffee and come upstairs for our devotions.

From what I can gather, our experience is unusual. At church recently, several couples about our age shared their spiritual life with couples who were engaged to be married. Harriet and I were surprised that not one of them took time to pray and study Scripture *together*. Each said they had a "quiet time"—but separately. From back in the audience I raised my hand and said, "My wife, Harriet, and I have our quiet time *together* every morning—not separately. When we went on a Marriage Encounter weekend sixteen years ago, we learned the importance of having a specific time every day for unstructured talk, Scripture reading, and prayer. It puts Christ at the center of our relationship. I think that is a better way of doing it than separately."

For couples who have never taken this step, here is a practical way to make it easy and fun to put God at the center of your marriage while nurturing your love for each other and your children. Each morning, wake up fifteen minutes earlier than necessary and read one page of a book, *Heirs Together of Life*[2] and a daily Bible reading suggested by its authors, a retired pastor and his wife. They say that the book's aim is to help couples understand "what the Creator has designed for marriage and the home." The book selects key verses from Genesis to Revelation, packed with biblical wisdom on the godly home. They then show its relevance in their own home where seven children grew to know and love the Lord. Eight readings, for example, examine every chapter of the Song of Solomon, noting that "God made men and women to desire each other!"

---

[2]Charles and Norma Ellis, Banner of Truth Publishing, P.O. Box 621, Carlisle, PA 17013. If you mention that you read about it in *Marriage Savers,* the price is $7.50 (not the regular $10.95) with no charge for postage.

"In the training of children, the Book of Proverbs is highly beneficial," they comment. "It is dangerous for the parent to present his own ideas as truth. To be able to point to objective truth, God's truth, is wonderful. How helpful it is for a child to grow up with Proverbs in his heart." For example, they point to Proverbs 18:2: "A fool finds no pleasure in understanding but delights in airing his own opinions." I took the book's advice with my kids. When they were in serious error, I'd go through Proverbs, pick out the quotes that made the point, and quote them. To a boy who was lazy in doing homework, Proverbs 6:9–11 was powerful:

> How long will you lie there, you sluggard?
> When will you get up from your sleep?
> A little sleep, a little slumber,
> A little folding the hands to rest—
> And poverty will come on you like a bandit
> and scarcity like an armed man.

RELIGIOUSLY COMMITTED PROTECTED AGAINST DIVORCE

It is a mistake to think that the family unit can be a substitute for involving your family in a local church. Recently, a reporter interviewing me asked, "Don't you think a person can be a good Christian and not go to church?" My quick answer was "No. At least I need the spiritual nurture I get at church. And that's where we have found our closest friends." The Reverend Everett Fullam, former Rector of St. Paul's Episcopal Church in Darien, Connecticut, and my former pastor, used to say, "Thee and me make a pretty small circle."

As noted earlier, those who are active in practicing their faith are more than *twice* as likely to stay married as the nonreligious, according to a National Survey of Family Growth sponsored by the National Institute of Child Development. Some 17% of couples attending church once a year or less will separate or divorce after five years versus only 7% of those who attend monthly or more often. And after fifteen years, 37% of nonchurchgoers are no longer married versus only 14% of those attending monthly.

"Couples who are religiously committed are protected against divorce," says Dr. David Larson (a research psychiatrist formerly at NIMH quoted in chapter 1 on the fact that divorced people are twice as likely as married people to die in any year from heart disease, cancer, or stroke, four times as likely to die in an auto crash, or by suicide, etc.). "If you want to die early, don't go to church. Play golf on Sunday," he quips.

A decade ago, the Connecticut Mutual Life Insurance Company conducted a study that found that the most religiously committed people are the happiest people in their homes and at work and the least likely to get divorced! To determine their level of religious commitment, people were asked if they not only attended religious services regularly and prayed but also felt that God loves them, and if they read the Bible, attended church social events, had "something you call a religious experience," encouraged others to turn to religion, and listened to religious broadcasts. Those who "frequently" did seven to eight of these religious practices were called "intensely religious." Obviously, the "least religious" were those who "frequently" took none of these steps.

Compared to the least religious, the most religious were five times as likely to say that "living with someone of the opposite sex without being married is morally wrong." Some 60% of the intensely religious, if unhappily married, would "try to reconcile the problem at all costs," while only 33% of the least religious would do so. The most religious were also much more likely (64%) to say that they receive much more satisfaction from their relationship with their "immediate family compared with other aspects of [their] life," while only 39% of the least religious agreed. Though the most religious had lower incomes than the least religious, they were almost twice as likely to feel they received recognition for their efforts at work (62% versus 37%) and to feel that their work "contributes to society" as the least religious felt (91% versus 53%).

George Gallup reported similar results in a 1992 book, *The Saints Among Us.* He reported that 13% of the nation are living saints, people who live "noticeably different, more authentic Christian lives. They often spend significant time helping people burdened with physical and emotional needs. They are more giving and more forgiving."

However, the saints are twice as likely to be poor, black, and over fifty—as white, middle class, and younger. Yet 93% of these saints say they are "very happy." They are less likely to get depressed or suffer stress. It is one more proof, as if any were needed, that God's upside down economics really do work: "Give, and you shall receive."

PREACHING IS NOT ENOUGH; CONSCIOUS INTERVENTION IS NEEDED

If only 60% of the most intensely religious would try to save their own troubled marriage, it is clear that organized religion has a long way to go to make a case for the biblical view of marriage.

Clearly, better preaching will not be enough to spark most people to create a lifelong commitment that can weather any storm.

What's needed to save many more marriages is a conscious strategy by church leaders to intervene at different stages of people's lives with teaching that can be life-changing. There are key stages in everyone's life when there are "teachable moments" that can be used to give people a vision of how to avoid divorce. To be "marriage savers," churches must work on two parallel tracks, or the train of lifelong marriage won't even move out of the station. The church must teach in two ways:

- what Scripture says about people in each age bracket—whether it be about a teenager, an engaged couple, a married person, and even a divorced person;
- what *practical steps* each person can take to increase the odds that he or she will pick the right mate and build (or rebuild) a solid marriage.

Here's just one example of how people of faith are saving marriages in the most difficult of situations—deeply troubled marriages. Sometimes a pathology sets into some marriages, of one bitter exchange leading to name-calling that touches off yet more explosions. The spiral only seems to go down, with both parties concluding that the situation is hopeless. There are thousands of couples across America, however, whose marriages were once on the rocks but survived and thrived. Those couples now are reaching out to help others with grievous problems, to save their marriages. In 78 metropolitan areas or states, these "marriage savers" are running weekend retreats called "Retrouvaille" (French for "Rediscovery"). In Jacksonville and Fort Worth, for example, about half of the couples who attend are already separated or divorced. *Yet, 80% of those marriages are being saved!* To learn more, read chapter 10.

A BLESSING MACHINE OR A BLESSING?

The church, which too often is only a wedding-blessing machine, can in fact be a real blessing to every person it marries and to every married couple in its membership.

When the church is truly functioning as it should, it will help you, your loved ones, and your friends, avoid divorce.

Let's begin by looking more closely at the first teachable moment in most people's lives—the often-terrifying teenage years.

FOUR

Helping Keep Your Teenager Chaste

Train a child in the way he should go, and when he is old he will not turn from it.

—Proverbs 22:6

I had been told all my life that sex before marriage was wrong but no one ever told me why.

—A teenager, writing to Josh McDowell[1]

Why does a book called *Marriage Savers* begin with teenagers? When 1.1 million teens get pregnant a year, they are *not* learning discipline needed for lifelong marriage. Rather, promiscuity is preparing them for divorce or welfare! In 1991, five hundred eighteen thousand teens had babies, most of them out-of-wedlock.

But there is *good news* that you may not have heard, based on research of more than three years with 7000 seventh-to-tenth graders who were virgins when first questioned by Dr. Stan Weed, president of the Institute for Research and Evaluation, a private research company in Salt Lake City.

First. You can make a big difference in determining whether your teenager becomes sexually active. For example, you can be more influential than the person whom your teen dates if you encourage your teenager to be sexually chaste. Conversely, you will get a negative result if your attitude is, "Hey, I know you are going to be sexually active, so please use this contraceptive." Peer influence is important but not as significant as *positive, parental* influence!

Second. Even if your son or daughter has been sexually active, you as a parent can have a greater positive influence on their *future* sexual behavior than might be predicted by their history. If your daughter has had sex, your

---

[1] *Why Wait?* Josh McDowell and Dick Day, Here's Life Publishers, San Bernardino, CA, 1987.

influence as a parent can outweigh that history. You can make a case with her to stop having sex (secondary virginity), but you *must* talk to her.

Third. The influence of church involvement is virtually as important as your own influence as a predictor of their sexual values. Kids who attend church regularly and who say that their faith is important to them are much less likely to be sexually active. That *doubles* your impact on their value system because, as a parent, you can help your child find a church youth program that *he or she* finds exciting.

Fourth. The degree to which your son or daughter is consciously thinking about the future increases the odds of *not* wanting to become sexually involved, out of a fear that those long-term goals will be threatened, says the study. If so, you can obviously help spark the future orientation in your teen to increase that teen's interest in college by, for example, visiting college campuses with your child.

These four factors—parental sexual values, parental influence, a teen's faith, and his/her future orientation—can combine to create in your child higher values that incline your teenager to be sexually inactive. Conversely, if your parental values on sex are low, if your child is spiritually inactive and has few aspirations, that teenager is *three* times as likely as the kid with higher values to become sexually active.

There is more good news for parents. If you can influence three other aspects of your teenager's life in a positive direction, the odds of that teen's losing his or her virginity in a given year *are less than five percent!*

You can have an indirect influence on these three areas of your teen's life: his peer environment, whether he/she is dating one person steadily, and is drinking. How? Search for a church youth group that your teenager loves to go to. That may mean switching churches and going to a larger church with a solid youth program. Those kids will provide positive peer pressure. There will be more group activity, less one-on-one dating, and probably no one interested in binge drinking.

Now, let's assume the reverse—that your teen has friends who are a bad influence, who are sexually active and drinking to excess—and that your boy or girl is drinking, going steady, and has a low value system. How likely are such teenagers to lose their virginity in a year? *Nearly 50%!—ten times* the likelihood of becoming sexually active than for the one who has high values, positive peers, and is not drinking.

All of this analysis is based on fresh study by Dr. Stan E. Weed, CEO of the Institute for Research and Evaluation.

THIS IS COMMON SENSE

Isn't this simply *common sense* on these issues? Didn't your own mother or father tell you about the importance of going to church, having good friends, and not drinking alcoholic beverages? Isn't this what your pastor might say, but without any facts to back him up?

For a generation now, parents have been nervous about asserting traditional values. Why? Perhaps because they don't know how to answer a teenager's challenge, "Why should I remain a virgin?" This chapter offers objective information that you can use to bolster your case for chastity. But parents must regain the courage of common-sense convictions.

For example, pornography *is* harmful. I know something about the subject. I covered the deliberations of the Attorney General's Commission on Pornography, got its *Final Report*[2] published, and wrote its forty-page introduction and summary. One of the Commissioners whose mind was changed (more by the mail he received from individual citizens than by the sociological evidence) was Dr. Park Dietz, a psychiatrist with a master's degree in public health *and* a Ph.D. in sociology! Surely, if anyone has the credentials to assess the importance of common sense versus social science, it is Dr. Dietz. Yet in this personal statement about the impact of pornography, he says about social science what many parents feel in their gut about parenting: *Look for common sense.*

> Social science is too new on the historical scene to have developed adequate data on every important social problem, too little funded to have amassed all the data desired, and too positivistic to tell us what we should do. . . . The 1970 Commission on Obscenity . . . went so far in attempting to rely on social science evidence that a majority of its members took the absence of experimental evidence of causation of antisocial behavior or sexual deviance as a basis for urging the deregulation of obscenity. . . .

> Every time an emperor or a king or queen or a president or a parliament or a congress or a legislature or a court has made a judgment affecting social policy, this judgment has been made in the absence of absolute guidance from the social sciences. The Constitutional Convention of 1787 had no experimental evidence to guide its decision-making. When the First Continental Congress proposed the First Amendment in 1789 and when it was ratified by the states in 1791 and made a part of the Constitution, the empirical social sciences had not yet been conceived.[3]

Therefore, parents, you should always feel free to make common-sense assertions to your kids about the relationship of teen sex to marriage. For example, when my kids were teenagers, I used logic in making a case against premarital sexual activity. "Do you want to be faithful to the woman you marry?" I would ask. My boys nodded, yes. I'd respond, "Then you should

---

[2]*Final Report of the Attorney General's Commission on Pornography,* Introduction by Michael J. McManus, 1986, Rutledge Hill Press, Nashville.
[3]Ibid., page 487.

consider your teen years as training in chastity for a future faithfulness. To the degree that you can be sexually abstinent *before* you are married, the eas-ier it will be to be faithful to your wife afterward."

At the time, I had no proof. However, a major 1992 study shows that those who have lost their virginity before marriage *are 60% more likely to divorce than those who marry as virgins!* See the evidence on pages 92–93.

EMPIRICAL EVIDENCE ON TEEN SEXUALITY

Thanks to a major 1992 study cited next, our knowledge about how to increase the odds that teens will remain chaste is a light-year ahead of where it was even in 1990.

Fortunately, there is now freshly documented evidence on the factors that will influence a child to become sexually active, or to remain sexually abstinent. This information is essential in attempting to assess the effective-ness of any sex education program designed to increase abstinence by teen-agers. It was developed by Dr. Stan E. Weed, CEO of the Institute for Research and Evaluation. He gave questionnaires to 7000 students, 80% of whom were virgins when first questioned in 1988–89 and 1989–90, and who attended var-ious junior and senior high schools in city, suburban and rural areas in Utah. Some had taken abstinence-based sex education programs, while others had taken no course. The funding for his path-breaking research came from the Office of Adolescent Pregnancy Prevention in the federal Department of Health & Human Services and from the Utah Department of Education.

By anonymously questioning seventh, eighth, and tenth graders who were virgins, on their values, attitudes toward parents, friends, and church, and dating and drinking experience, Dr. Weed isolated those factors he thought most likely to predict which students would become sexually active in the next year. Then he returned to those students a year later to see who had, in fact, lost their virginity. Some students were questioned in 1988–89 and then requestioned a year later. Others were questioned the first time in 1989–90 and then in 1990–91. The requestioning provided a longitudinal look at what values and experiences were, in fact, most likely to predict the tran-sition from virgin to nonvirgin.

This data from a "control group" that had received no sex education could then be compared with students who *had* participated in one of three programs that aim to increase the likelihood that students will remain chaste. His primary goal was to measure the effectiveness of three different sex edu-cation programs being used in the state to see which had the greatest impact in reducing predicted teen sexuality: "Sex Respect," "Teen Aid," and "Values and Choices." Such a study is nationally unprecedented and of fundamental importance to any parent or school board trying to decide what kind of "sex education" should be offered in schools.

As noted above, his first step was to determine what factors are most important in predicting whether a teenager will become sexually active. Dr. Weed's hypothesis is that from a student's perspective, there were five possible variables of importance:

1. *The student's value system.* Questions were asked to measure each student's current sexual values. For example: "If someone asks you to have sex, what would you do?" Another: "How likely is it you will have sex before marriage?" These questions measure *intent*. Those students clearly indicating intent to be sexually active were considered to have "low values" and those saying they would remain a virgin until marriage were assigned "high values." Dr. Weed says, "Those who say they would have sex, probably certainly will. One's intention is a good measure of future behavior."

2. *Peer environment.* Sample questions were: "How many of your friends have had sex?" "Is there support from your friends to be abstinent before marriage?" "How much pressure do you receive to be sexually active?"

3. *Personality.* As a measure of a person's vulnerability and rebelliousness, teens were asked to react to such statements as: "If someone tells me I shouldn't do something, it makes me want to do it all the more."

4. *Drinking.* Examples of questions: "How often do you use alcohol?" "Have you been drunk? If so, how often in the past month?"

5. *Sexual knowledge.* This variable is how much students *know* about the facts of sexually transmitted diseases, the effectiveness of condoms, male and female physiology, and so forth.

Guess which of these preceding items is irrelevant in predicting future sexual activity. Go on, circle an item before I give you the answer! Test your knowledge of the world of teenagers.

Did you guess sexual knowledge? I bet you did not. Why?

Perhaps 90% of sex education programs now in America's schools are based on the premise that if the kids are given "the facts" about the likelihood of catching Sexually Transmitted Diseases (STDs) such as AIDS, or if they know which forms of contraception are most effective, they will make better and more responsible decisions about sexuality.

The fact is, Dr. Weed asserts, that "*The most knowledgeable kid is just as likely to be sexually active as the least informed!* And the informed are *no more likely* to use contraceptives." It makes no sense. What matters is not the information but the values communicated. If the teacher says, "*You* have to decide what's right for you," the student thinks, "It's not a bad thing to do." Knowledge does not drive behavior—at least sexual behavior.

Nor are differences in personalities very significant. The rowdy student is not much more likely than a quiet one to be sexually active.

What matters most are:

- whether the teenager has higher values or not;
- whether his peers are positive or negative;
- whether he drinks a lot, and
- whether he has dated early, often, and regularly with a person of the opposite sex.

Half of those teenagers who make the wrong choices as compared with *only* 5% of those with the most favorable combination of high values and actions will lose their virginity in a year, according to Dr. Weed's research.

Independent confirmation of this thesis is a sex survey conducted by *Who's Who of American High School Students,* which found that a stunning 72% of the best students have *never had sex.* They graduate as virgins!

With those factors as background, the impact of sex education *depends entirely on the content of the sex education.* ✖

With the course called "Sex Respect," students "showed a very significant shift in favor of abstinence. "Teen Aid" is significant but less so.

"'Values and Choices' made no significant change," said Dr. Weed, "but all are vastly better than what is found in nine-tenths of American schools. They actually tend to *increase* teen sexual activity." Later in this chapter, I'll provide more detail on "Sex Respect," "Teen Aid" and "Values and Choices," after we have looked at how active American teens are sexually and what sex education most kids are exposed to.

THE VAST INCREASE IN TEENAGE SEX

Most sex education is worthless. After twenty years, as sex education has reached the vast majority of U.S. teenagers, they have become not less but much *more* sexually active. Premarital sexual activity among adolescent females has almost doubled in the last two decades, with a sharp increase since 1985. Sex education was supposed to reduce the fire of teen sexuality, not pour gasoline on it!

By 1988, according to the U.S. Centers for Disease Control, 51.5% of females aged fifteen to nineteen had engaged in premarital sex by their late teens as compared to 29% in 1970, the biggest increase being among the youngest teenagers. In 1970, less than 5% of fifteen-year-olds had experienced sexual intercourse. That shot up fivefold by 1988 to 26%! For eighteen-year-olds, it rose from 39 to 69%.

"Even more disturbing than the high numbers of young women experiencing premarital intercourse is the increasing number of partners they have," said Charmaine Yoest of the Family Research Council, a private lobby for the family in Washington. Of sexually experienced fifteen- to seventeen-year-olds, 26% have had four or more partners. Among eighteen- and nine-teen-year-olds, 34% had four or more partners. In fact, many eighteen-year-olds today have had as many sexual partners as women aged forty have had over their entire lives!

Now, it must be said that I have not *yet* proved that this increased sexual activity is due to the increasing spread of sex education. The growth of the two in parallel could be a coincidence. But it is not, as will be demonstrated.

First, however, let's look at the consequence of the vast increase in sexual activity of teenagers. It has had major negative consequences:

— *Fertility*: The U.S. has the highest teenage fertility rate of any modern nation (*double* that of Great Britain, *triple* that of Scandinavian countries, and *ten times* that of Japan): one million teen pregnancies a year, or 3000 a day!

— *Births* to unmarried teenagers have increased astronomically: up 56% in the 1950s; another 119% in the '60s. Due to an increase in abortions, the increase of out-of-wedlock births slowed in the '70s but still jumped 38%, and another 19% in the '80s. There were only 59,000 births of children to unmarried teens in 1950, and 337,000 in 1989. Thus, of the 518,000 babies born to teenagers in 1989, two-thirds were out-of-wedlock. Half of these children-having-children never complete school, and most end up on welfare. Half of all women on welfare had their first child as a teenager.

— *Abortions* to teenagers doubled from 191,000 in 1972 to 419,000 by 1978 and have remained at about that level each year of the 1980s. Abortion terminates about 40% of teenage pregnancies, according to the National Center for Health Statistics.

— *Sexually Transmitted Diseases* are skyrocketing among teens. Genital warts alone infect three million teenagers. More than a dozen other STDs including chlamydia, herpes, syphilis, and gonorrhea are growing rapidly. If left untreated, STDs can lead to infertility, heart disease, arthritis, brain damage, and even death, but four out of five women infected by gonorrhea or chlamydia show no symptoms. One result is that STDs render 100,000 women infertile annually, and about 10,000 teenagers contract AIDS, which is always fatal. When a person has three or more sexual partners in a lifetime, the odds of getting cervical cancer jump fifteen times, according to University of Michigan gynecology researcher Dr. Thomas Elkins.

— *Behavioral Problems*: According to a study published in *Pediatrics*, early sexual activity leads to serious behavioral problems. Of 1500 girls studied, nonvirgin girls were 2.5 times more likely to have used alcohol than virgins, 6.2 times more likely to have smoked marijuana, and 4.3 times more likely to have attempted suicide. Boys were seven times more likely to have been arrested or picked up by police. Admissions of adolescents to hospitals for depression have tripled.

— *Suicide* among teenagers (fifteen to nineteen years old) has tripled from 3.6 to 11.3 per 100,000 between 1960 and 1988 and has accounted for 10% of deaths of those aged 1–24 years in 1987, said the *Morbidity and Mortality Weekly Report*, 1989, Communicable Disease Centers, Atlanta. And "Sexual matters often predominate among the risk factors for adolescent depression and suicide," said a supplement of the May 12, 1982, *Medical Tribune*.

THE FAILURE OF SEX EDUCATION

Such horror was to have been avoided by sex education, which expanded dramatically, in an attempt to reverse, not accelerate, these trends. Four-fifths of states in the 1980s required or encouraged the teaching of sex education. Of course, sex education can mean anything from teaching students abstinence to the biological facts about reproduction or the promotion and demonstration of contraceptive devices, said the Family Research Council.

Family Planning Perspectives is not a magazine of right-wing critics but of Planned Parenthood's research arm, the Alan Guttmacher Institute, yet its articles document the failure of the approach:

1. A study by Deborah Dawson, published in *FPP*, July/August 1986, reported that "prior contraceptive education increases the odds of starting intercourse at 14 by a factor of 1.5." She added, "The final result to emerge . . . is that neither pregnancy education nor contraceptive education exerts any significant effect on the risk of premarital pregnancy among sexually active teenagers—a finding that calls into question the argument that formal sex education is an effective tool for reducing adolescent pregnancy."

2. A 1986 poll conducted by Louis Harris for Planned Parenthood reports that teens who have had a sex education course have a fifty percent *higher* sexual activity rate than those who had no course, or one omitting contraceptives.[4]

3. A study published in the May/June 1982, *Family Planning Perspectives* by William Marsiglio and Frank Mott, found that "prior exposure to a sex education course is positively and significantly associated with the initiation of sexual activity at age 15 and 16."

---

[4]"American Teens Speak: Sex Myths, TV and Birth Control"

4. Analyzing the Marsiglio/Mott study, Dr. Jacqueline Kason found that fifteen-year-olds were 40% more likely to begin sexual activity if they had had sex education; sixteen-year-olds were 25% more likely.

A few pages ago I noted that the "biggest increase" in teen sexual experience "has been among the youngest teenagers. In 1970, less than 5% of fifteen-year-olds had experienced sexual intercourse. That shot up fivefold by 1988 to 26 percent." I've quoted from Planned Parenthood's *Family Planning Perspectives* that fifteen-year-olds who took standard sex education are 40–50% more likely to become sexually active than those who never took it. And in 1992, the Centers for Disease Control reported that of students who engaged in sex in three preceding months, only 45% used condoms. That's evidence that typical sex education is positively harmful and a major factor in increased teen promiscuity.

Why? What is the content of sex education?

CONTENT OF MOST SEX EDUCATION PROGRAMS

Most sex education in public schools is based on a Swedish approach that assumes teenage sex is inevitable, that teachers should take a neutral stance on morality, and teach contraceptive use to reduce teen pregnancy.[5] *When teaching contraception increased teen pregnancy, sex educators got birth control clinics opened nearby, then moved them into the schools, and ended up simply handing out condoms. All to no avail.* A second premise is that if teens know about the dangers of AIDS, STDs, pregnancy, they will be persuaded to practice only "safe sex" with a condom. Former Surgeon General C. Everett Koop discovered how wrong those ideas were after he mailed out an AIDS pamphlet to every household and found that it had no impact on young people: "They knew everything after reading the booklet, but it did essentially nothing to change behavior." Why? As Stan Weed proved, what matters is not knowledge of sex—but *values*, one's sense of what is "right" or "wrong."

Dr. Alfred Kinsey, the father of American sexology, disagreed. He saw no "right" or "wrong" sex. His 7-point "Kinsey Scale" used in most sex classes, shows sex as a continuum, ranging from heterosexuality, given a 0— to homosexuality, given a 6. In the middle in the "balanced" position of 3, is bisexuality. This desensitizes students, leading them to think that all sex is "normal," and worth trying. They are not told that Kinsey's estimate that 10% of males are homosexual is based on a group of men, 25% of whom were inmates of prison (where more men practice homosexuality), or that hundreds of Kinsey's subjects were rapists and child molesters.

---

[5]That premise is flawed. Even with soaring rates of teen sexuality activity cited earlier, *half* (48.5%) of girls aged 15–19 have *not* had intercourse. An equally logical case can be made that teenagers do not want to be sexually active and would like help to continue to be abstinent.

Explicit Materials are used in many of the classrooms. They shock young people. In 1985–1990, film strips of boys and girls masturbating, and male actors engaging in anal intercourse, or women in lesbian scenes—were shown in Greenwich, Connecticut public schools (until some parents objected). New York City's new curriculum asks teachers to recognize that "children may live with lesbian/gay parents." *First graders* read from books such as *Heather Has Two Mommies* and *Jennifer Has Two Daddies.*

Family Planning Clinics was the next "answer." When teen pregnancies continued to rise, Planned Parenthood convinced the federal government that the problem was that teens could not afford birth control. So Washington funded 5000 "family-planning clinics" with \$2 billion between 1971–1981 that were often placed near high schools. By 1982 they reached 1.5 million teens a year with free condoms, birth control pills, IUDs and so on. (About \$150 million a year is still budgeted by the federal government, matched by \$250 million of state funding.)

Why didn't the pregnancy rate go down when more teens used birth control? The belief that they could enjoy "safe sex" induced a higher percentage of teens to be sexually active. And they are notoriously irregular users of contraceptives and are more impulsive and risk-taking. Even 14% of older women get pregnant when condoms are the contraceptive.

Result: Teen pregnancy rates climbed 48% from 1971 to 1981.

Teen abortions were the next phase of "sex educators." Free abortions for teens did lower teen births. Planned Parenthood bragged about the success. But a 1986 study by Stan Weed and Joseph Olsen found that while there was a drop of 80 births per 1000 teenage clients—there were also 120 more abortions per 1000 teenagers! Thus, there was actually *an increase of 40 pregnancies* per 1000. "Pregnancy rates were not going down as a result of family-planning involvement but to a more frequent termination of pregnancy through abortion," Weed and Olsen wrote.

School-based clinics became the next fad of sex educators. They said that if contraceptives could be handed out in school so kids did not have a stigma of going to a family-planning clinic, more would use them. Knowing that this would be controversial, sex educators disguised their purpose. The federal law providing initial funding said that they were to give "nutrition and hygiene counseling, health-care-related to sports . . . alcohol and drug-abuse education" in addition to family planning. By 1980, there were 12 school-based clinics and 162 in 1990, at a cost of \$125,000 each.

But did they work? Not at all. *Family Planning Perspectives* published a study that looked at five years of experience of school-based clinics in Dallas, San Francisco; Gary, Indiana; Muskegon, Michigan; Jackson, Mississippi; and Quincy, Florida. "None of the clinics had a statistically significant effect on school-wide pregnancy rates," the report concluded. In fact, that conclusion misstates the study's data! A close reading of the tables show that pregnancies rose by one-quarter in schools with sex-based clinics!

Did sex educators concede defeat? Of course not. Everything was carried to its logical extreme in the 1991–92 academic year.

Free condoms were handed out by New York City schools. Thrilled that the new market might open eventually, condom makers donated an initial 45,000 condoms—the famous "Trojans" made by Carter-Wallace and Schmids "Ramses." A Coalition of Concerned Clergy and Parents told the school board that the condom failure rate is 18% with teens and cited a UCLA study that *the HIV virus leaked through Trojans.* Yet the school board voted 4–3 *against* allowing parents to block the handing out of condoms to their children. The impact of condom handouts is unclear at this writing.

ABSTINENCE-BASED SEX EDUCATION

In 1981, when Republicans seized control of the U.S. Senate for the first time in a generation and Ronald Reagan recaptured the White House for the Republicans, Alabama's then-Senator Jeremiah Denton pushed through a bill to promote sexual abstinence for America's teenagers. Derided by liberals as the "chastity bill," the legislation created the Office of Adolescent Pregnancy Programs in the U.S. Department of Health and Human Services. Though its funding has been small—$7.8 million in 1992, for example (and threatened with termination in recent years), the agency has funded the development of sex-education programs aimed at promoting abstinence.

To varying degrees, several of these curricula have been successful. Parents concerned about keeping their children chaste should look upon the remainder of this chapter as an introduction to how your public schools and your church can be allies in your battle to protect your children from premature and excessive sexual activity now being promoted in most sex-education programs. I will review four abstinence programs now in public schools: "Sex Respect," "Teen Aid," "Postponing Sexual Involvement," and "Values & Choices" (plus, "Why Wait?" that was designed especially for church youth groups by Josh McDowell). Both Sex Respect and Postponing Sexual Involvement have been independently evaluated, and help reduce teen pregnancy by 50% or more. Since these programs work and deserve wide use, they deserve a closer scrutiny. Teen Aid and Values & Choices are similar to Sex Respect in focus but are less effective and will get less space.

"Why Wait?" appears to be effective and has been used by an astounding 60,000 church youth groups, but it has not been independently evaluated.

What has this to do with marriage? As Sex Respect says in its *Teacher's Manual*: "Teens are being taught that they can act on any impulse and not have to face the consequences. How can we create a healthy society when its citizens have not learned self-control?"

What marriage can thrive if the couple has not learned self-control?

"SEX RESPECT"

"Sex Respect"[6] was developed by Coleen Kelly Mast, a former parochial school teacher, for use with Illinois public school teens in the Bradley-Bourbonnais High School. One of the strengths of her program is that there are materials for the student, the teacher, and the *parent*!

In the Parent's Guide, written to spark family dialogue, she says that a goal is to "save their teens the heartaches of broken love affairs, the burden of teen-age pregnancy, and the pain and suffering caused by sexually transmitted diseases."

The first chapter of the teen text begins:

> Just as we had to learn to crawl to stand, and to balance before we could walk, so we have to learn abut the mental, spiritual, and emotional parts of our sexuality before we are mature enough to handle the physical part, or sexual intercourse.

That is a difficult message to sell to this generation!

I received a report from the Public Health Service dated January 3, 1992: "Sexual Behavior Among High School Students—United States, 1990." It is based on interviews with 11,631 students and shows that by the ninth grade, 40% of young people have had sexual intercourse, and by the twelfth grade, 72%! Of even greater concern, 25% of ninth graders and 55% of twelfth graders have had sex in the last three months!

But the Sex Respect program is effective. How?

In the Teacher's Guide, Mrs. Mast recognizes that "Adolescence often is characterized by a young person's rejection of the controls of authority figures." Even so, her course is aimed at helping teachers and parents *to speak with one voice*, making the same case for abstinence—a case that is remarkably subtle:

> Teens have a much better opportunity to understand that saying "no" to sex and impulsiveness now fosters saying "yes" to love and maturity later. . . .

Further down, she adds:

> This program is about RESPECT. We teach respect without controversy, even though it is a challenge: respect for parents; respect for teachers; respect for other family members; respect for the property of others. The fact that vandalism provides psychological relief does not reduce our insistence on curbing it, because vandalism is not good for society. Why then should we be reluctant to provide sex education that is based on respect for oneself and others, and that will, in turn, benefit society?

---

[6]Taken from SEX RESPECT: *The Option of True Sexual Freedom* by Coleen Mast, copyright 1986, Respect Incorporated, P.O. Box 349, Bradley, IL 60915.

Mrs. Mast also deals frontally with the central question: "Why not teach birth control?" In response she offers both reasoning and statistics to make a case that:

> When teens are taught contraception in the classroom, they are led to believe that this is a legitimate option for them. We don't instruct in Driver's Education on "how to speed without getting caught," or "how to get traffic tickets fixed." Since sex outside marriage is not healthy for the teens in our classes, why offer them advice on "how to do it?"

She then ticks off persuasive data and analysis, some of which, in a sense, repeats material quoted earlier in this chapter but in succinct one-liners that could help advocates with school boards be more persuasive:

> Teens who have been given birth control education have a 50% higher sexual activity rate than teens who have not.[7]

> Teenagers who use the pill with a high rate of compliance reported an 18% pregnancy rate within the first year of use.[8]

> Birth control addresses only one symptom of the problem of teen sexual activity. . . . Birth control does not address teenage loneliness, insecurity, and need for intimacy.

> Sexual abstinence is the only certain method of avoiding teen pregnancy. . . . Birth control education weakens the message of abstinence. . . . It gives a double message of "how to say no" and "how to say yes," to an age group that needs only clear guidelines.

> Most birth control methods offer little or no protection from sexually transmitted diseases.

> Fifty percent of women who have had abortions say they were using birth control and it failed.

> Birth control does not stop the emotional bonding that joins the young man and woman during genital activity:
> * Breakups are more devastating for the teens.
> * Their ability to bond later to a spouse is hindered.
> * Memories of past sex acts are recalled later and used to make comparisons.
> * Genital bonding can fool young people into marrying the wrong person.

This point of view is communicated directly to the teen in the Sex Respect materials, often with humor. The material is laced with cartoons. One

---

[7]Louis Harris Poll for Planned Parenthood, "American Teens Speak: Sex, Myths, TV, and Birth Control."

[8]Martin, Fisher, et al. "Comparative Analysis of the Effectiveness of the Diaphragm and Birth Control Pill During the First Year of Use Among Suburban Adolescents," *Journal of Adolescent Health Care*, Sept. 1987, 393.

is a box with these words over a license plate: "Sex Is Like Driving. You Need a License for Both." The reader then sees the license itself, which says "I'LL WAIT."

SECONDARY VIRGINITY

There is another way to view how many high school kids are having sex—how many are *not*. While 54% of the 11,600 students interviewed in 1990 said that they have had sexual intercourse, some *45.8% are still virgins*. A course like SEX RESPECT will give many students the knowledge and skills to remain chaste, but what about those who have already been sexually active? SEX RESPECT makes a case for them to be sexually chaste—so-called *secondary virginity*. An excerpt:

"Secondary virginity is the decision to stop having sex until after marriage and the acting out of that decision. Any person who wants it can have it by:

- deciding to change
- detaching one's self from old habits, from people, places and situations that weaken self-control
- developing new, nonphysical ways to share.

"So even though you may have lost your physical virginity, you can still return to its advantages. Don't buy the myth that once you've given in to them you can no longer control your sexual impulses. After all, if you gain ten pounds during Thanksgiving break, it doesn't mean that you have to gain another ten during spring break. . . . You can stop. It won't be easy, but neither is studying for a test rather than cheating, cooling off instead of punching someone. . . ."

"TEEN AID"

"Teen Aid"[9] is quite similar to Sex Respect in its approach to promoting sexual abstinence. Developed in Spokane by a group helping pregnant women with their babies, its aim was to help them avoid a second out-of-wedlock pregnancy. It argues that postponing sexual involvement frees teenagers from sexually transmitted diseases, guilt, or disappointment, and the trauma of abortion, or out-of-wedlock birth. But its focus is broader than sexual abstinence, covering such added topics as nutrition, alcohol abuse, exercise, fetal development, and self-esteem.

There is a 240-page textbook that is optional, a workbook, and a "Parentgram," which students take home to spark family discussion about values on such topics as abortion, drugs, and abstinence.

---

[9]Published by Teen Aid, Inc., 1330 N. Kalispel, Spokane, WA 99201.

In Jacksonville, Florida, the biggest city using Teen Aid, a teacher told *The Florida Times-Union*: "Our kids have a perception that everybody is doing it. We give them permission to abstain and make some assumptions that they are capable of that." Parent Jim Jenson agreed: "I think they're showing you good ways of giving them positive support for abstinence."

Some parents, however, recoiled at the term, "secondary virginity." One said, "I just don't think fourteen-year-olds who already have a baby are going to see secondary virginity as an option." A teacher disagreed: "It says, 'I can start over again, and I can regain the advantages of abstinence.'"

Teen Aid sparks discussion beyond the sex issue to what qualities a successful family or a good friend have and what decisions can be made now that would produce such friends or family.

Teen Aid stresses that having sex carries certain responsibilities, such as the chance of pregnancy, and therefore is best done in marriage. By contrast, dating is seen as a time to focus on recreation, companionship, and friendship. It does not say when dating should begin, leaving that decision up to parents, but it does encourage parents to set dating standards and to share their own values.

There are problems in making a case for abstinence in the public schools, no matter how good the curriculum is. The *Florida Times-Union* story on April 28, 1991, quoted some teachers who worry that Teen Aid imposes values on parents who may have been teen mothers and fathers themselves. One said, "Parents do not want people telling them how to raise their kids." And despite its absence in the curriculum, some teachers *want* to teach about birth control to those who refuse to abstain. "I'm just not sure that I can avoid the subject by beating around the bush," said Sheila Smith, a teacher at Mandarin Middle School. "If a child asks me about contraception, I feel obligated to answer."

On abortion, Teen Aid calls the fertilized egg a baby, unborn child, or a new human—not a "fetus." Why? "We want them to see there's a direct responsibility between the act of intercourse and having a child," said Mrs. Benn. The curriculum ties that subject in with heredity and genetics. Students talk about how they resemble relatives but are very different.

Thus, Teen Aid is a close cousin of Sex Respect.

"VALUES AND CHOICES"

"Human Sexuality: Values and Choices"[10] is a fifteen-session curriculum written for seventh and eighth graders, with three sessions aimed at their parents. It, too, got its initial funding from the Adolescent Family Life Program and was developed by the Search Institute in Minneapolis, with

---

[10]"Values and Choices," published by Search Institute, 122 W. Franklin Ave., Minneapolis, MN 55404

backing from the Lutheran Brotherhood. Values and Choices uses videotapes in each class to spark discussion and contains similar material on abstinence, such as helping kids recognize sexual pressure, and then—learning how to say "No" in a variety of positive ways.

But it differs from Sex Respect and Teen Aid in several respects:

First, it attempts to decrease students' support for the "sexual double standard." One unit is devoted to the condemnation of sexism and sexual stereotyping, which are said to "limit choices and human potential."

Second, its choices focus is more "open-ended" in allowing students to "identify choices in specific situations and possible consequences accompanying each choice." Thus, it is not as directive or clear about "what is right and wrong," what is positive and what is harmful.

Third, and most important, the course offers information on "birth control methods"—as well as information on "the advantages of abstinence." Dr. Michael Donahue, Search research director, told me in an interview that Sex Respect is an "abstinence-only curriculum. The Values and Choices strongly emphasizes abstinence, but it does recognize the fact that not all teens are abstinent. So it includes information on contraception." A key theme is "sexual responsibility." (This is a direct contradiction to the premise upon which a federal grant was given—that the course would only promote abstinence.)

As Sex Respect predicts and as the long-term research proves, providing contraceptive education so dilutes the abstinence approach that there is *no* net gain in reducing teen pregnancy among users of Values and Choices.

EVALUATION OF ABSTINENCE COURSE

Dr. Stan Weed's evaluation of the three programs: Of 7th, 8th, and 10th graders with "lower values," those at greatest risk of becoming sexually active—37% did lose their virginity within a year. But of those with lower values who *did* take a course making a case for abstinence, only 22% had had sexual intercourse a year later. That's about 40% lower than the control group that had no abstinence course.

And of the three courses, "Sex Respect showed a very significant shift in favor of abstinence," says Weed. "Teen Aid's impact was also significant but did not do quite as well. Teen Aid had a larger number and greater variety of teachers committed to the program philosophy. With teachers who were strongly committed to the program objectives, students in this course did nearly as well as those in Sex Respect. Values and Choices had no significant change on rejecting permissiveness or in the intent to have sex."

More important was this finding from another study: "After two years, *those taking Sex Respect in junior high had pregnancy rates that were half of those students not in the program but attending the same schools.*"

"POSTPONING SEXUAL INVOLVEMENT"

Another course promoting abstinence, "Postponing Sexual Involvement" (PSI),[11] deserves attention, for three reasons:

1. Its technique is substantially different from those outlined above: The teachers are not professionals but eleventh and twelfth graders!
2. It is more successful than Sex Respect, sparking a much higher percentage of kids to postpone sexual involvement.
3. It has worked with the most difficult students to reach—inner-city black kids.

PSI[12] was initiated by Dr. Marion Howard, a professor in the Department of Gynecology and Obstetrics at Emory University and clinical director of the Teen Services Program at Grady Memorial Hospital, the inner-city hospital that serves Atlanta's poor. It was begun with Ford Foundation funds, not money from the federal government. (Therefore, it was not compared to Sex Respect, *et al*, in Weed's research.)

Dr. Howard created a sex-education program in the mid-1970s for Atlanta's public schools. It was quite similar to what most schools are now offering: five classroom periods of discussions on human sexuality, human decision making, family planning advice, and contraceptives to all who wanted them. It flopped.

Dr. Howard concluded, "Simply providing young teenagers with such information was not effective in changing sexual behavior." They were not more likely to remain chaste or to use contraceptives.

As she put it, in a book I highly recommend to parents of teenagers, *How to Help Your Teenager Postpone Sexual Involvement*:

> The completion of mental, psychosocial, and moral growth and development occurs years after the onset of fertility. Young people are at a real disadvantage, therefore, when forced to cope with social and peer pressures on sex. Adolescents tend to focus on the present. If adolescents in the eighth grade are thinking ahead, it is most likely about what they are going to do on the weekend. . . . Although most adolescents know that sex can lead to a pregnancy, they often focus on more immediate feelings. "The other guys will think I'm cool if they know I've had sex." "Maybe if I have sex with my boyfriend, it will keep him interested in me."

Therefore, Dr. Howard concluded that the best way to reach young teens is through "role models—teenagers slightly older than those being given the program—to present factual information, identify pressures, teach

---

[11]*How to Help Your Teenager Postpone Sexual Involvement* (Continuum, 1988)

[12]"Postponing Sexual Involvement" is a project of Teen Services Program, Grady Memorial Hospital, P.O. Box 26158, Atlanta, GA 30335-3801

assertiveness skills, and discuss problem situations. Teenage leaders have been shown to produce greater and more lasting effects than adults. Slightly older teenagers illustrate that those who "say no" to the pressured behavior can be admired and liked by others.[13]

PSI began in 1983 with eleventh and twelfth graders leading five classes with eighth graders. A male and female work as a team and are paid for their time, teaching classes for all eighth graders in nineteen separate Atlanta schools, reaching 4,500 students each year.

A key focus, based on a survey of more than 1000 sexually active girls, is what 84% of teens most want to know: *"how to say 'no' without hurting the other person's feelings."*

Its premise is that:

—Young people under 16 are often pressured into doing things they really do not want to do. Pressure to have sexual intercourse comes from peers and from glamorous images presented in the media.

—Young people need awareness and skills to be able to resist.

To measure the effect of PSI, 536 low-income minority students were interviewed— 395 who took the course in 1984–85 and 141 kids in schools without it. They were interviewed before taking the course and afterward.

The astounding result: *"By the end of the 8th grade, students who had not had the program were as much as five times more likely to have begun having sex than were those who had had the program: twenty versus four percent."*[14]

Dr. Howard found that *only one percent* of girls became sexually active by the end of the eighth grade out of 240 girls taking PSI, compared to 15% of 109 students in control schools who took no course. That's a stunning 15 to 1 ratio!

There was even a big impact on boys, though not as great. "By the end of eighth grade, boys who had not had the program were more than three times as likely to have begun having sex as were boys who had had the program (20 percent versus eight percent)," wrote Dr. Howard.[15]

Even with tallying boys and girls together, "Students who had missed the program were as much as 5 times more likely to have begun having sex than were their fellow students" in PSI (20% versus 4%).

Clearly, Postponing Sexual Involvement *does* postpone sexual involvement!

I know of no more effective abstinence program in America's public schools.

---

[13] Article in *Family Planning Perspectives*(Jan./Feb., 1991).
[14] Dr. Howard in *Family Planning Perspectives*.
[15] Ibid.

The impact fades with time but remains significant. A year later, at the end of the ninth grade, only 24% of PSI students had lost their virginity compared to 39% of control students.

What's more, Postponing Sexual Involvement has a more lasting impact.

In a February 1992, interview, Dr. Howard said that those eighth graders are now high school seniors and have had "a one-third reduction" of pregnancies compared to students outside the PSI program. How does she know? Her hospital, Grady Memorial, has followed the girls, keeping record of abortions, or teen births. Grady delivers 80% of babies born to Atlanta's teenagers. Furthermore, "More of the boys said they did not father a pregnancy. But that is harder to validate," she said.

Fortunately, Postponing Sexual Involvement is spreading rapidly. More than half of the school systems in Georgia that have sex education, now use PSI. It is being used in Raleigh and Durham, North Carolina, Fairbanks, San Jose, Cincinnati, and there have been 3,800 inquiries in all. Many church youth groups are also using it.

PSI is also much cheaper to implement than any of its competitors. There are no textbooks to purchase as in Sex Respect. There is a videotape that is for use in training student mentors who teach the classes, and written outlines for them. Total cost to buy PSI in any school system (or a church) is only eighty dollars.[16]

JOSH MCDOWELL'S "WHY WAIT?" SERIES

In each of the abstinence courses outlined thus far there is a central flaw. None tap the wisdom or power of Scripture. Of course, they were designed for public schools, where the Bible can not be taught as truth. Sex Respect and Postponing Sexual Involvement make a good secular case for biblical values though Scripture is never quoted. They could be used in a church setting with a church youth group.

If you are to help your teenager remain chaste, your church should be an ally in the battle and provide your youth groups with material that is explicitly Christian. St. Paul wrote "It is God's will that you should be sanctified, that you should avoid sexual immorality; that each of you should learn to control his own body in a way that is holy and honorable, not in passionate lust like the heathen" (1 Thess. 4:3).

However, a "Teen Sex Survey in the Evangelical Church" commissioned by Josh McDowell Ministry (of Campus Crusade for Christ) found that three-fourths of church youth learned little or nothing about sex at church, even in such conservative denominations as the Church of the Naza-

---

[16]To learn more, write Emory/Grady Teen Services Program, Box 26158, Grady Memorial Hospital, 80 Butler St., S.E., Atlanta, GA 30335.

rene and the Lutheran Church, Missouri Synod. One study estimates that 43% of church kids have had intercourse by the time they are seniors in high school. To fill that void, Josh McDowell has developed a program called "Why Wait?"[17] It combines videotapes, books, and discussion guides.

"Why Wait?" grew out of his talks with students across America. Josh has probably spoken in person to more high school and college students than any other American: to eight million on college campuses alone, on behalf of Campus Crusade for Christ. His provocative subject often is "Why Wait?"

The question came in a letter he received from a girl who wrote Josh:

> I just couldn't take the pressure any more. My boyfriend kept pressuring me for sex. The longer I resisted, the more I kept thinking, "What am I waiting for anyway?" You know I didn't have an answer. It seemed everyone else was enjoying it so I finally gave in. Now I know why I shouldn't have had sex, but now it is too late.

Evangelical churches were also concerned. Their National Sunday School Association commissioned a "Youth Survey" asking 3000 teenagers what kind of help they most wanted from their churches. "Counseling for sexual problems ranked first among 21 items," says Josh McDowell.

Therefore, McDowell put together two first-class sets of videotapes of talk, skits, music, and pungent youth reaction. Parts were made before live audiences. One is for parents, the other for teens.

"NO! The Positive Answer" is a four-part series (15 minutes each) aimed at teenagers. It has now been seen by an astonishing 60,000 church youth groups and more than two million kids.

Much of its content came from an essay contest that Josh sponsored for teens to speak out on their pressures, fears, and victories in the sexual arena. Their voices are woven through the videotapes. And they are moving:

> Dear Mr. McDowell,
>
> Can you help me? I'm thirteen and I've just ruined my life. I thought Mike really loves me, but last night we had sex for the first time and this morning he told my girlfriend that he didn't want to see me anymore. I thought giving Mike what he wanted would make him happy and he'd love me more. What if I'm pregnant? What am I going to do? I feel so alone and confused. . . . I can't talk to my parents, so please write me back. . . .

In speaking to teens, McDowell is dramatic, lively, even funny—but always biblical (unlike the earlier abstinence programs) and practical.

In one tape he says to high schoolers: "You've been lied to. How many of you have ever seen the price of sex on television? Have you ever seen anyone get a sexually transmitted disease on television?" The camera shows that not one hand went up. "That's *fiction*!" he shouts. "Today, just today, 33,000

---

[17]Josh McDowell Ministry, Box 1330, Wheaton, IL 60189. 1-800-222-JOSH.

Americans will get a sexually transmitted disease—twelve million this year!"

In another video he explains why "NO" has "two positive elements—to protect you and provide for you." He asks students to imagine that they trained for years as swimmers and made it to the Olympics, but when they show up for the ultimate race, the swimmers are lined up on four sides of the pool. "All jump in. It is not a race but a demolition derby!"

"That's why pools are divided into lanes. The lanes are there to protect you from hitting others. So God has given rules to protect you and provide for you. He wants to protect your most important sex organ—your *mind*! Hebrews 13:4 says, 'Let the marriage bed be kept pure.' But heavy petting and beyond will go into your long-term memory." He tells of one young man who said that sex with his wife was hurt by memories of old affairs: "Josh, I have ghosts from former relationships. I experience reruns in my mind." He talks about how biblical rules protect young people from distrust, suspicion, heartbreak—not to mention 1.1 million teen pregnancies a year, AIDS, and STDs.

PARENTS HAVE MORE TO LEARN

The video series for parents is called "How to Help Your Child Say NO to Sexual Pressure." It has eight thirty-minute sessions, costs one hundred twenty-nine dollars, and has been shown to parents in 30,000 churches. It is significant that the series for parents is four times as long as the one for teens (four hours versus one hour). Parents have more to learn!

A survey of 1,400 parents, *Family Life and Sexual Learning of Children*,[18] revealed that only 15% of mothers and 8% of fathers had ever talked to their children about premarital sex. As one teen wrote Josh: "If only all parents could understand that we teens want to learn about sex from our parents, not from school or from the streets. Unfortunately, many parents shy away from the subject of sex."

Why? Some parents are embarrassed. Perhaps they themselves are not proud of their own sexual ethics and feel hypocritical in talking to their children. With more than half of marriages ending in divorce, many parents know that they have not been the role models that they should have been. Others may feel tongue-tied because they don't know enough Scripture data that can persuade skeptical kids.

My wife and I found it easier to talk with our first son, who was proud of his chaste stand, than with our second and third sons. We put all three in good church youth programs, where youth leaders who were closer to their age might have more credibility than old Mom and Dad. But with our third son, Tim, who was so attractive that the phone rang off the wall with girls

---

[18]Roberts, E. S., Kline, D., and Gagon, J. *Family Life and Sexual Learning of Children*, Volume 1, Cambridge, MA. Population Education, Inc., 1981.

calling him up, we felt that we had to do more. When we heard that Josh McDowell was speaking at a Christian family camp-out, we took Tim and a friend to hear him in the summer of 1987, when he was sixteen. Tim was impressed, as were we. So we bought three audio cassettes of Josh McDowell, who was far more articulate and persuasive than we could be, and asked Tim to listen to them with us over the next month. He did so, somewhat reluctantly but graciously. I said, "When you hear Josh McDowell, I want you to think it is I speaking. I agree with everything that he says."

We also persuaded our church to show both video series—to teenagers and to parents. One father, who did not know I was responsible for his seeing it, told me later, "It gave me a way to talk to my daughter about sex—a bridge that either of us can now cross to talk to each other."

The one weakness of the McDowell materials is that they have not been independently evaluated by someone like Stan Weed. However, this is the kind of comment I have heard from pastors: "It was by far the best thing we have ever done," Rev. Kevin Dunlop of the First Church of the Nazarene in Anderson, Indiana, told me: "Attendance grew each week. The first night we had 30, and by the end, it went to 70!" A guidance counselor at Newbury Park Adventist Academy in Newbury Park, California, wrote: "Why Wait?" is such an excellent curriculum. It's creative, it's biblical, it's relevant, and it's awesome." A pastor in Grinnell, Iowa, said: "The video segments are short, sweet, and very strong; the music is great. The series is the most effective tool on the subject of premarital sexual relationships between youth I have ever used." A Baptist pastor in West Columbia, South Carolina, said that the series is "the *best* I've ever used. The video had an excellent mix of talk and music. Its production values are high."

Josh McDowell has also co-authored a series of superb books to help. *Why Wait?* and *How to Help Your Child Say "No" to Sexual Pressure* are superb books to help you instill moral convictions within your children. Remember, parents, that *you* can have a greater impact than your kid's peers.

THE MEDIA IS THE ENEMY

Your biggest enemy as parents, mentioned only briefly up to this point, is the ghastly message of sex and mayhem that your child is exposed to on television, in the movies and videotapes, in music and pornography.

According to Nielsen data, by age eighteen, the average American child will have watched 22,000 hours of television. That's *double* the 11,000 hours spent in school! And what are they seeing? You know, in a visceral way, but here are the numbers from the American Academy of Pediatrics, which is concerned about the amount of violence children are exposed to:

— 200,000 acts of violence
— 14,000 sexual scenes and innuendoes.

Watching prime time TV on Saturday and Sunday nights, for example, are twenty-five million two- to five-year-olds; twenty-nine million six- to eleven-year-olds; thirty-two million teenagers.

Why does any parent permit it?

The Surgeon General has cited hundreds of studies showing that violent films and TV are partly responsible for a vast increase in U.S. violence. Dr. Brandon Centerwall, an expert on media violence, writes: "TV is a factor in 10,000 homicides each year." Dr. Tom Radecki, a psychiatrist who created the National Coalition on Television Violence, says that entertainment violence is responsible for 25–50 percent of all domestic violence in the United States. He cites studies that show that kids with a heavy TV diet are more likely to solve problems with peers by punching them. Long-term studies show that heavy TV watchers are much more likely to become pregnant while unmarried, delinquent as teenagers, and criminal as adults.

This should not be surprising, given that content of most films, in which for example, heroes win through murder, such as "Robocop 2" (which has 147 violent acts per hour), or "Total Recall" in which Arnold Schwarzenegger is killing dozens of people via a chainsaw, breaking necks, and blowing a hole in his wife's head, saying, "Consider this a divorce."

Then there is the degrading "music": "As Nasty As They Wanna Be" by 2 Live Crew, which depicts women being urinated upon and called "bitch" as they are forced by men into anal, oral, and genital sex. It sold two million copies. "The hard-core rap music is demeaning," says Keith Clayborne, a black newspaper publisher. "It uses curse words, and it's violent in nature. It teaches our kids bad behavior."

Even *Playboy* and so-called soft-core porn magazines "legitimize rape," said the Attorney General's Commission on Pornography. The eight major men's magazines have sales that are five times higher per capita in Alaska and Nevada than in other states. And rape rates are *six times higher* per capita in Alaska and Nevada than in North Dakota. X-rated films give the impression that women want to be raped. So it is no mere coincidence that 27% of Kent State coeds *have* been raped.

When our boys were young, television was much less violent and sex-laden. Compare *Gunsmoke*, for instance, with *ROC* (a homosexual wedding), or *Doogie Howser, M.D.* (looking favorably on teen intercourse). Even so, our TV set was OFF to our kids except for news, Walt Disney programs, and an occasional special program. The result: Beginning at age four or five, each learned to play a musical instrument, which gave them a self-esteem rare in young boys; all were involved in sports, and made good grades. We refused to allow R-rated movies, or to allow them to drive at age 16. When they protested, saying that no other parents were so strict, I cited data that the odds were one in three that they would have a major accident at ages sixteen or seventeen.

They knew that we were more strict than their friends' parents, but they knew also that we sacrificed time and money for them. So they survived—no, *thrived*.

"HELP YOUR CHILD SAY *NO* TO SEXUAL PRESSURE"

Much of this chapter has focused on policy: how to get better sex education in public schools and in churches. As I said at the beginning of the chapter, however, there is much the individual parent can do with a son or daughter. The question is *how*? A little pamphlet from Josh McDowell offers specific suggestions that are both simple and powerful:

Parents must build four bridges of communication with their child:

- By expressing ACCEPTANCE, we build a sense of SECURITY.
- By expressing APPRECIATION, we build a sense of SIGNIFICANCE.
- By expressing AVAILABILITY, we build a sense of IMPORTANCE.
- By expressing AFFECTION, we build a sense of LOVABILITY.

A young person who has a strong sense of security, significance, importance, and lovability is less likely to become sexually involved. He or she does not have to seek these things through sexual encounters.

"Take some time to think of ways you can build these bridges in your relationship with your child," said McDowell. "Here are a few possibilities:

- "Work together on chores and use the opportunity to talk.
- "Watch a TV program with your child (even if it is not your choice) and discuss it.
- "Increase the number of meals your family eats together, perhaps changing a time slightly to accommodate one member's schedule.
- "Pick 'cues' to remind you to express affection: Saying good-night, leaving for or returning from school, sitting down to dinner, checking a young child's homework—all these could be cues for a little kiss, a hug, a pat, a whispered, "I love you.' "

IN SUMMARY

It may seem odd to suggest that the first step to be taken in saving marriages is with teenagers, but our modern world is chewing up teenagers and spitting them out. Evil surrounds them and is far more pervasive than when teenagers of my generation were growing up. Pornography, for example, hardly existed in the 1950s. Now it is everywhere. Divorce was rare when I was a kid. Most public schools are teaching sex education that actually promotes promiscuity. And worst of all, the *majority* of young people will live in a single-parent home before they are eighteen, giving them a twisted idea of marriage. The world seems determined to infect the bodies, the minds, and the souls of our children, making it almost impossible for them to learn self-restraint and selflessness needed for *lasting* marriage.

But there *is* hope. It can be found at three levels:

First, you as a parent can turn off the TV and do more things with your teenagers. When I realized that I had not built bridges of communication to my younger sons, I began taking them to play golf on weekends. For the first time, we were on a peer relationship, treating each other equally as we shot about the same scores. It was fun!

Second, you can get the "Why Wait?" videos to equip you to speak frankly, persuasively with your daughter or son about sex. No one can be more influential in communicating the importance of chastity. In fact, why not watch them with your teen? (They can be rented at a nominal sum from any Christian bookstore.)

Third, you could be more ambitious and get your church to show the "Why Wait?" videos— both those targeted at the kids and those aimed at parents to help scores of young people learn how to resist the seductive pressure to be sexually active premaritally.

Finally, new sex-education curricula have been developed for public schools that can cut teen rates of sexuality by 50% or more. While the battle will be tough, it has already been won in several thousand school districts. If parents from a cross-section of local congregations in your town are enabled to review the materials outlined here, I think that you can easily pick a course and use allies to help you persuade your local school board.

The outcome is up to you.

FIVE

Getting Serious—Help for the Seriously Dating Couple

There is a time for everything and a season for every activity under heaven . . . a time to embrace and a time to refrain (from embracing).

—Ecclesiastes 3:1, 5

I'm in love!

—The author, after his
second date with Harriet

For most people there is no more thrilling time in life than when one falls in love and dates someone so seriously that one keeps thinking: "Should we get married?"—and the world becomes an enchanting place!

My mind turns back to that period of my life. I met Harriet on a blind date in 1964. Her sister, Theodora, was dating Tim Nelligan, who shared a townhouse with me in the Georgetown area of Washington, D.C. I was a young *TIME* magazine correspondent, thoroughly intoxicated with Washington and my work covering the substance of what President Johnson called "The Great Society." While more senior correspondents reported upon the politics of selling Congress on the first major federal aid programs in education and health (such as Medicare), I had the privilege of interviewing anyone from the President on down on how these programs might change lives.

Theodora's sister, Harriet, also worked for Time, Inc., as a secretary in New York, so Tim and Theodora thought that we ought to meet each other the next time Harriet came down to visit her parents, so they planned a double date with us to go to a concert.

She was having dinner with her family when we arrived. My first thought was, "Boy, she is pretty!" She shook hands with unusual vigor for a woman, and with a dazzling smile. Harriet laughed frequently and merrily. When she got into my little Corvair, something popped and hit my windshield with a snap. Harriet laughed and said, "Hand me my doo-hinkey! They don't make snaps like they used to!" It was some sort of a garter-belt attachment that women wore in those days. I thought, *This is one self-confident, put-together woman, who laughed, when another would have been mortified.*

Later we went dancing at my townhouse in Georgetown with her sister and Tim. After they left, I made a fire and we talked and talked. I wanted to kiss her but dared not do so because I didn't want her to think my interest in her was only physical. By the time I drove her home, to my astonishment, it was 6:00 A.M.! Harriet told me later, "I just floated in. When my mother asked me why I was so late, I said, 'Mother, I've just met the most fascinating man in my life!' She was still unkissed by me!

Things were different on our second date—much more passionate. And I cast aside all sorts of caution and asked her as we were dancing again, "Do you think you might consider marrying me?" She replied, without hesitation, "Yes, I will!"

BACKGROUND ON OUR MARRIAGE

I always felt blessed by my marriage to Harriet. We had three sons in 1966, 1969, and 1971. She had always encouraged me to pursue my career dreams, though they were highly unorthodox as well as risky. However, my work caused stress on our marriage. Some background may be helpful.

I moved to Connecticut to create a series of "Television Town Meetings," in New York. I had secured an agreement from all eighteen TV stations in New York to air the same programs over five weekends that would frame "choices" of public policy for citizen debate and balloting. That commitment was unprecedented.

But no station was willing to put up the money to produce them. And the sponsor of the project, Regional Plan Association, thought the project too risky to put me on its staff. Therefore, I had to raise money not only for my salary, but for RPA's staff to help develop the content for five one-hour programs. At the time we moved to Connecticut, I had raised funds for only two months' work. I thought that with shows on every station, companies would jump to sponsor them. No way! Not with controversial TV shows on poverty, housing, and so forth. Ultimately, I raised small grants from many corporations, foundations, and the Federal Government.

We tried to harness the collective power of the news media to present "choices" for solving urban problems in Town Meetings. The project, which we called "Choices for '76," involved four elements: shows aired on eighteen TV stations over five weekends in 1973; twenty-six newspapers published ballots for citizen response; and many also wrote articles on the pros and cons of the issues. Some 20,000 people were organized in small groups to respond. Finally, we published a paperback book with a few pages on each of the fifty choices.

Under this pressure, I became a workaholic, reading and writing until midnight or later. And I worked six and a half days a week. I was not a good husband to Harriet, or a good father who took time with his boys.

When regular paychecks stopped, things got worse. In 1974–75 I helped other cities create similar projects. That may sound impressive, but consultancy checks were highly irregular. Harriet remained patient and encouraging, but I was putting her under strain.

And my dream expanded to create "American Town Meetings" that would involve network television and a news magazine. Alas, neither *TIME* nor *Newsweek* nor ABC, CBS, or NBC were interested. This created a major career problem! Rather than give up, I convinced an organization spawned by the bicentennial, the Citizen Involvement Network, to back my efforts to at least research and write background papers on the pros and cons of national choices that *might* be the basis of "American Town Meetings."

An iffy plan! Worse, the work was in Washington, D.C., while I lived in Connecticut! Its future was too uncertain for us to move.

Fortunately, Harriet's folks lived near Washington and put up with me on weekday nights. But my life became grim. I boarded a train at 2:00 A.M. Monday in Stamford and tried to sleep, arriving at 8:00 A.M. On Friday after work I'd return home, arriving at 11:00 P.M.

Harriet would have a lovely candlelight dinner awaiting me. We'd talk into the night. I often fell asleep in my chair, exhausted. Saturday was a day of working on background papers. We had a little above-ground pool out back, and Harriet often asked me to take the boys for a swim. "I don't have time," I'd often say. On Sunday we'd go to church, and I'd begin my train commute, again.

That went on for many months, but it ended late in 1975. The Citizen Involvement Network decided that it did not want Town Meetings to spark citizen involvement in the bicentennial. (Thankfully, I did find new work in New York, researching.)

A NOTE OF HUMILITY

After three more decades of life I now see so much more clearly that St. Paul was right to say, "Flee from sexual immorality" (1 Corinthians 6:18). Moreover, I prefer the bluntness of the King James Version: "Flee fornication."

Those who obey that Scripture can avoid pain at three levels:

1. *No Doubts*: Those who have not been sexually active before meeting the person they want to marry will never have paralyzing doubts about their capacity to be faithful to a spouse.

2. *Restraint Is Easier*: Those who are virgins when they meet the person they want to marry will find it easier to keep their physical relationship within proper bounds.

3. *No Pregnancy*: Obviously, women will not become pregnant before marriage—and thus will be spared inevitable embarrassment, especially with their families.

EVERYBODY'S DOING IT: THE WORLD'S VIEW

The Centers for Disease Control say that premarital sexual activity among adolescent females nearly doubled from 28.6% in 1970 to 51.5% in 1988. Among fifteen-year-olds alone it shot up sixfold from 4.6% to 25.6%! And 75% of nineteen-year-old females were no longer virgins. What about males? The Urban Institute conducted a National Survey of Adolescent Males in 1988 and found that by age nineteen, 79% of males "reported having had sexual intercourse compared to only 73% of the 1979 sample." And these are only teenagers!

What are the sexual practices of single Americans in their twenties?

According to Dr. Joan Kahn of the University of Maryland, the percentage of white women who were virgins at marriage plummeted from 43% in 1965–1969 to only 10% by 1980–1983 (the last year with data). In the same time, black female virgins dropped from 12% to 5%. Unquestionably, less than a tenth of singles now are virgins. And more than half of marriages are preceded by cohabitation. If "everybody is doing it," clearly, America's standards have changed. Is it a good thing?

"LIVING IN SIN? A BISHOP RETHINKS HUMAN SEXUALITY"

No one is more eloquent for this unbiblical point of view than Episcopal Bishop John Shelby Spong of the Diocese of Newark, who thinks that *the church* should bless fornication among cohabiting couples.

Bishop Spong wrote a 1988 book with the shocking title: *Living in Sin? A Bishop Rethinks Human Sexuality.* One chapter begins:

> I call upon the churches of this land to revive a concept of betrothal and to install it as a valid option and a sign of serious commitment, even though it falls short of the legal status of marriage. By "betrothal" I mean a relationship that is faithful, committed, and public but not legal or necessarily for a lifetime. . . . In fact, the contemporary practice of engaged couples comes close to defining what I mean by betrothal . . . . A liturgical form for such a betrothal would be fitting. That liturgy would include a declaration that the couple intends to live together in love and faithfulness for a period of time in a bonding relationship. The commitment would be recognized by the general public and by the church.
>
> The conception and birth of children would not be appropriate to this relationship of betrothal. A child born of both intention and by love deserves to have the nurture available in and the security provided by a legal bond of marriage, with permanence of commitment being the expectation of both the father and the mother . . .

His words seem reasonable and soothing, but his advice is not only unbiblical—it is impractical. There are many inconvenient facts about each of his lines of reasoning:

1. Birth control has been available for generations, and abortion now snuffs out the lives of 1.5 million pregnancies a year. Yet illegitimacy has soared fourfold since 1960, from 224,000 out-of-wedlock births to one million in 1990. Spong acknowledges that "conception and birth of children would not be appropriate" to betrothal. Yet 891,000 cohabiting couples *do* have children. How would betrothal make any difference? If anything, it might induce *more cohabitation*, which would generate more illegitimacies. To bless fornication would encourage more—not less—irresponsible behavior.

2. The male partner in cohabitating couples doesn't hang around long when a baby is on the way. The million illegitimate births a year lead to few marriages or common-law marriages. Some 4.9 million women who had children out of wedlock are bringing them up alone. Does Spong seriously suggest that more men would stick around if they had a "betrothal certificate?" Why would they? How would betrothal provide "an option to casual sex?"

3. Furthermore, as chapter 2 notes in detail, *cohabitation does not work* as a trial marriage. Spong says that betrothal would make legitimate "exploratory testing of a relationship" in a "trial period of living together." His clear assumption is that betrothal will build more stable marriages—that conventional wisdom is flat-out wrong. *The National Survey of Families and Households*, in its report, "The Role of Cohabitation in Declining Rates of Marriage," is clear: "Cohabiting unions are much less stable than those that begin as marriages. Forty percent will disrupt before marriage, and marriages that are preceded by living together have 50% higher disruption rates than marriages without premarital cohabitation."

If the odds were known, who would be foolish enough to gamble?

Nevertheless, Spong's Diocese endorsed a report by its Task Force on Changing Patterns of Sexuality and Family Life, which said that "The Church has generally been opposed to the actions of couples choosing to live together without ecclesiastical or civil ceremony. . . . The effect of the opposition has been to separate those couples from the ministry of the Church, to the detriment of the quality of their relationship. These persons might well benefit from church affiliation."

In a 1987 column, I wrote "What rot. [This] pandering after bodies in pews . . . will drive biblically oriented Episcopalians away." And, in fact, the Newark diocese *has* lost 22,000 Episcopalians under Spong—a *third* of its people, a bigger hemorrhage than from any other Episcopal Diocese.

A BIBLICAL RESPONSE

Neither the Newark Diocese nor Spong in his book, quote Scripture to justify the position they have taken. It is simply dismissed: "The Bible is misunderstood and misused when approached as a book of moral prescriptions directly applicable to all moral dilemmas," said the diocese.

"The central point of reference for the thinking Christian is the life, ministry, death, and Resurrection of Jesus Christ. . . . When a choice is between observance of the law or active, inclusive love, Jesus embodies and teaches love."

In my 1987 column, I retorted: "Nonsense!" Did not Jesus denounce the woman at the well?: "You have had five husbands, and the man you have now is not your husband." And I quoted Dr. John Rogers, then president of the Trinity Episcopal School for Ministry: "The Newark statement is biblically contradictory. To imply that Jesus is love—without rules and commandments—is unfair to Jesus. He said, 'If you love me, you will keep my commandments.'"

Dr. Rodgers says, "This is an ethic of intimacy which blesses the culture, rather than criticizes it. . . . Instead of criticizing and transforming the church, it is collapsing under the mind of the age. The ethic is incredibly vague and is a formula for the abuse of women. The place for the sex act scripturally is heterogeneous, monogamous lifelong marriage."

For example, Jesus showed compassion for the woman caught in adultery, whom the Pharisees said that the Law of Moses commanded be stoned for such a sin. In John 8, he said to them: "If any one of you is without sin, let him be the first to throw a stone at her." They all walked away, leaving Jesus with the woman. He said to her, "Has no one condemned you?"

"No one, sir," she said. "Then neither do I," Jesus declared. "Go now and leave your life of sin." Thus, he continued to condemn the sin while loving the person.

Bishop Spong and his Newark Diocese turn Scripture about sex on its head. The issue is not whether unmarried people living with each other can benefit from the church—but whether there is any such sin as fornication, and if so, what is the job of the church *vis-à-vis* with sin: to rationalize and endorse it, or, biblically, to oppose it? Surely, when bishops and churches praise evil, evil will only grow. Besides, shacking up needs no church fan club. It soared sixfold from 11% in 1970 to two-thirds of newlyweds now.

Webster's New Collegiate Dictionary defines sin as "transgression of the law of God." I add to that my belief that sin always harms someone—always the sinner and often those around him or her. The issue is not simply biblical or theological. It is also one of ethics that can be demonstrated without regard to Scripture.

"PURITY . . . SEXUALITY AND THE SINGLE CHRISTIAN"

The most eloquent advocacy for chastity I have seen is a book, also written by an Episcopalian, a Christian reporter, Julia Duin, called *Purity Makes the Heart Grow Stronger: Sexuality and the Single Christian.* (Isn't it ironic that a pretty, single reporter in her thirties wrote a book with that title, while a *bishop* wrote *Living in Sin?*)

Some excerpts from Miss Duin's book:

> We all know that sex doesn't bestow instant maturity, and I think the opposite can be true: Premarital sex exposes our immaturity and inability to wait for the best. Christ did not need sex to be a man. Being a man involves courage, taking risk, leadership, decisiveness, tenderness, and gentleness as well. . . .

> One way I've found to bloom instead of wilt on the vine is by looking for romance—not the courtship kind but the destiny kind. This kind of romance is the expectation, anticipation, joy, hope, and desire we experience as we lay down our lives for other people.

As I write, Miss Duin has not married and is still a virgin. Her purity shines like a beacon.

COHABITATION DOES NOT WORK

As parents or people who have influence upon young people, we need to tell them that cohabitation will set them up for a failed marriage.

In 1983, *Newsweek* reported that only 16% of college students thought it harmful "for a man and woman to live together before marriage" while 61% said it would be "helpful." If the students were right, cohabitation might deserve consideration. What's astonishing is that Spong and his diocese and other mainline denominations (such as the Presbyterians, Evangelical Lutherans, and United Methodists) that are flirting with the idea of blessing cohabitation, have not looked at the evidence of its palpable harm, as reported by many studies:

(1) *Psychology Today* reported in its July/August 1988 issue, a Swedish study: "Yale University sociologist Neil Bennett and colleagues found that cohabiting women were 80 percent more likely to separate or divorce than were women who had not lived with their spouses before marriage."

(2) A 1983 study by the National Council on Family Relations of 309 newlyweds, found that those who cohabited first were less happy in marriage. Women complained about the quality of communication after the wedding.

(3) The *National Survey of Families and Households* reported in 1989: "Unions begun by cohabitation are almost twice as likely to dissolve within 10 years compared to all first marriages: 57 percent to 30 percent."

Marriage is one shoe that you cannot try on before you wear it!

Now let's examine what happens to couples who don't live together but are sexually active while in a dating relationship.

WHAT'S WRONG WITH SEX IN A DATING RELATIONSHIP?

Sexually active people are much more likely to divorce! Joan Kahn and Kathryn London studied 2,746 women in the National Survey of Family Growth and measured the odds. "Among white women first married between 1965 and 1985, virgin brides were *less* likely to have dissolved their marriages through separation or divorce than women who had not been virgins at marriage," they reported in the *Journal of Marriage and the Family* in November 1991. How much less likely? The numbers are stunning:

Nonvirgins have a divorce rate that is 53% to 71% higher than virgins. As the chart below based on their research indicates, this impact was about the same with virgins who married between 1965–1969 and with those marrying between 1980–1983. The column is the year of marriage; the second, the divorce rate by 1988 of those who were virgins at the time of marriage; and the third, the divorce rate of non-virgins from the same age cohort; and the fourth, the higher percent of divorces among non-virgins.

	Divorce Chart		
Years of Marriage	*Divorced/Separated Virgins*	*Divorced/Separated Nonvirgins*	*Percent Higher*
1980–1983	14%	24%	71%
1975–1979	21%	34%	62%
1970–1974	30%	46%	53%
1965–1969	30%	50%	67%

The authors, Dr. Kahn of the University of Maryland and Dr. London of the National Center for Health Statistics, say that "Women were more likely to have been virgins at marriage if they came from intact families, went to church regularly as teenagers (especially, fundamentalist Protestants), and were subject to strict rules while growing up." If those factors in the background of virgin brides are excluded, or "controlled" in sociological jargon, "virgin brides are *not* significantly less likely than non-virgins to separate or divorce."

This finding states the matter upside down. Of course, virgins are more likely to be religious, and be brought up in strict homes. There are several lessons from this important new study:

First. Both men and women have a reason to remain chaste before marriage. This is unprecedented sociological evidence that those with biblical standards can *increase their odds of a lasting marriage*. To put it differently, non-virgins increase *their* odds of divorce by about 60%.

Second. Parents should make a copy of this table and show it to their teenagers as evidence that there is a long-term payoff to playing the game of life by God's rules. And parents should be encouraged to expose their children to the best religious education they can get, to be strict on the age at which dating is allowed, cars are available, and so forth.

Third. Pastors have got to begin preaching on the long-neglected issues of chastity for the unmarried. As the authors of this study report, the percent of women who marry as virgins plunged from 43% in the late '60s to a mere 10% by 1985–87. Unfortunately, the study did not look at the issue of male virginity and divorce. Paul wrote to the Thessalonians, "It is God's will . . . that you should avoid sexual immorality, that each of you should learn to control his own body in a way that is holy and honorable, not in passionate lust like the heathen."

Pastors can now cite evidence from the National Center for Health Statistics, that women who don't cherish chastity will have divorce rates 60% higher than those who do. That's real world evidence of the wisdom of Scripture. Paul wrote to the Corinthians: "Flee from sexual immorality. All other sins a man commits are outside his body, but he who sins sexually sins against his own body" (1 Cor. 6:18). Chastity is a basic biblical principle (1 Thess. 4:3–8; Eph. 5:3–12).

Equally important is research by Father Andrew Greeley, a sociologist and novelist who is doubtless America's best-known priest (thanks to his lively novels). He asked the General Social Survey of the National Opinion Research Center in Chicago to study the relationship of sex to marital fidelity and happiness. In his 1991 book, *Faithful Attraction*, based on GSS data, Greeley reports that *half of all adults (48%) have had only one sexual partner— their spouse!*

That figure includes 65% of all women and 30% of the men. What's changed is increased sexual activity by women. In 1970, 78% of all women had experienced sex only with their marriage partner.

THE RESEARCH OF DR. JIM A. TALLEY

Few people have seen these risks up close more than has Dr. Jim A. Talley. For over two decades he worked with singles and was the "singles minister" for fifteen years at the large, 3,800 member First Baptist Church of Modesto, California. In those years he counseled 10,000 single adults, many of whom were "single again" after a divorce. In 1972 when he joined the staff, divorces were rising rapidly. They had doubled in a decade from 393,000 in 1960 to 845,000 in 1972 (and would reach nearly 1.2 million by 1980).

Jim felt that the problem for many couples was that they "were being swept into marriage by 'eromania' (romantic love) and never took the time *to develop the skills required to make a relationship work.* People tend to seek romance, somehow believing that a lasting relationship will be part of the package. So in today's disposable society, alliances are often hastily devised and easily discarded at the first signs of conflict or disillusionment, as people search for the magic of instant love."

In his book, *Too Close, Too Soon*, written with Bobbie Reed, Talley notes that "men and women have a tendency to approach intimacy differently. For men, physical intimacy often precedes emotional involvement; however, women usually relate emotionally before they are physically close to a dating partner." This creates inevitable misunderstandings.

> If a woman believes that physical contact follows emotional intimacy, then she may assume her partner to be as emotionally committed to the relationship as she. . . . She may start expecting a marriage proposal once her partner initiates physical intimacy. Perfectly logical to her; possibly terrifying to him. The relationship may end at this point. The man, completely surprised by the depth of his partner's emotional attachment to him . . . may withdraw, explaining that he isn't ready for a serious relationship.

> True intimacy takes time to develop as trust is built into each facet of a relationship by a series of shared experiences. . . . Recognizing and accepting the fact that physical and emotional intimacies tend to have different priorities for men and women is the first step in resolving those differences. The second step is to exercise mutual patience.

Of course, patience is *not* the characteristic of most modern romances—sexual intimacy is the norm, and it is like putting rocket boosters on a Ford, shooting it down a highway at high speed. Dr. Talley uses another image to describe the danger:

> Premarital sex creates instability in the relationship. It is like trying to build the second floor of a building on a few sticks in the ground. There is guilt, an unrealistic expectation of marriage, when neither made that commitment, and an intensity in the relationship without a foundation of friendship to hold it up.

But how, in today's sexually saturated culture, can a seriously dating couple put on the brakes, find patience, remain chaste, while building a relationship that could grow into a lasting marriage?

Dr. Talley's answer is what he calls "Relationship Instruction."

THE SERIOUSLY DATING COUPLE: A TIME FOR COUNSELING

Originally, Talley was trying to help engaged couples but found that they didn't pay much attention. He would sit down with young engaged couples and say,

> Falling into love with and being sexually attracted to a member of the opposite sex is no guarantee for a successful marriage. A marriage is more than romance and sex. It is an ongoing relationship. Yet too often, relationships do not survive the harsh realities of everyday life. Relationships

between men and women are complicated interactions that take a significant amount of time and energy to develop. You have set your marriage date too soon. You are going too fast. You must slow down.

But they had already set that wedding date. The sacred wedding date. A hall had been reserved. Invitations had gone out, or were about to. "I could wave red flags, but that train was going to the station no matter what," he now recalls. "It was as if their ears could not hear. They could not process what I was saying. I felt like a man standing in front of an eighteen-wheel diesel truck. If I put my foot under the front tire, they would release the brake and roll over it. I wanted them to discuss their relationship after they already had a full head of steam. My counseling did absolutely no good."

Therefore, he concluded the ideal time for counseling is at an earlier stage—before engagement, when a couple is ready to become emotionally intimate, at the time the couple is "seriously dating." He writes in *Too Close, Too Soon*: "Principles, concepts, expectations, and potential dangers are all easier to learn and accept before we become emotionally involved with a specific dating partner. In fact, the thought response to advice or counseling becomes less positive in direct proportion to the level of involvement in the relationship. During the early stages of a friendship, singles are usually open and responsive to advice on how to keep the relationship under control."

"RELATIONSHIP INSTRUCTION"

Therefore, he designed "Relationship Instruction" for the seriously dating couple to help them learn how to build a relationship before they are ready to make a lifelong commitment. What is Relationship Instruction? It can be viewed at several levels: It is a course, character development, and a discipline:

(1) *A Course* that has been taken by 5000 couples, can be taken anywhere at any time using both a paperback text, called *Too Close, Too Soon*, and a *Relationship Instruction Workbook*, written by Talley. It is best taken with an instructor, who can be a pastor, a counselor, or best of all, a solidly married Christian couple. After an initial meeting with the instructor, the man and woman, each of whom has his or her own *Workbook*, do an hour of homework one week. The next week they meet, exchange workbooks, and discuss them. Then, the following week, they meet with the instructor, who first reads the *Workbooks* and then discusses them for an hour with the couple.

Meeting every other week for eight sessions, the course takes four months. Furthermore, the couple agrees in advance to complete the Relationship Instruction course even if the dating relationship does not continue. Talley says "This is to prevent either one ... from getting hurt and to test [your] commitment level."

(2) *Relationship Development*: One week, each person writes a three-page biography on the most important influences in his or her life. Another explores the meaning of "love" as understood by our culture and Scripture. A third asks each person to write out short-range and long-range goals—personal, professional, spiritual, volunteer, and so forth.

The assignment another week is to explore the differences between men and women in such areas as logic versus intuition; initiator versus responder; conquers by force or wit versus conquers by love; steady versus changeable; future-minded versus present-minded. Another explores one's "self-esteem" and the characteristics that Scripture uses to describe a "godly man" and a "virtuous woman." Thus, the course helps the man and woman learn about each other and helps both put Christ at the center of their relationship. Yet both agree in advance that "No wedding proposal or date should be discussed" during the four months, in order to "protect the relationship from unrealistic expectations."

(3) *Discipline on Sex and Time*: The instructor asks each person to sign a commitment to limit his and her physical involvement and their time together. This discipline is quite stringent. In their first meeting with the instructor, the couple is asked to agree to keep strict limits on the time spent together.

On sex, the instructor asks them to "be honest about the physical part of the relationship."

"THIS IS DIVORCE INSURANCE!"

My first reaction, as Jim Talley told me about it, was "Wow! It is one thing to ask a couple to commit to chastity, but the time limits seem utterly unrealistic. I remember that when I first started dating Harriet, I wanted to be with her all the time. Your suggestion of a limit of twenty hours in the first month is only one date a week! Has anyone agreed to such severe limits?"

He replied, "I know of more than 1000 couples who've taken Relationship Instruction.[1] Many of them were previously married but divorced. They don't want to make a mistake in a second marriage." Indeed, I interviewed such a couple. Andrea, a divorcée, who married twice-divorced Bob, said, "It helped us put on the brakes. People who've been married before can easily jump the hurdles of the heart and head straight into the physical part." Bob added, "I had serious doubts. But after two failures, I needed help to prepare for marriage."

Still, the tough time-limits seemed extreme. I asked, "Jim, why are they needed?"

---

[1]My original interview was in 1985. An updated estimate is that 5000 couples have taken Relationship Instruction.

"My experience suggests that on average, a couple will be in bed after 300 hours alone together. I try to stretch that time out, with 140 hours in the relationship period, and another 160 hours during engagement so that they end up in bed for the first time on their wedding night!"

I asked, "What's been the impact of Relationship Instruction on those who took it?"

His reply astonished me: "Well, of over one hundred couples I've personally counseled, about half did not get married. But of those who did, I know of only one separation and a possible divorce." And that's over a decade!

"Two out of one hundred couples? That's less than a *five percent divorce rate*!" I said, "What you've created is *divorce insurance*!"

Of course, there probably are divorces or separations of couples who moved away from Modesto that Jim Talley did not know about. Assume that the failure rate is five times what he knows about. That is still only a 10% divorce rate compared to a 60% marriage-dissolution rate detailed in chapter 2.

RELATIONSHIP INSTRUCTION IS A CLEAR MARRIAGE SAVER

Talley outlined another major value of "Relationship Instruction" in an interview on February 29, 1992: "Virginity is not renewable, but celibacy is," he said. "Once you have messed up your virginity you cannot make this over. But you can renew a commitment to celibacy and live a godly and moral life. I've had people tell me, 'The simple thing of signing a commitment has enabled me to be faithful and to stay within the guidelines.' One man said, 'By signing my name and making a commitment, I stopped sleeping around. It was the first step back toward reconciliation with my ex-wife.' "

Relationship Instruction could become as important in a local church as classes for the engaged. While there are scattered pastors who offer Talley's course, I know of no other pastor or church that has a program aimed at seriously dating couples—let alone one who would dare make demands that couples sign a contract, pledging:

- chastity, an old-fashioned idea!
- the limiting of time together,
- to take a four-month course and complete it even if their relationship ends.

Why should it be surprising that a church ask seriously dating couples to adhere to biblical standards? For a generation or two, churches have been almost embarrassed by scriptural standards. Why? Have they been proven wrong?

Absolutely not! The cohabitants have been proven foolish.

The church must be condemned for its silence on the 3000-year-old wisdom that God has left in Scripture. I just opened my Bible to find one verse to make the point, an example in Ephesians that sounds like a word to America's churches in the 1990s:

> Continue to work out your salvation with fear and trembling, for it is God who works in you to will and to act according to his good purpose. Do everything without complaining or arguing, so that you may become blameless and pure, children of God without fault in a crooked and depraved generation, in which you shine like stars in the universe as you hold out the word of life. . . (Phil. 2:12–16).

I asked Jim Talley why the churches have failed to take a stand with the truth they know, in guiding young adults. Clearly, with three out of five marriages failing and millions not getting married at all, today's young generation is lost, wandering on its own.

Talley replied, "Each pastor has tried to hold up the standards, but when he does, the couple he is talking to will go down the street and get married where there is a lower and lower standard. So there is nothing left at all. It is so bad you can't comprehend it. In Oklahoma City, there were 10,000 divorces last year!"

PERSONAL EXPERIENCE WITH RELATIONSHIP INSTRUCTION

In the last few months, Harriet and I have had direct experience with the value of Relationship Instruction. Along with three other middle-aged couples, we volunteered to lead small group discussions in our church[2] with engaged couples attending eight weeks of classes. Two of the couples in our small group were not yet engaged. For them, the discussion about money, marital sex, and husband-wife conflict resolution seemed a little abstract inasmuch as they had not yet decided whether to get married.

Therefore, I told them about Relationship Instruction, which seemed more appropriate for their current status as seriously dating couples: "On the one hand, you'd have to sign a contract with us in which you'd have to agree to keep your sexual involvement to "French kissing" or less, not discuss engagement for four months (which you might find to be a relief!), limit your time together, and complete the course, even if you stop dating each other!

"On the other hand, the process involves learning how to put Christ at the center of your relationship and really getting to know each other at a much deeper level. For example, you study Scripture that relates to marriage. One week you have to write a three-page autobiography in your workbook on what were the most important influences in your life, and another week you outline your long-range goals. You'd meet with Harriet and me every

---

[2]Fourth Presbyterian Church in Bethesda, Maryland.

other week. We'd read your workbooks, ask questions, and share our own experience on how we handled different problems in our marriage. It is a very rigorous process. Frankly, about half of the people who take Relationship Instruction do not get married.

"But there is one big payoff. The man who designed the course and gave it to more than one hundred couples, says that of those who have married, he knows of only one or two divorces. Taking Relationship Instruction is like taking out "divorce insurance," I asserted.

Both couples agreed to meet with us. I'll tell their story.

"MICHAEL AND ANNE"

To protect their privacy, I'll call one couple, Michael and Anne. Michael is thirty-three, is in the media and has never married. Anne is twenty-six, a very pretty health worker, and also never married. When I asked the level of their physical involvement, it was "Fondling sexual organs." Somewhat surprised that it had gotten that far, given their willingness to take the course, I asked them how they felt about limiting their sexual involvement to "French kissing."

Anne spoke first: "I have never had sex. God gave me a desire to wait. I have done everything but intercourse—which is almost equal to having had the sexual experience. But you are sharing a very intimate part of yourself. For a woman, emotionally you are giving so much of yourself. If God takes that person out of your life, it becomes very traumatic. That can be completely avoided if you and he limit the physical end of the relationship."

Michael, whose hair is rather long and artistic, spoke sheepishly: "I, unfortunately, have had sex with young ladies before. The relationship always ended at that point. You know you could attempt to appeal on a different level, but in having sex, you were, in a shallow way, pleasing each other. But the relationship stops growing emotionally. Since we are not married, we were not teammates but were playing on opposing teams. So the relationship would die."

Anne added, "We have begun to be too physically active, of touching to the point of climax. It can be dangerous emotionally if that person is not the person you have married. You have lost that person's respect, and you lose respect for yourself. A sexual relationship can steal your joy. And you feel foolish because you have given up something you were trying to save for the right man."

Michael said, "We got carried away, and both of us feel guilty. I feel bad. Though I am trying to please her, the long-term effect is guilt."

Anne added, "In my last relationship, we each had someone holding us accountable, but we did not have a written system (as in Relationship Instruction). It worked for a month or two, but it was easy to wriggle around. I got back to the same stumbling block."

Anne knows two people who allowed premarital sex to lead to pregnancy. One was a woman from her college youth group. "She was with a Christian man. Now they have nothing to do with each other. And she has a two-year-old baby girl! They did not marry. It is as big a problem among Christians as it is for non-Christians."

The other person is a man who got a girl pregnant and wasn't sure whether to marry her. He did so, "but the marriage is long and painful," said Anne. "He has left her twice but keeps reconciling."

Michael, who had attended Oral Roberts University, confessed, "I got frustrated with Christian women and dated non-Christian women. I felt it was disobedient. And I got what I deserved—a broken relationship." In that period, his "biggest fear" was "that I was going to die before I would have sex!" The fear was unwarranted!

But that had made him more determined "to keep my relationship with Anne. I knew that she was pure. I knew that if I was dating someone who had been sexually active before, it would be easy to fall into that same trap. I am trying to build a solid spiritual foundation."

Michael remembers seeing his "parents kiss fewer than ten times. They were not very affectionate. Their marriage was like a business arrangement." Clearly, he had higher hopes for his own marriage, but for a decade after college he had lived a life that was short of his dreams at two levels. He was not dating Christians all the time, nor was he living a pure life. Now that he was achieving both goals, he welcomed Relationship Instruction "because it helps with the discipline of keeping the relationship pure. And there is no guilt in this relationship, because we are not sexually active. And there is no fear of Anne's getting pregnant."

AN EARLY-MORNING PHONE CALL

Early one Saturday morning, two months after we began meeting with Michael and Anne, Harriet and I got a phone call from them that woke us up. They were clearly embarrassed and stumbled around for words.

I said, "What's wrong?"

"We went to further than we should have sexually again last night. We promised to call you if it happened, and here we are," said Michael. Anne added, "It's very embarrassing. We are disappointed with ourselves. But I want you to know we feel good abut calling. We want to get back on track. We apologize for calling so early, but we did not want to put if off."

"How did it happen?" I asked.

Michael replied, "Well, I fixed her a fancy duck l'orange dinner. It was seduction duck—and it worked," he said, laughingly. "We had wine and a fire in the fireplace and it was very romantic. It got to be quite late, so she slept on the couch, instead of going home. And . . . we were trying to please each other . . ." His voice dribbled off.

She added, "And because it was late and I lived far away it was easy to rationalize sleeping on the sofa. What is helping us—is having to call. We feel that we have done real well, up to this point."

I asked, "Is this the first time that you have exceeded that far?"

They said it was.

"Well, first I want to thank you for having the courage to call us up. I know that was difficult. But it shows you care and are trying to abide by the biblical standard. Harriet and I admire you for that. We will talk about this in more detail later. But I want to say now that the first mistake you made, Anne, was to stay at his home overnight. That should never happen again."

"You are right," Michael said. "It won't happen again."[3]

"The second point I want to make is that you are apparently ignoring the commitment you made on the amount of time you are spending with each other."

Michael protested, "But you yourself said you thought the limits were on the extreme side."

"That's right, I did. But now I see more clearly why Jim Talley has suggested that there be time limits."

SUMMARY THOUGHTS ON RELATIONSHIP INSTRUCTION

For our eighth-and-last Relationship Instruction session, Anne and Michael, to our delight, brought over a surprise Chinese dinner. Over dinner and afterward, we asked them to reflect on the value of the process.

Anne began, "First, we have needed someone to be accountable to, and we appreciate the time that the two of you have given us and your openness. Second, the *Workbook* gave us something concrete to do. You begin by having to do the homework—reading *Too Close, Too Soon*, then turn to writing things out. And the *Workbook* helps you to put your thoughts on paper. To allow the other person to read them means that you had to be vulnerable, as he reads what you really feel. Then you have another form of communication in having to talk about what you have written" (first with Michael, and then us).

Michael added, "When you see it written down on paper, it seems more serious. it is easier to look at the whole picture. Writing my autobiography, for example, was a unique experience. When you put it in writing, you have made a commitment, which is a deeper feeling than if you had simply talked about it."

Neither of them had thought seriously about future goals before writing them down. Michael, for example, would like to own his own business within five years, so he concluded that he ought to begin *now* to do freelance

---

[3]She did spend one more night on the sofa, but both say the sexual issue was kept in bounds. In April 1992, they became engaged to be married.

work on Saturdays and vacation days to determine if he could accomplish it and thus create the capacity and customers to go on his own.

Michael talked about the sexual issue: "When we exceeded Level 7, it was very difficult to pull back. It took self-discipline. But I understand there is a bigger goal here. We are much better off for having kept within the guidelines."

Anne said that the *Workbook* was helpful in getting each to identify "tangible strengths and weaknesses" in each other, and "in identifying a lot of problem areas that we worked through to an adjustment. I now feel secure in feeling like we really know each other, know how we feel about different issues. And even today, if a conflict comes up, now I feel I know how to communicate about it. It was a more traumatic experience before. Now it is not threatening."

She added that Relationship Instruction has "prepared me with a clearer understanding of what a Christian marriage can be. It would have been incomplete if any aspect had been missing—the counseling by you people, the accountability this gave us, or the Workbook. My perspective on our relationship previous to taking the course was much different."

An anxiety has been replaced with confidence. "I feel sorry for the couples who don't go through this kind of preparation in advance of marriage. Some of the engaged couples don't know what they are walking into. We did it the right way."

After the Saturday morning call, Michael and Anne realized that they needed to cut down on their time spent together. "We made a greater effort to spend time with groups," he told us. "For example, on Valentine's Day, I would normally have had a romantic evening alone. But we were out of time! So we gave a Sweetheart Couple Potluck Dinner with five couples. The men planned and cooked lamb shish kebab and rice while the women sat by the fire and gossiped. We barbecued outside with our coats on—a nice kind of bonding with men! It was a creative group time."

PREPARE—ANOTHER REASON FOR SUCCESS

There is one more reason that Michael and Anne got so much out of Relationship Instruction and why all of the couples pastored by William Gunnels[4] did so well. Both Pastor Gunnels, Harriet, and I added an important element to Relationship Instruction—a set of 125 questions given to each of them in a questionnaire called PREPARE.

---

[4]Pastor William Gunnells used Relationship Instruction materials at Hinson Memorial Baptist Church in Portland, Oregon, and at Buckhead Community Church in Atlanta. Like Jim Talley, he was a full-time singles minister until January 1992 but is now in secular work.

PREPARE can predict with 86% accuracy that couples taking it will get divorced!

More important, it identified with startling clarity, problem areas in each couple's relationship. That enables a counselor to focus immediately on whatever issue is troubling the couple. And PREPARE has materials that can help *any couple* learn absolutely crucial skills in conflict resolution.

Further, there is for married couples a companion "instrument" called ENRICH. PREPARE/ENRICH is important enough and complex enough to deserve its own chapter.

SIX

A Crucial Need: Weigh Your Relationship's Strengths and Weaknesses

A dating relationship is designed to conceal information, not reveal it.

—Dr. James C. Dobson, *Love for a Lifetime*

Test everything. Hold on to the good. Avoid every kind of evil.

—1 Thessalonians 5:21–22

D r. James Dobson, the popular host of "Focus on the Family," America's most widely aired radio show (2,000 stations) is correct to say that deception is involved in dating. As he explained in his book, *Love for a Lifetime*:

> Each partner puts his or her best foot forward, hiding embarrassing facts, habits, flaws, and temperaments. Consequently, the bride and groom enter into marriage with an array of private assumptions about how life will be lived after the wedding. Major conflict occurs a few weeks later when they discover that they differ radically on what each partner considers to be non-negotiable issues. The stage is then set for arguments and hurt feelings that never occurred during the courtship experience.

Have you ever wondered why the divorce rate in Japan is about one-fourth that in the United States? Perhaps one reason is that most Japanese choose partners who will be approved by their families, while American couples choose their marriage partners without any regard for family approval. Apparently, the Japanese families have a clearer vision for who is a suitable partner for a child than the adult child has on his own!

Why? Romance *is* deceptive.

Consider this: Of the 1,183,000 U.S. marriages that ended in divorce in 1988, the median length of those that dissolved was seven years, lumping together half of all marriages ended within *seven years*! In fact, two out of ten ended before the third anniversary.

Dr. David H. Olson, a family psychologist at the University of Minnesota, says:

These findings suggest that many married couples experience serious marital conflicts very early in their relationship. Many of these relationships can be assumed to have contained the seeds of eventual break-up from the beginning. Few engaged couples successfully anticipate the conflicts they will encounter in their marital relationship. Also, some sort of intervention might have been helpful if the potential trouble spots could have been identified. In addition, many couples do not have the communication skills necessary to resolve these conflicts.

Therefore, any person contemplating marriage needs an objective way to assess the character, background, temperament, and attitudes of a potential spouse on issues ranging from money and children to jealousy and substance abuse. Furthermore, the man and woman need an objective way to assess their strengths and their weaknesses *as a couple*. Finally, they need help in learning basic communication skills, particularly in conflict resolution.

In fact, these issues are shared by every seriously dating couple, every engaged couple, and every couple whose marriage is frustrating, disappointing, or in serious trouble.

PREPARE/ENRICH

To meet these needs, Dr. David Olson, former president of the National Council on Family Relations, created a questionnaire called PREPARE (*Pre*marital *Personal and Relationship Evaluation*) to be given to couples who are not married. Over the past decade it has been used by half a million couples.[1] More than 100,000 a year now use this instrument. A similar but different instrument called ENRICH has been used by 250,000 married couples to diagnose marital problems. Nearly 20,000 clergy/counselors are trained to administer PREPARE/ENRICH.[2] (ENRICH's use is described in chapter 8.)

In both PREPARE and ENRICH, 125 questions are asked separately of the male and of the female in ten crucial areas. It takes about thirty minutes and is computer-scored resulting in an excellent couple profile that a pastor or counselor can interpret. The ENRICH questionnaire is similar to PREPARE but also asks an already married couple questions about the satisfaction the husband and wife have with their marriage.

Dr. Anna Beth Benningfield, president of the American Association for Marriage and Family Therapy in 1993, calls PREPARE/ENRICH "a well-designed and easily administered inventory. Its primary value is not so much in providing new information to a couple but in helping them begin to talk

---

[1]Of the 500,000, about 400,00 were administered by local churches where the couples celebrated their weddings.

[2]For a list of those trained to administer the questionnaire in your area, write PREPARE/ENRICH, P.O. Box 190, Minneapolis, MN 55440-0190.

about the areas of strength and areas that will require some work and some negotiation, some accommodation."

Individuals are asked if they "Agree Strongly," "Agree," or if they are "Undecided," "Disagree," or "Disagree Strongly" with statements like these:

Realistic Expectations:

1. I believe that most disagreements we currently have will decrease after marriage.
2. I expect that some romantic love will fade after marriage.

Personality Issues

3. I really like the personality and habits of my partner.
4. I am concerned about my partner's drinking and/or smoking.

Communication

5. I can easily share my positive and negative feelings with my partner.
6. My partner is less interested in talking about our relationship than I am.

Conflict Resolution

7. We openly discuss problems and usually find good solutions.
8. We have some important disagreements that never seem to get resolved.

Financial Management

9. We have decided how to handle our finances.
10. I wish my partner were more careful in spending money.

Leisure Activities

11. I enjoy spending some time alone without my partner.
12. At times I feel pressure to participate in activities my partner enjoys.

Sexual Relationship

13. I am very satisfied with the amount of affection I receive from my partner.
14. My partner and I sometimes disagree regarding our interest in sex.

Children and Marriage

15. I think parenting will dramatically change our relationship and the way we live.
16. I have some concerns about how my partner will be as a parent.

Role Relationship

17. My partner and I agree on how much we will share the household chores.
18. We disagree on whether the husband's occupation should be a top priority in deciding where we live.

Religion and Values

19. We share the same religious values.
20. We sometimes disagree on how to practice our religious beliefs.

FAMILY ROOTS: COHESION AND ADAPTABILITY

In addition, PREPARE asks questions to probe the nature of each person's "family of origin" (with whom they grew up). Every person brings to his or her marriage, assumptions about what a marriage is, based upon his or her family of origin. "People either re-create the type of family system they had as a child, or they react by doing the opposite," writes Olson. "Thus, if a couple came from quite different family systems, this may create some conflict for them as a couple."

What does Olson mean by "family cohesion"? It is the "emotional bonding that family members have toward one another," he says. For example, some families are disengaged with little closeness or loyalty, and every family member "does his own thing." At the opposite extreme are the "enmeshed" families with high cohesion and demands of loyalty, such as expected attendance of family members at dinner, all birthdays, and holidays. Questions asked of participants probe how often family members ask each other for help, how close they feel toward one another, and whether togetherness is a top priority.

What is meant by "family adaptability"? Olson says that's "the ability of a marital or family system to change its power structure, role relationships, and rules in response to situational and developmental stress." Questions probe for the assertiveness, control, and discipline of mother and father, negotiation styles, and role relationships. At one extreme, some families are rigid, run by a dictator with strict discipline and little role change. At the opposite extreme, some families have no one in charge, or dramatic role shifts, erratic discipline.

INTERPRETING PREPARE RESULTS

To take PREPARE or ENRICH, a twenty-five dollar fee is charged each couple. For that sum, the response sheets are tabulated anonymously by computer and a report is sent to the pastor or counselor who administered the questionnaire. No one is allowed to administer the PREPARE instrument unless trained to do so. The training is a day-long seminar.

To report results, counselors, pastors, or mentor couples are asked to schedule two feedback sessions with the couple. The first session focuses upon the sort of personality, communications, and financial or sexual issues outlined previously. The second is devoted to the "Family of Origin," which is reported in two different ways. The counselor may see conflicts on how they responded to questions about leadership and cohesiveness, but he can also show the couple how each of their families differ on a "Couple Map" that might indicate, for example, that the male's family is "rigidly enmeshed," while the female perhaps comes from an opposite extreme of being "chaotically disengaged."

In addition, each couple is given a pamphlet, "Building a Strong Marriage," which emphasizes that PREPARE is "*not a test*. No one passes or fails. These questions are simply designed to help you describe your relationship more completely." It states that the goals of the PREPARE Computerized Report and feedback session are:

- "The opportunity for you and your partner to talk about your relationship with another person who has an interest in the success of your marriage.
- "To provide you with information about how you and your partner view your relationship.
- "To help you identify the strength and the growth areas of your relationship that need more discussion."

More broadly, the booklet notes that "Most couples spend a great deal of time, energy, and money on their wedding ceremony, which only lasts a few hours. However, they often invest little time in building relationship skills that would help them have a more satisfying and lasting marriage."

Another value of the booklet is that it lists various books to enrich the couple's marriage and gives the names and addresses of eight national organizations that provide marriage enrichment weekends. (See Appendix.)

RELATIONSHIP STRENGTHS

When couples fill out their questionnaire for PREPARE, the questions flit from subject to subject, but in the computerized report that comes back from PREPARE/ENRICH, the questions are regrouped by subject area with the conclusions of the male and female placed side by side, and in each area the couple's agreements and disagreements are highlighted. Equally important, the percentage of their answers on which there is "positive agreement" is highlighted. On those issues in which the couples "agree with each other in a positive way on 70% of the items," the couple is told that they have a "relationship strength." Issues with less than 30% agreement are euphemistically called "growth areas."

CONFLICT RESOLUTION

Besides relationship strengths, a more fundamental issue is that of conflict resolution. I tell the couples we mentor that my most important lesson of conflict resolution in twenty-seven years of marriage is one I learned after a decade of marriage—the wisdom of Scripture that provided basic guidance on how I should deal with my conflicts with Harriet:

"Be angry but do not sin; do not let the sun go down on your anger" (Ephesians 4:26 RSV).

"In other words," I tell couples, "God expects us to be angry from time to time, but we are admonished not to allow the anger to last a long time. Certainly, in a marriage, a couple should never go to bed angry. We both try to acknowledge hurting the other's feelings and find a solution or compromise. We want to rebuild our relationship daily so that no problem festers. What this Scripture suggests is that *the relationship is always more important than any issue that divides a couple.*"

TEN STEPS FOR RESOLVING COUPLE DIFFERENCES

Fortunately, a built-in part of the PREPARE process, strongly urged by its creators, is an exercise to help couples learn how to resolve conflicts amicably. In Dr. Olson's well-organized materials for counselors, he writes, "The couple can often learn a great deal about resolving differences if you would help them work through some issue. This will enable them to learn that it is possible to better understand each other and to begin resolving some of their differences."

Every couple is given a "Building a Strong Marriage" booklet in which are "Ten Steps for Resolving Couple Differences:"

1. "Set a time and place for discussion.
2. "Define the problem or issue of disagreement.
3. "Define how you each contribute to the problem.
4. "List things you have done that have not been successful.
5. "Brainstorm and list all possible solutions.
6. "Discuss each of these solutions.
7. "Agree on one solution to try.
8. "Agree how each person will work toward the solution.
9. "Set a time for another meeting to review your progress.
10. "Reward each other as each of you contributes to the solution."

BETH AND JOHN: A CASE STUDY

One seriously dating couple Harriet and I mentored from church were Beth and John. We began by complimenting them on their "Relationship Strengths," such as a 90% agreement on religious issues. "For example, you both agree strongly that 'It is important' that you pray with each other," I said. "What that means is that you have a bridge either of you can walk across with confidence to solve any problem that may arise." However, one of their "Growth Areas" was "Conflict Resolution." They said they have "very different ideas about the best way to solve disagreements." They disagreed with the statement, "My partner always understands me," and said they had "serious disputes over unimportant issues." In another section, Beth indicated that he often gave her "the silent treatment." (This was a common pattern of young couples at church—agreement on religious issues but absolutely no skills in communication or conflict resolution.)

I gave them "Ten Steps for Resolving Couple Differences," and noted #1 was to "Set a time and place for discussion." I said, "Right now, let's talk through 'the silent treatment' issues. They grinned weakly and shifted uncomfortably on our couch. "Now, #2, each of you define the problem."

Beth: "There're times when I get the silent treatment, when I bring up a problem. Or he'll say something is 'fine' to put off dealing with it."

John: "She takes a lot longer to say what she means than I will—40 words what I hear in five words. The rest sounds like nagging. . . . Sometimes, I need time to think about what she says. I'm not sure what to say."

I said, "Beth, answer Step #3. How do *you* contribute to the problem?"

Beth grinned sheepishly, confessing, "I contribute to it when I give up, put on my answering machine. I pretend I'm not there and don't talk to him." I replied, "So you give *him* the silent treatment?" Both laughed.

"John, how do you contribute to the problem?" I asked.

He replied: "I put Beth off, rather than fully resolving it."

I asked for "solutions" tried in the past that did not work. He said his job as a TV newsman meant "I have to get up at 4:00 A.M. She brings these things up at 8:00 P.M. or 8:30 P.M. when my energy level declines."

Next, I asked them to "brainstorm," listing all possible solutions.

John: "I need to talk, when I may not feel like it."

Beth: "Pray about it." John nodded. "If we are on the phone, where it is easier for him to clam up, I could drive over to his house. Or better, postpone the issue to when he is not tired."

Almost joyfully, they decided to try a blend of these solutions. What seemed to matter was that each was willing to bend a little and try. Two months later, I asked how it was going. She smiled brightly, "It is no longer a problem. I used to feel frustrated. He would clam up. I did not understand why he was responding that way. Before, I would have raised my voice and blurted out all my frustration in accusatory tones. Now, instead of talking on the phone, I go over and in a calm tone discuss how I feel."

He added, "I will not be silent again." He said the issue had been like a "brick wall, that we did not know how to cross. The Ten Steps of Conflict Resolution are like a ladder, which we used to climb over it. We can now look at other walls, and know that we can climb the ten-step ladder to overcome the problem."

IMPORTANCE OF "FAMILY OF ORIGIN"

Beth and John came from quite different families. Beth's father divorced her mother, partly because she suffered from mental illness. "It started six months after I was born," Beth said. "She had shock treatment. A couple of times she was hospitalized and was gone for a long time. I would stay with an aunt." Later, "I was the mother" to a brother and sister seven to ten years younger. "I learned a lot and got more responsibility because my mother was a manic-depressive. There was no clear leader in our family. Tasks were handled in a disorganized fashion. My father lived down the street and got together with us for breakfast every morning. He has provided for us and blames the divorce on her illness and her low self-esteem. The marriage was putting too much pressure on her."

As the oldest daughter, Beth acknowledges that *she* "was the mother." However, her own mother and father took advantage of her. They often refused to attend school events of importance to her sister. So Beth felt obligated to go—even at age twenty-six and after she had moved out of the house! This created conflict with John, who felt that she was devoting excessive time to her family instead of to him.

These issues surfaced when Harriet and I reported the results of PREPARE to them. Harriet said, "Your parents never really allowed you to be a normal teenager and still expect you to be the mother to your brother and sister. They stole your adolescence." As Harriet spoke, Beth's eyes welled up with tears, and she had to leave the room to regain her composure. Later, Harriet gently suggested that "Since your mother has recovered from her mental illness, and your father from his drinking, you might suggest that they ought to begin going to these school events." Beth nodded, gratefully. She later did so and thus helped nudge her parents into a more responsible role while she broke free from excessive cohesion.

In many respects, John's family was just the opposite—enmeshed rather than disengaged—and with a domineering mother. "She was overprotective," he recalled. "She would not let me play Little League baseball because she was afraid I would get hurt. She kept me from doing anything. Once I left Pennsylvania to go to college, I never returned home to live—not even in the summers. I remember being told, 'Once you are out of the house, you have to make it on your own. We don't have to support you anymore.' I took that to heart. They paid my tuition the first year. The second year was very hard for them. So for the third and fourth year I was on a work fellowship, and they did not have to support or pay for me.

"When I go home now she still treats me like a little boy. I feel controlled by my family. There was a lot of love in my family, but it was dysfunctional. I grew up seeing how a family should *not* operate. I would like to learn the right way." Yet Beth said that *he* has the same "controlling" aspect to his personality. Not until he had discussed PREPARE results with Harriet and me on families of origin, did he realize that he was repeating the pattern of excessive control that he had been critical of in his mother.

WHEN SHOULD PREPARE BE ADMINISTERED?

Dr. David Olson, who created PREPARE, told me in an interview that "The best time for a couple to take PREPARE is when they are *thinking* about marrying this person, so they can think about whether 'this is a relationship I want to invest my life in.' Then they can start working on the issues. They should take it again about six months before marriage to see if they have dealt with these issues. If they have not, they had better focus in on them, for they will *only get worse* after marriage! Typically, what happens is that a problem comes up when they are most idealistic and most in love, and it doesn't get resolved. But it will get worse over time unless they do something to face it."

We found PREPARE to be an ideal companion to the Relationship Instruction for the seriously dating couple, described in chapter 5. However, it is most often given as part of engagement counseling. Indeed, it would be an excellent exercise for the very first counseling session by a pastor or counselor with an engaged couple.

I should add that there is a version of PREPARE for those couples with children from a previous marriage. It is called PREPARE-MC (Married with Children). The issues facing such couples are so much more complex and difficult that PREPARE-MC is strongly recommended by most pastors who've used it. "It can help couples focus on the fact of the likely impact of children from previous marriages," says Rev. Earl Andrews, Associate Pastor of the giant, 6,250-member Frazier Memorial Methodist Church in Montgomery, Alabama. "Oftentimes, people will minimize the impact of children from previous marriages, in the flush of romance."

PROFESSIONAL ASSESSMENT OF PREPARE

What do pastors and family counselors think about the PREPARE instrument itself? Pastor Earl Andrews said, "I have used it about twenty times. Its strength is that it enables the couples to identify where they stand on twelve important areas of life in a very concise and convenient manner. What would take them weeks and months to do in casual conversation they are able to effect through answering 125 questions. So often in casual conversation, we camouflage the truth about ourselves because the other person might not like us. This instrument does better at pulling out who we are than any other instrument I have used. I generally point to three areas of strength and three of growth. Many couples have gone out subdued, by realizing they have many areas to work on."

Dr. Wesley Hartzfeld has administered PREPARE to fifty couples a year for five years at The Chapel, a large nondenominational church in Akron, Ohio. He noted that even "in a Christian marriage, ego gets in the way" of trying to solve problems. For that reason, he requires every engaged couple to take PREPARE or PREPARE-MC "so they can learn communication skills during that important engagement period. . . .

"Generally, all couples do *not* do as well as they think they will. As a counselor, I am not alarmed by that. My hope is that it will be a motivation for them to work on their relationship. Even couples who have known each other a long time don't do much better on the test than those who've known each other a short time. They may be aware of the issues, but they are *not* confronting negative issues in the relationship.

"I agree with those who do surveys that money—financial management—is always a key issue I look for on a PREPARE test. Almost never does a couple do well in that category. There are usually a lot of differences in the way they handle money or the environment in which they grew up. PREPARE helps them realize their differences and talk about them. PREPARE is also an accurate indicator, most of the time, of the type of environment the couple experienced, and how it will impact them."

A 1979 doctoral dissertation by David G. Fournier reports the reaction of two hundred PREPARE counselors. More than 80% described the instrument as "extremely" or "very" useful. Most stated that the questionnaire was "very accurate for most" or "somewhat accurate for all" of the couples they counseled. Nine-tenths found the Summary Analysis of couple results very helpful. Most all counselors who use PREPARE once, will use it routinely. No premarital questionnaire is as widely used as PREPARE.[3]

The fact that nearly 20,000 counselors have taken a one-day training course to administer PREPARE is far more eloquent a testimony of its validity from a counselor perspective than from any doctoral dissertation.

CAN PREPARE PREDICT MARITAL SUCCESS OR DIVORCE?

The most remarkable element of PREPARE is that it can predict with astonishing accuracy which couples will divorce! Dr. H. Norman Wright,[4]

---

[3]Another premarital instrument that gets high marks from counselors is called "Taylor-Johnson Temperament Analysis." Unlike PREPARE, it compares personality types of individuals: nervous versus composed, depressive versus lighthearted, sympathetic versus indifferent, for example. Each person describes himself or herself and then describes the partner. Both then look at each other's descriptions and talk about them.

[4]Chapter 7 urges engaged couples to use Dr. Wright's workbook, *Before You Say "I Do."*

America's well-known writer on marriage and how to prepare for it, says that PREPARE has come up with a predictive element. With 86% accuracy, it can predict the result—which couples are the ones who will divorce. Does he trust the predictions? Yes. "I have been using the tool ever since its inception (fifteen years ago). It is so insightful, it is being used all over the world."

As evidence, PREPARE/ENRICH sends summaries of two studies to pastors or counselors using PREPARE. One by Blaine Fowers is of 148 couples who took PREPARE in 1980 and were contacted two years later. "Using PREPARE scores . . . it was possible to predict with 86% accuracy those couples that eventually got divorced and with 78% accuracy those couples who were happily married," said the Fowers study.

"The average prediction rate for both groups was 81%. The PREPARE categories that were most predictive of marital success were *realistic expectations, personality issues, communication, conflict resolution,* and *religious orientation.*" Couples with low scores (growth areas) in these categories and very few relationship strengths were the ones who got divorced, and those with high scores were happily married. A decade later, virtually the same results were reported in the July 1989 issue of *Journal of Marital and Family Therapy.* This is a remarkable achievement. There is no other premarital instrument (questionnaire) that is so prescient in forecasting which marriages will dissolve or endure. But the pamphlet given to couples, "Building a Strong Marriage,: clearly states: "PREPARE will not predict the success or failure of your marriage." I asked Dr. Olson about the contradiction, saying, "Either it can predict with 86% accuracy who will divorce or it can't. Why not encourage pastors to warn those with low scores that they are in danger?"

Olson replied that the study proved how "scientifically valid the instrument is." But "we did not come up with a way to predict for *any particular couple.* How do you know what will happen to an individual couple? I would present the issues to the couple and encourage them to work and resolve as many of them as they can. We might predict that a couple might do well, but some can improve their relationship by resolving major issues. *This is, in fact, our goal.*"

ONE IN TEN COUPLES BREAK THEIR ENGAGEMENT!

In fact a tenth of those who take PREPARE decide *not* to marry. Counting those postponing marriage, it is as high as 15%, says Olson.

The Fowers study showed that "couples who delayed were very similar to those who later got divorced. . . . This indicates that couples who canceled their marriage made a good decision because they would have had a high probability of ending up being unhappily married. PREPARE, therefore, provides a useful preventive function by helping some couples decide not to marry that have a high probability of divorce."

Far more important, however, is the fact that *most* couples find, as John and Beth did, that PREPARE strengthens their relationship. This has even been proved in a study by Dr. Joan Druckman, Dr. David Fournier, and Dr. Beatrice Robinson. Couples who took PREPARE and had a two-hour feedback counseling session to report results, "significantly increased their adjustment and satisfaction" in the areas of Communication and Financial Decision Making, "became more empathetic after marriage," and "became more independent and less controlling."

ADVICE TO PREMARITAL COUPLES, PARENTS, AND COUNSELORS

Thus, PREPARE (and PREPARE-MC plus ENRICH described in chapter 7) is an outstanding diagnostic tool. It has distinct values both to couples and to clergy or counselors helping to prepare a couple not just for a wedding but for a lasting marriage.

A. From the couple's perspective:

1. Most couples find that PREPARE strengthens their relationship. "It has made me aware of some strengths and weaknesses in our relationship and of areas we need to discuss more," said John.

2. The PREPARE process, which involves three counseling sessions (one when the instrument is administered, and two to report results), demonstrates to a couple the value of open, honest communication—particularly about differences that tend to be sidestepped in the glow of a romance. Problems that are ignored will only get worse after the wedding.

3. The exercise using "Ten Steps for Resolving Conflict" teaches an invaluable strategy for solving problems before they grow too large.

4. PREPARE-MC stimulates needed discussion for second marriages involving children.

5. Studies of couples who used PREPARE reveal that two common-sense perceptions are correct. Couples satisfied in their marriages tended to know each other longer before marriage. And "successful couples had parents and friends who also reacted more positively to the marriage than did the dissatisfied group," says Dr. Olson.

6. A tenth of couples conclude that their relationship is so weak that a divorce is likely, and they decide not to marry.

However, the percentage of couples who break their engagements *should probably be higher* in light of the fact that 60% of new marriages are failing.

My advice to couples who take PREPARE is to take notes on what you are told. Keep track of which are your growth areas and which are your relationship strengths. Also write down the specific issues that deserve future discussion between you. If you have a high percentage of "Growth Areas" and few "Relationship Strengths," at the minimum, you should postpone any wedding (if a date has been set) and work on resolving the conflicts, misunderstandings, or unrealistic expectations that are revealed by PREPARE. Then, six months or so down the road, take PREPARE again to check your relationship's blood pressure before you make a decision whether to walk down the aisle with that partner.

While it may feel like a test, PREPARE is a vastly more important assessment than any SAT or College Board test you ever had. At one level it is a diagnostic tool that can help you improve your relationship. *Most people are able to do so.* PREPARE is also the most objective snapshot you are ever likely to get of your relationship at a moment in time. *It reveals the potential of your relationship for future marital happiness or misery.* Regardless of how big the problems seem to be, invest the energy, effort, and conflict-resolution skills you will learn in the process to try to overcome the difficulties but be prepared to end the relationship if it does not improve after some months of effort. It would be not a tragedy but a *blessing* to look elsewhere for a future husband or wife.

B. From the perspective of the clergy or counselor:

1. PREPARE and PREPARE-MC (and ENRICH) will provide a wealth of diagnostic information that can enable you to target your counseling on the areas where each individual couple needs the most assistance.

2. They are clinically proven to be reliable instruments to enhance a counselor's or a pastor's ability to work with premarital or married couples.

3. They are efficient and effective in discerning both relationship strengths and problems, euphemistically called "growth areas."

4. My church trained ten mentor couples to administer PREPARE in their homes, opening up a whole new ministry for older, solidly married couples to be "marriage savers" working with either seriously dating couples or engaged couples. Paul, in writing to the Ephesians, says that the job of the pastor is "To prepare God's people for works of service" (4:12). *What more important work of service is there than building strong marriages?* Thus, a pastor's ministry can be multiplied. The result will be many saved marriages.

However, a pastor or a mentor couple faces an ethical problem in deciding what should be said to a couple with a high percentage of conflicts and misunderstanding but few strengths. The problems should be directly presented and discussed. The first suggestion of PREPARE's Dr. David Olson is that additional counseling sessions be scheduled with the young couple to give a subtle but clear indication that they do not feel that their relationship is strong enough to move ahead. For example, in additional meetings, they might try to apply the conflict-resolution model on several issues rather than use the model only on one issue. Often couples with weak relationships will discover through more intensive counseling that they probably should not risk marriage.

But what about those who seem determined to plunge ahead despite many red flags? Of course, the decision by any couple to get married is their own, assuming that they have reached the age of eighteen. But that should *not* be an excuse for one to stand back and say, "Hey, it's not my problem. I told them I was concerned."

I often ask pastors this question: "What percent of those you counsel decide to break their engagements?" Usually, the answer is "None," or "Very few." No wonder we have a 60% marriage dissolution rate! Remember Malachi's warning:

> For the lips of a priest ought to preserve knowledge, and from his mouth men should seek instruction—because he is the messenger of the LORD Almighty. But you have turned from the way and by your teaching have caused many to stumble (Malachi 2:7–8).

Dr. H. Norman Wright, author of thirty books (such as *So You're Getting Married, Communication: Key to Your Marriage,* and *Romancing Your Marriage*) told me in a recent interview: "In the last year and a half, I have worked with thirty-five couples in premarital counseling. I charge them $350 for the testing and six sessions and will go as many sessions as is necessary for no additional cost. I want to make sure we are doing all we can.

"But fifteen couples broke up their engagements and did not marry."

Pastors, check those numbers: Of the thirty-five couples he counseled, fifteen broke their engagements! That's 42%! What did he do? First, he administered PREPARE. Then he gave them the Taylor-Johnson Temperament Analysis. He met with them at least six times, and he said, "I am requiring couples to visit a divorce-recovery workshop during premarital counseling. *That* opens some eyes. They go and hear the turmoil some are going through, and they come back. I say, 'none of those couples there ever believed when they got married that they'd be facing divorce. What will you do to assure this will not happen to you?'

"You have to have a plan," says Wright.

I argue that if you as a pastor or a counselor do not have at least a fifth of your engaged couples break their engagements, you are failing in your task. That is still less than half of the percentage of couples who break their engagements with America's most noted marriage counselor.

C. From the perspective of a parent:

Harriet and I are the parents of three sons aged twenty-one to twenty-six, in whom we have invested years of effort and thousands of dollars to equip them to be happy, fulfilled, contributing Christian citizens. No decision they will make is as important as whom they decide to marry—except, possibly, for *how* they marry. The one gift that we can offer them is the opportunity to grow through deepening experiences such as PREPARE and a range of vigorous options described in chapter 7 that includes solid counseling and attending a weekend retreat for engaged couples, like the "Engaged Encounter." PREPARE costs only twenty-five dollars. For value received, it is a pittance that Harriet and I are glad to pay. And if there were a counselor like Norm Wright nearby, we'd gladly pay for the three-hundred-fifty dollar course as a gift. It is a far more important investment in their future fulfillment than the thousands likely to be spent on a wedding.

Parents, *urge your son or daughter to take PREPARE with their beloved*—and offer to pay the bill. There is no greater opportunity for you as a parent to be a Marriage Saver of a child's marriage. If they tell you that they are not interested, make them promise, at least, to read this chapter you have just completed (plus the next one!).

If you want to save the marriage of your loved ones, you have to be willing to stick your neck out and *make a case for what is right*, using this precious time of engagement to deepen their skills of communication, conflict resolution, and learning how to make Christ the third partner of their marriage. There are only a few times in one's lifespan when direct, outside intervention can have a life-changing impact. Clearly, one of the most important and certainly the easiest time to be of help is with the seriously dating or engaged couple. At that age, couples are both more idealistic and more open and willing to learn. Fortunately, young people know that the odds are not good for new marriages to succeed. Therefore, most of your sons and daughter will welcome a gift that can be of great help, such as a check for PREPARE and, equally important, a check for them to attend Engaged Encounter. When they go for counseling, urge them to take notes, as suggested earlier. *Couples should invest less time and money in the wedding and more energy in building their relationship.*

"A wedding is but a day, but a marriage is for a lifetime."[5]

---

[5]The slogan for "Marriage Encounter"

SEVEN

Marriage Prep—Help for the Engaged Couple

This manual has been developed to help you remove the risk element from marriage.

—*Before You Say "I Do"*
by Wes Roberts and Norman Wright

Put to death, therefore, whatever belongs to your earthly nature: sexual immorality, impurity, lust, evil desires. . . . Do not lie to each other, since you have taken off your old self with its practices and have put on the new self, which is being renewed in knowledge in the image of its Creator.

—Colossians: 3:5, 9–10

WEDDING IN AMERICA IN THE 1990s

America was still deep in a recession March 9, 1992, when *The New York Times* published a story in its business section with the headline: BRIDAL MAGAZINES FIND CUPID IS RECESSION-PROOF. Several paragraphs paint a clear picture of America's excessive preoccupation with weddings:

"We're going gangbuster for the first issues of 1992," said the associate publisher of *Elegant Bride*, whose advertising pages were up 51% for the first two issues of the magazine. Meanwhile, *Brides and Your New Home* sold more than 500,000 copies of its February-March issue.

"There is a huge appetite out there for pages and pages of pictures of wedding gowns and answers to endless questions about how to discourage children from attending a wedding (hold it at night), how to remind your bridesmaids without seeming pushy that it is customary for them to give the bride a shower (subtly, in a phone call to your maid of honor) and whether you have to invite your hated first cousin (no). . . .

"Engagements, which used to average eight months, are now more likely to be 12 to 16 months—all the more conducive to plan an elaborate wedding—average cost: $16,000 and climbing, followed by an extensive honeymoon. People are getting married at an older age with brides around 25 to 26 years old and grooms a few years older, which means they have more money to spend," continued the *Times* article.

"The bridal books are trying to play all of this to their advantage. Several include supplements in a plastic bag with each issue. *Modern Bride* has included a fashion supplement, a shower organizer, and a wedding gift planner with recent issues. 'Polybagging is the hot thing now,' said William F. Bondlow, publisher of *Bridal Guide*. 'With our March-April issue, we included a groom supplement for the first time. . . .

"*Bride's* tried another kind of gamble. After changing its name to appeal to the home-furnishings market as well as the traditional brides' market, it split the magazine into three parts: the first and largest section devoted to the wedding, the second to the honeymoon, and the third to furnishing the new home." "Advertisers love it," said its publisher.

Brides' surpassed itself with its February-March 1991 issue, which weighed in with 1,046 pages," concluded *The New York Times* article.

Three facts in this story are shocking to me:

1. In one month, brides' magazines sold 1,150,000 copies! There are only 2.4 million marriages in a year. So each bride must read several magazines on weddings.

2. A single magazine of 1,046 pages focused on the froth of weddings—gowns, bridesmaids, honeymoons, "polybagging"—and almost nothing on what really matters: *the marriage* and how to make it work.

3. Some $16,000 is spent on the *average* wedding.

LIKELIHOOD AND CAUSES OF DIVORCE

Yet, according to the Gallup Poll, if you have *ever* been married, "the odds are now 50-50 that you've either been divorced, separated, or seriously close to separation. If you're between the ages of 35 and 54, those odds increase to two out of three."

Women are more apt to be unhappy in their marriages. Contrary to common assumption, women are much more likely to initiate the separation that leads to divorce. Of divorced women interviewed, 55% say it was their initial idea to separate, while only 44% of men took responsibility.

Clearly, during engagement, *a woman should spend less time on the wedding and more time in building a relationship that can endure with her future husband*.

Women are historically skilled at creating a home. They are the nurturers. That is why engaged women are reading magazines about their future married state. Unfortunately, in putting their exclusive attention on details of the wedding, honeymoon, and so on, they are making a big mistake. Their focus is essentially on the events of the day rather than on *spiritual* or *relational* issues with lifetime consequences. The result is that *women*, more often than men, are more unhappy in marriage. So, *women* initiate most divorces.

Engaged women can make a basic decision to reduce time on planning the wedding so that they can increase time to explore different forms of marriage preparation that offer them the greatest long-term prospects for strengthening their relationship with their fiancé. This chapter will outline what, I believe, are the nation's most effective strategies.

To understand their significance, you must first have a clear perception of what *are* the causes of divorce. I am grateful to George Gallup who has made available these results of polls reported in 1989.[1]

The major problems in most divorces are not profound, intractable difficulties, such as physical abuse (which sparked 5% of divorces) or drug or alcohol abuse (which caused 16% of breakups). Infidelity is a cause of only 17% of dissolutions.[2]

The overwhelming cause of divorce is "incompatibility," which is responsible for 47% of divorces. Related to that were arguments over money, family, or children (10%). (Another 5% cited no cause.)[3]

However, stated differently, *three-fifths* of marriages (57%) failed due to poor communication, or to poor conflict-resolution skills.

"The problems that ultimately lead to the breakup of a marriage become apparent quite early in the relationship. More than one-third (38%) who have divorced report that they were aware of the problem *at the time of marriage or soon thereafter*," said the Gallup study. Two experts react:

Dr. Paul Meier, co-founder of Minirth-Meier Clinics, says that "As a trained Christian psychiatrist, I can honestly and emphatically say this excuse (incompatibility) is no more than a cop-out used by couples who are too proud and lazy to work out their own hangups. Instead of facing them, they run away by divorcing and remarrying. Then there are four miserable people instead of just two. Why spread misery? Bad marriages are contagious."

Dr. Mavis Hetherington, a professor of psychology at the University of Virginia, says that many ignore relationship problems when dating: "When people are courting, they tend to be optimistic about the relationship. If their

---

[1] A random sample of 989 adults who have ever been married were interviewed out of a total sample of 1,213 adults, eighteen and older, December 27–29, 1988. For results based on the sample of 996 respondents, one can say with 95% confidence that the error attributable to sampling and other random effects could be plus or minus three percentage points.

[2] "Substance abuse causes divorces more commonly initiated by the wife (20%) than by the husband (13%)," said Gallup. If infidelity is involved, who sparks the divorce? Surprisingly, *the wife's* adultery causes more divorces (26%) than the husband's (17%)!

[3] Of course, there is overlap. Some drinking or adultery may stem from incompatibility. And some incompatibility may be due to character flaws.

partner has a behavioral problem, they tend to minimize its seriousness and to think they can alter or correct it. As romance wears off, as the flowers stop coming, these problems become more apparent."

GOOD COMMUNICATION:
THE HEART OF SUCCESSFUL MARRIAGES

Conversely, another Gallup Poll reported in 1989 came to this critical conclusion: "In an era of increasingly fragile marriages, a couple's ability to communicate is the single most important contributor to a stable and satisfying marriage."[4]

Only 40% of married and "romantically involved couples rate their ability to communicate as "excellent." Another 47% say that their communication is "good," while 12% say that it is only "fair" or "poor."

"Yet the quality of the relationships among couples with excellent communication is strikingly better than among those with less satisfactory communication," says Gallup.

Overall Relationship: For example, "Eighty-four percent of those whose communication is excellent say they are completely satisfied with their overall relationship, but only half of those with "good communication" and a tiny fifth with "fair or poor communication" have solid marriages."

Choose Same Partner Again: "Similarly, almost all (97%) of the respondents who rate their communication with their partner as excellent say they would choose that person to be their partner again, compared to 89% of those with good communications, and only 56% of those with fair or poor communications."

The same pattern can be seen in three other areas: Couples with excellent communication do a better job in meeting one another's emotional needs, in satisfying each other sexually, and in developing a level of trust.

Emotional Needs: Only a third (31%) of people say their partner always meets their emotional needs. But half (49%) of those with excellent communications do so compared to only a fifth (21%) of those with good communications, and a tiny 8% of those with fair or poor communications.

Satisfying Sex: "A majority (56%) of married or romantically involved adults report being wholly satisfied with the sexual relationship they share with their partner," write the Gallups. But three-fourths (76%) of those with excellent communication are pleased with their sexual relationship, while

---

[4]These findings are based on telephone interviews with 1,037 adults, eighteen and older, who are married, widowed, or unmarried and involved in a romantic relationship. The survey was conducted between September 24 and October 9, 1988. Like the earlier Gallup Poll, error attributable to sampling and other random effects could be plus or minus four percentage points.

only 47% of those with good communication agree, and a small 24% of those with fair or poor communication."

It will be a surprise to Hollywood movie makers that *good sex grows out of good talk*—not spectacular bodies, adultery, or premarital sex.[5]

Trust: Finally, "The level of trust in a relationship also appears to be closely tied to couples' ability to communicate," say the Gallups.

"More than nine out of ten (92%) whose ability to communicate with their partner is excellent say they trust him or her all of the time. Somewhat fewer (77%) persons who rate their ability to communicate as good say they can always trust their partner. Less than a majority (39%) of those with fair or poor communication have complete trust in their partner," the Gallup Report concludes.

HOW ENGAGED COUPLES CAN IMPROVE COMMUNICATION SKILLS

Clearly, therefore, the most important single goal of the engaged couple should be *to improve their communication skills.*

That is not easy. Why? "The frustration is that they are in love! The engaged have the illusion that communication is real easy, that they can talk about anything. Their attitude is, 'Leave us alone,'" says Father Tom Lynch, pastor of St. James Catholic Church in Stratford, Connecticut, and former national director of Family Life, for the Catholic bishops.

And the couples who *are* bewildered by their fights don't know what to do. They cannot improve communication skills on their own—it would be similar to trying to learn to read and write without going to school.

Unfortunately, virtually no public school and no university teaches "Husband-Wife Communication 101." How sad and ironic that one can go through America's entire school system, mastering diverse and abstruse fields such as molecular biology, law, Renaissance art, or even psychology— and yet not learn the basics about how to create the greatest joy and satisfaction in life: a *lifelong* marriage.

Marriage Savers is attempting to change all that.

Recall that:

— Chapter 4 gave suggestions for helping teenagers learn to communicate in a healthy way with the opposite sex;

— Chapter 5 put a spotlight on one way to improve communication for the seriously dating couple by taking a course called Relationship Instruction.

---

[5]Is there any chance that Hollywood might read this book for guidance on how to construct realistic plot lines? Probably not. But it is time for Christian writers to write novels and movie scripts of people who are believable.

— Chapter 6 featured another strategy to do so, in which a seriously dating couple or an engaged couple meet with a counselor to fill out 125 questions called PREPARE—to help them evaluate their relationship. The questionnaires are compared by computer, and the couple meets with the counselor for two or more feedback sessions to review the strengths and "growth areas" of their relationship. The counselor helps couples improve their "conflict resolution" skills.

Therefore, my first suggestion to the engaged couple is that they take PREPARE—the most widely administered "premarital instrument" (to use sociological jargon) in the United States. Some 100,000 of the 2.5 million people who got married in 1992 used PREPARE. That's impressive.

However, 2.4 million couples did *not* take PREPARE. Fortunately, there will be many pastors and counselors in your community who can administer PREPARE. Some 20,000 instructors have been trained nationally. If you are getting married in a church, ask your pastor if he or she can administer PREPARE for you and do the follow-up counseling.[6]

FIVE MORE STRATEGIES FOR IMPROVING COMMUNICATIONS

There are five other ways for an engaged couple to improve communication skills that the rest of this chapter will explore:

1. *Learn Male-Female Communication Differences*: Much of marital conflict stems from the radically different way that men and women communicate. Every engaged couple should read America's number-one best-seller, *You Just Don't Understand* by Dr. Deborah Tannen. It has sold a million copies.

2. *Premarital Counseling*: Find the most rigorous program for engaged couples in your town and take it. Chances are that it will *not* be in your own church. Most churches have little or no marriage preparation, but Roman Catholics have been more creative in innovating strategies that stretch out engagements, teach important content, and improve communication by means of "Pre-Cana," "Engaged Encounter," and "Marriage Encounter." And some Protestant churches, generally the larger ones, have rigorous programs with solid biblical content and demands for chastity often lacking in Catholic programs. *What's needed is a merger of the best of both strategies.*

3. *Attend "Engaged Encounter:"* This is the most effective single step that one can take to improve communication skills. It is a weekend retreat for

---

[6]If your clergy are not trained in its use, for a list of qualified counselors in your area, write PREPARE/ENRICH, P.O. Box 190, Minneapolis, MN 55440-0190. If you are a Catholic, ask for the name of a Catholic priest to administer it. If a Baptist, ask for a Baptist pastor, and so on. Or you may want names of professional family therapists or counselors who are unaffiliated with a church.

engaged couples, organized and run by clergy and solidly trained lay people. Regrettably, relatively few engaged couples go on such a retreat.

4. *Use a Workbook Designed for Engaged Couples*: One of the best ones, reviewed at the end of this chapter, is *Before You Say "I Do"* by Wes Roberts and H. Norman Wright.

5. *Work with a Mentor Couple*: Ask an older couple with a solid marriage to meet with you as you do your workbook. They can read what each of you have written, ask questions, and give you the benefit of their years of married life in how to face problems in your relationship.

YOU JUST DON'T UNDERSTAND

"There are gender differences in ways of speaking, and we need to identify them and understand them," writes Dr. Deborah Tannen in her #1 bestseller.[7] "Without such understanding, we are doomed to blame others or ourselves—or the relationship—for the otherwise mystifying and damaging effects of our contrasting conversational styles." Her husband sees the world "as many men do; as an individual in a hierarchical social order in which he was either one-up or one-down . . . Conversations are negotiations" where people seek "the upper hand" or to "protect themselves" from being put down or pushed around. "Life, then, is a struggle to preserve independence and avoid failure."

But she sees the world like a woman, "as an individual in a network of connections. In this world, conversations are negotiations for closeness in which people try to seek and give confirmation and support, and to reach consensus . . . Life, then is a community, a struggle to preserve intimacy and avoid isolation."

She tells about Josh, who invited a high school friend home for the weekend and told his wife, Linda, that they'd eat out on Friday night. She is upset that he just "informed her" of his plans rather than discussing them. She would never make plans without talking to him. Josh replies, "I can't say to my friend, 'I have to ask my wife for permission,'" which implies that he is not independent or is a child. Linda is hurt that he thinks more of his friend than of her. He thinks that she's trying to control him.

It took me years to understand a conversational difference between Harriet and me. She would describe a conflict she had with another child's mother or with a boss, and I'd listen intently. Then I'd suggest a solution: Tell her this, or tell him that. She'd blow up: "My purpose in telling you was to share my frustration and to have a listening ear. If I don't talk to you, whom am I going to talk to?" I was just trying to suggest how to solve the problem— a role any male would understand. She didn't *want* to solve it, only describe it! Tannen says that our miscommunication is typical: "If women resent

---

[7]Deborah Tannen, Ph.D. *You Just Don't Understand*, Ballantine Books, 1991.

men's tendency to offer solutions to problems, men complain about women's refusal to take action to solve the problems they complain about."

Engaged couples who read this book will see that much of their verbal conflict is rooted in simple male-female difference.

CHURCH PREMARITAL COUNSELING: NONEXISTENT, OR USELESS

Less than a fifth of all marriages in America were preceded by marriage preparation courses, according to an earlier-cited Gallup Poll. And what was offered had negligible impact: "Attending marriage preparation courses or participating in pre-marital counseling sessions do not seem to prevent the ultimate breakup of a marriage. Divorced couples and those who are still together are equally likely (15 percent and 18 percent, respectively) to have had advance preparation or counseling for marriage."

This is a scandal at two levels:

1. *Every* church should offer premarital courses for the engaged.
2. The courses should offer substantive help for young couples who want their marriages to be successful. To achieve this goal, churches will have to make a bigger investment of prayer, thought, energy, and time to help engaged couples.

As noted earlier, organized religion clearly has *access* to most engaged couples:

- In 1960, 83% of all couples marrying for the first time, did so in a church or synagogue, and there were only 393,000 divorces.
- In 1988, when 73% of all first marriages were still being blessed by clergy, there were 1,183,000 divorces.

Clearly, most churches are little more than blessing machines. The preachers mumble pious words in liturgy with the immortal words captured these days on videotape, words that in 60% of all marriages will come back to haunt the couple. As he asks the groom:

Will you take this woman to be your wife, to live together in the holy covenant of marriage? Will you love her, comfort her, honor and keep her, in sickness and in health, and forsaking all others, be faithful to her so long as you both shall live?

The groom replies, "I will." The bride also agrees to the statement. Then the minister asks them to repeat the vows. The bride says:

I take you to be my husband, to have and to hold from this day forward, for better or for worse, in sickness and in health, to love and to cherish, until we are parted by death, as God is my witness, I give you my promise.

The words *are* beautiful. I remember that tears came to my eyes the day I said them to Harriet, October 16, 1965. In those days, premarital counseling was rare. We were married by an Episcopal bishop who had been Harriet's local minister when she was a girl, but he was of no more help to our marriage than the caterer. He performed a ceremonial function that day that was essential, but so was the food and drink essential for the wedding party afterward.

Of course, the bishop asked us to meet with him beforehand, which we were happy to do. We saw him once. The chat took about fifteen to twenty minutes.

It was harmless. And *useless. Worse, it was a grave disservice.*

Why?

A FOUR-PRONGED MODEL TO EVALUATE PREMARITAL INSTRUCTION

First, we were taught nothing about the problems that we would likely face in marriage on such substantive issues as finances, in-laws, sex, raising children, and so forth. What could have helped us was some classes for engaged couples to acquaint us with some of the realities of married life—particularly on the most likely problems and solutions.

Second, Harriet and I were not trained in any communication or conflict-resolution skills that could have helped us deal with whatever problems might arise. Here the primary need is not lecture but experience-based verbal and written communication exercises, which, like Relationship Instruction described in chapter 5, equip the couple to transform their romance into a lifelong, rewarding marriage. As noted above, there is no better way to begin than by a questionnaire like PREPARE, given to the male and female and interpreted by a counselor or mentor couple.

Third, we were given no indication of how to make Christ the third partner, indeed, the *center* of our marriage. The church should not assume that the two people asking to be married are mature Christians. The odds, in fact, are quite likely to be the opposite. No group in the population is less active religiously than single young people. "You have to assume you are working with a group, many of whom are unchurched. At that moment, there is a great opportunity for evangelization. It is the teachable moment." Says who? Some Baptist? No. That's Don Paglia, co-director of the Catholic Archdiocese of Hartford's Family Life Office and president of the National Association of Catholic Family Life Ministers. I am not suggesting a hard-sell course on "Do You Know Jesus?" that might turn off many who have long been outside the church—but a more subtle approach. Classes and curricula can be designed for engaged couples on what Scripture says about love and marriage. And they can learn the importance of praying as a couple, with Jesus at the center of the marriage.

Finally, Harriet and I could also have benefited from meeting privately with a solidly married couple to whom we could turn for mentoring both during engagement and afterward. In every congregation there are many couples who have been married twenty to thirty years, who would gladly pass on their wisdom to help young couples build solid marriages. They can be trained by the pastor equipped for this important ministry.

To the good, in recent years, many churches have begun to strengthen their marriage preparation. While only a fifth of couples say that they had premarital instruction, according to Gallup, that includes a lot of middle-aged (like us) and older couples who got nothing. Probably well over half of all churches now offer some counseling for engaged couples, but for many Protestants it is generally little more than two or three counseling sessions focused on the wedding and some generalized questions about "any problems" the couple may be having. Larger churches tend to be more demanding, but smaller churches offer no training in communication skills, no mentoring couple, and no biblical instruction. Catholics have pioneered with several of these elements, but not generally with biblical teaching, nor are most facing the cohabitation issue.

At present, I know of only one local church that prepares engaged couples with the fourfold model of marriage preparation outlined above:

- *teaching* on the substantive issues of marriage;
- *equipping* the couple to communicate and resolve conflict;
- *evangelizing* the couple to help put Christ at the center of their marriage;
- helping each couple learn about marriage via a mentor couple.

I urge engaged couples to search for a church that offers as many of these elements as possible, regardless of the church in which you will be married. You may be wed in a particular church where you have grown up, but you should feel free to take marriage preparation classes elsewhere. (One of the couples whom my wife and I are mentoring right now does not attend our church but came for the premarital classes, even though they had already been married a few months.) You should consider getting the best combination of the four premarital components *as divorce insurance*. And, for reasons detailed below, you are most likely to find these elements in a Catholic church. That will shock Protestant readers. But, to participate in marriage preparation, Catholics don't require you to convert to Catholicism, or to marry in a Catholic church.

I urge church leaders, pastors, and parents of single adults to measure the quality of your church's current premarital program by using the preceding four yardsticks. A bottom-line measure of your church's effectiveness is to answer this question: What percent of your engaged couples decide to *break their engagements*? If your program is rigorous, many weak relationships should break apart *before* the wedding—not afterward!

Don't be just a blessing machine, because the producers of today's ghastly marriages *are* the producers of tomorrow's divorces.

THE "COMMON MARRIAGE POLICY" OF THE ROMAN CATHOLIC CHURCH

No American denomination is doing a more thorough job of preparing engaged couples for marriage than does the Roman Catholic Church. Protestant denominations ought to study the Catholic model and develop a similar or better program to increase the odds of Protestant marriages' succeeding. Catholics recognize that the church must take the initiative to make demands on couples to help them grow closer to each other and to the Lord. Of 142 dioceses in the United States who responded to a survey in 1991, 124 of them (87%) have a Marriage Preparation Program for the 336,000 couples married in Catholic churches.

These dioceses have what is often called a "Common Marriage Policy." In the past, couples knew who was the "Marrying Sam"—the priest who had lax marriage standards. Now, no matter which local priest a couple approaches, these challenging demands will be made in common:

1. *Minimum Preparation Period*: From the time of an initial appointment with a priest, most dioceses require six months of marriage preparation. Some stretch out the time for a whole year. None are fewer than four months. To many couples this is disheartening. Once they get their courage up to tie the knot, many want to do it quickly. But *the longer a couple knows each other before the wedding, the greater are the odds of success in their marriage.*

2. *Premarital Questionnaire*: An instrument such as PREPARE (such as the "Pre-Marital Inventory" or PMI, or "FOCUS") is administered by a priest or deacon, early in the engagement. Its content may be tailored for Catholic couples, with church-related questions. The priest or deacon will meet with the couple to go over results, with a particular focus on areas of conflict that the questionnaire surfaces.

3. *Layperson-Led*: Partly due to the shortage of priests and to the fact they are celibate, "Coordinating Couples" or "Sponsoring Couples" take on the primary task of preparing Catholic engaged couples for marriage. A single parish might have two dozen couples who meet with the engaged on a one-to-one basis for five "Evenings for the Engaged." More frequently, sponsoring couples meet with the engaged for five to ten hours during "Pre-Cana Workshops," held almost every weekend somewhere in the diocese.

4. *Marriage Instruction Classes*: There are several different ways that instruction is carried out. Two are noted above: Pre-Cana Workshops, generally involving couples from a dozen or more parishes in a "deanery"; second, Evenings for the Engaged are held in the homes of sponsoring couples. A

third option and by far the best, is an intensive "Engaged Encounter" weekend retreat. It is so rigorous that about a tenth of attendees conclude that they should break their engagements!

5. *Religious Ceremonies for the Betrothed*: In Rhode Island when a couple decides to prepare for marriage, an "Initiation Ceremony" introduces the couple to the entire congregation. Later comes an "Engagement Ceremony" with candles symbolizing the light of Christ. This is done before the whole church during a Sunday Mass, underscoring the importance of this rite of passage. At St. James in Stratford, Connecticut, the parents of both couples pray over their children, bless them, and give them an embrace of farewell on the night before the wedding.

THE PREPARATION: PRE-CANA WORKSHOPS

"In our diocese, it is known from the youngest age that before a couple enters the Sacrament of Marriage, there is a preparation time," says Msgr. Joe DiMauro, Director of Family Life in the Camden (New Jersey) Diocese. *"The theme is that a wedding is a day. A marriage is a lifetime.* We constantly stress in high school that *it takes time to prepare for anything*—especially something as crucial as marriage."

How much time is required? "At least a year. Ordinarily, in our neck of the woods, a couple contemplating marriage can't rent a hall in less than a year. Catering services are booked well in advance of a year.

"Formation begins with the witnessing priest or deacon. A lot of time is spent going over the (Pre-Marital) Inventory—several hours together. The couple meets with the priest or deacon to plan the wedding celebration itself—the Scripture to be read, the prayers they would like, etc. In these formational sessions, they are forming a relationship with the priest, whom we encourage to get to know them personally.

"There are ten hours of instruction, which can be over three weekends, but the best form is a weekend retreat in Engaged Encounter." The Pre-Cana Workshops do require "work" by each couple, both writing and discussing. "It is not just a lecture," said Msgr. DiMauro. "Discussion is very much a part of the format. There are four unmarried couples with one married couple" at each table.

"We have a workbook, 'Perspectives on Marriage,' that couples take home," said Don Paglia, co-director of Hartford's Family Life Office. "It is adult learning, with short talks by married couples or priests. Then we use the workbook for individual or couple exercises. We have role-playing case studies, table discussions." A married couple sits at a table of engaged couples and encourages the group to talk about their answers to questions posed by the workbooks.

ONE CATHOLIC COUPLE'S PERSPECTIVE

What does it feel like to go through Catholic marriage preparation? In Phoenix, several years after their marriage, I interviewed Alan and Paula Sears, who are now parents of three children.

Alan Sears, a Baptist, was so impressed by the premarital process that he converted to Catholicism! Alan is the last person I would have imagined marrying a Catholic girl and converting. I first met him in 1985 when he was the Executive Director of the Attorney General's Commission on Pornography. In his early thirties, married, father of two children, and a very active Baptist, he was a national leader in the Southern Baptist Convention, the nation's largest Protestant denomination, and a long distance from Catholicism. In fact, he was chairman of the issues committee of the Southern Baptist Convention (SBC). I saw him at the SBC's often-chaotic annual meetings, managing the process of submitting issues to be voted upon by the whole Convention of 45,000 people.

Nevertheless, his wife left him and married another man. Alan moved to Phoenix, where he directed a nonprofit agency that offered free legal help to citizen groups or prosecutors fighting pornography. After several years, he met Paula, and they were married.

Initially, they met with Father John—both individually and together. He gave them FOCUS, a premarital questionnaire called a "compatibility test." It asked questions such as:

"Are you afraid of your fiancé?"

"Have you ever been struck by him/her?"

"Would you tell your partner 'No' if he/she asked for anything?"

"How many children do you want to have?"

"Will they make your life wonderful?"

The Sears met with Mr. and Mrs. Bill Kelsey, parents of teenage kids, to go over their answers to the questionnaire during an "Evening for the Engaged" that lasted four hours. The Kelseys congratulated Alan and Paula for the results, which showed relationship strengths. And they probed the areas of conflict or disagreement, giving them an agenda of issues to discuss. The Kelseys told them that they had met with "numerous couples" who scored so poorly that they recommended that the couples not get married. Alan and Paula were impressed that a married couple whom they had never met was willing to devote so much time to them. (Usually, Evenings for the Engaged are spread over three to six nights.)

For several months they attended a series of classes, with a different teacher every week. The first was a priest who abruptly announced, "If you want to get married in the church because your relatives told you to do so, please get up and leave right now! Don't commit a fraud. Don't get married in the church so Mommy will be happy. Go to a Justice of the Peace and have a secular wedding."

An accountant lectured on money. He said, "The largest area of disagreement for couples is financial. Often they get too big a house.[8] He introduced the couples to books by one of America's finest writers on Christian family economics, Larry Burkett, who bravely makes a case for tithing, for example. Such sessions did not always go smoothly. When the accountant suggested that each person should show his spouse their bank account and reveal details about income, a truck driver declared that his wife had no right to know "what is going on with my money. I make it. I spend it."

A priest who was a "Twelve-step" member of Alcoholics Anonymous lectured on the danger signs of alcohol and drug dependency. He described the "co-dependent personality" as an enabler who protects the substance abuser, facilitating his/her mounting alcoholism. He confessed how easy it was for him to conceal his own alcoholism and noted simple warning signs of a problem. He emphasized that addiction can generally be spotted *before* marriage and could be dealt with before becoming crippling. Every church in America has members of Alcoholics Anonymous who would welcome the opportunity to warn engaged couples about the dangers of ignoring early signs of alcoholism.

How does Alan Sears sum up his experience with Catholic marriage preparation? "It gave us a feeling that we really understood what we were getting into and that we could make it work. Looking back in retrospect, it did prepare us. Our expectations were realistic."

Isn't that what every church in America would like to hear from the couples that they married? However, to elicit such a response from those who marry in your church will take a comparable investment of energy by each congregation and denomination. *Engaged couples must be cherished.*

THE MENTORING COUPLE'S ROLE

One of the most important innovations of the Catholic Common Marriage Policy is the help given by a "mentor couple" to engaged couples. No one is better equipped to help young couples begin married life than a seasoned, mature couple with a solid marriage. Every church has many couples who would gladly take on the mentor role. Such people are the *greatest untapped resource for saving marriages* in the United States.

What are mentor couples uniquely qualified to do? Be a practical role model to other couples; give precious time; demonstrate the church's love of the new couple; become a part of the church's life.

---

[8]Harriet and I made this mistake. We thought we had to have a house with three bedrooms, when we had only one child on the way. But after two years, we moved to a smaller, two-bedroom townhouse.

True, mentor couples, usually called "coordinating couples" by Catholics, came into existence partly due to the shortage of priests. However, an engaged couple can more easily identify with a married couple willing to be candid about mistakes they made, or how they handled different problems of marriage, than with many pastors. In most Protestant churches the clergy usually do the counseling. Many consider it one of the joys of the job. But the pastor, who is sort of "paid to be good," is less likely than a lay couple to acknowledge pains or flaws in his own marriage, therefore, he is less "real." By contrast, lay couples are quite likely to be transparent and, consequently, credible. Furthermore, no pastor involves his spouse in counseling, whereas a mentor couple combines wisdom from both the male and female perspective. Finally, most pastors simply do not have the time that volunteer couples can offer. A pastor who trains mentor couples can multiply his or her ministry manyfold. They are a source of the energy and time needed to make engagements truly meaningful.

EVENINGS FOR THE ENGAGED

I asked an airline pilot, a member of St. Catherine's Catholic Church in Greenwich, Connecticut, what the mentoring experience was like for him and his wife. In their late forties, the couple are parents of six children.

"First, it has been wonderful for our marriage!" he said. "When I suggested that couples ought to spend time every day in dialogue focusing on their own relationship, away from the kids, my wife interrupted, saying, 'What are you talking about? You don't meet with me every day!' She was right, and we schedule more quiet times now, as a result.

"We have a big church, so we meet with three couples at a time. The experience is quite similar with each group. On the first evening, the guys are constantly looking at their watches. They grumble, 'How long is this going to take? I got things to do.'"

The pilot then laughed, "But there is not one meeting with these couples in which someone is not breaking down in tears." One young woman after another is shocked to hear what their fiancés are saying:

"What do you mean, we will spend Christmas at *your* folks' house?"

"Who says that *you* will manage the checkbook?"

"Why do you think *you* will decide whether we should move?"

Clearly, the tough issues had not been put on the table by many couples until they were asked probing questions. With what result?

By the third "Evening with the Engaged," the pilot said, "All the couples love the experience because they are learning so much. They become like a pledge class of a fraternity—close to each other yet willing to look up to those who are older. The girls call each other up and say, "You won't believe what he said today." Or the guys will call each other and say, "Guess what she wants to spend money on now!" After the weddings, many of them keep in contact with us. They feel they have someone they can turn to if they get in trouble. It has been a very satisfying experience."

Steve Buttry, editor of *The Minot (ND) Daily News,* has quite a different experience. First, he and other mentor couples went through a rigorous weekend training session, covering the entire course itself, which is spread out over five Evenings for the Engaged. One of the tips they heard: "Make the course your own by using your own experience to illustrate how you dealt with various problems."

For example, the second Evening is on communications and conflict. Steve said, "We outlined constructive ways of fighting. We told the couples that *we* had to learn that we communicate differently. My wife came from a family where everything is discussed in the open—fireworks. My mom and dad aired things behind closed doors. I was not as expressive. If she made a big deal about something, I felt, 'She can have her way.' I learned eventually that was how she responded to *anything.* So I had to express myself more, and she had to learn that just because I am not saying anything does not mean I have no feelings. We had to learn each other's communication styles so it was not one-sided."

During the Evening for the Engaged on sexuality, the Buttrys passed out index cards and asked the couples to write down anonymously any questions they had about sexuality. People are bashful to ask what is on their heart if they have to do so in public but are glad to do so anonymously. What questions arose? "Is it important to follow church teaching on birth control?" How do kids affect your sex life?" "How do you keep your sex life fresh?"

The fourth Evening for the Engaged is on spirituality. Resentments surfaced quickly. "We are not both Catholics," one man says, fearing pressure on his Protestant wife. The Buttrys surprised them by saying: "We will not tell you about the Catholic Church. We are talking about the *domestic* church. Even if you are both from the Catholic Church, or are mixed, Catholic and non-Catholic, it is important to share what is meaningful to you spiritually, your spiritual doubts. Spirituality is one of the most important forms of intimacy. . . ."

Then, before the fifth session, one of the brides-to-be was killed in a terrible auto accident. Four other couples learned about it at their regular meeting in the Buttrys' home. "We felt we needed to deal with death as a group," Buttrey said. "They have a view of living for years, but we said, 'As a lifelong commitment, you are committing to go through the death of one of you, so we want you to finish two statements, writing out a sharing of your hopes and fears: "If I should die . . ." and "If you should die . . ." ' "

This happened several years ago in Kansas City when the Buttrys were in their first mentoring experience. They have used it in every session since.

ENGAGED ENCOUNTER

In Seattle, Washington, 1,200 engaged Catholic couples per year decide to go to a weekend retreat called "Engaged Encounter." It is like Weekends for the Engaged, but it lasts from Friday night through Sunday afternoon and is far more intensive—and far more effective. Sadly, in most dioceses, attendance is much smaller than in Seattle: 300 out of 5000 marriages in the Archdiocese of Hartford, for example. Nevertheless, it is one element of Catholic marriage preparation that has moved across denominational lines into Episcopal, Methodist, Lutheran, Reformed, and other mainline churches. An example is reported below.

Like "Marriage Encounter," the older and more established program that inspired Engaged Encounter (see chapter 9), the weekend consists of eighteen talks led by trained married couples and a priest (or in Protestant versions, a clergy couple) followed by private sessions between each engaged couple. In their private time the man and woman each write reflections in response to questions suggested by the lead couples. They read what each other has written and then privately "dialogue" about it. The relaxed atmosphere of an entire weekend allows them to examine all key issues they will encounter within marriage: conflict resolution, sexual relations, children, finances, friendships, church participation, marital goals, and so forth.

EPISCOPAL ENGAGED ENCOUNTER[9]

For example, several years ago, Art and Diane Moore, then national directors of Episcopal Engaged Encounter, took sixteen engaged couples to a ranch in Colorado. Diane began one session called "Encounter With Me" by saying, "Love is a decision. You have to decide to love that person over and over. You women will *not* feel the same way about him as you do today. In romance, you see no faults. But love is a cycle in which you go from romance to disillusionment to romance. You discover that you have to *decide* to love that person again . . . In the past, I never acknowledged that God had a place in our relationship. But that is what you ought to work for. What you want is a trio—the two of you plus God, which will make you a stronger couple."

The couples were then asked to spend an hour writing and talking about some searing questions: "What things do I talk to others more easily about than I do with you? What are the things that make me angry with you? What doubts do I have in marrying you?" Later, after a talk on the sacrament of marriage, they were asked to write answers to questions like these: "How is God working in our engagement? How will we reflect God's love after our wedding, to others and the world?"

---

[9]While Engaged Encounter began among Catholics, it has moved into Episcopal, Presbyterian, Lutheran, and other mainline denominations.

All of that was covered before lunch on Saturday! Afterward, they focused on the myriad of practical questions in marriage: whether to have children, when, how many, how to discipline them—careers versus family, and such money issues as, Who will pay the bills, how much will be saved?

Reactions? "This weekend showed me I have a lot of fears, mistrust, and difficulties risking honesty first with myself and then with my fiancé. It made me realize that commitment and love are things I have never taken seriously before. I always felt they just happened and were not experiences you make happen," said one. "It was a painful, emotional, draining, tearful, joyful, releasing, and finally peaceful experience."

To any engaged couple, I ask: Why would you *not* want such an experience? To the parents of engaged couples, I'd ask: "Why not pay the $150 or so to give your son/daughter and future spouse that experience?"

One other point must be added. Experience with Engaged Encounter across the nation indicates that nearly a tenth of those who attend, decide *not* to marry that person. Or they postpone their wedding. Is that a sign of failure? Hardly! With a 60% marriage dissolution rate for new marriages, the engagement process should be rigorous enough that weak relationships break up *before* marriage.

I challenge any pastor or church lay leader to answer some questions:

1. How does your marriage preparation compare with Engaged Encounter?
2. Would any engaged couple who completed your counseling sessions call them "painful, emotional, draining, tearful, joyful, releasing, and finally, peaceful?"
3. If the answers are "No," why give your couples second best?

PROTESTANT MARRIAGE PREPARATION

No Protestant denomination has the equivalent of the Catholics' "Common Marriage Policy," with common requirements, regardless of the church a couple goes to, such as a minimum period of engagement, the taking of a premarital test such as PREPARE or Taylor-Johnson, meeting with older "mentor couples," writing in an engagement workbook, or learning communication skills.

Some individual churches will make similar requirements and some exceed what the Catholics require in biblical study and personal morality. The larger churches tend to be more demanding with more requests for weddings than they can handle. The higher standards are seen as a way to strengthen the marriages of those who get married there.

However, most Protestant churches have only 100 to 300 members. In general, their demands of engaged couples are minimal: perhaps two or three counseling sessions, one of which is focused on the wedding itself. If a couple wants to be married in a month, that is usually okay if the church is available. There is no required reading, or training in communication skills, or a compatibility test. Such a church is a blessing machine, a wedding factory that *should be avoided* by engaged couples who want to learn how to build a lifelong marriage. Of course, if the bride grew up in such a church and her parents want the wedding there, that decision can be honored. But such a church deserves no more respect for its preparation for marriage than does a Justice of the Peace.

Couples caught in such a situation owe it to themselves to join a more rigorous program. Protestants should call the largest churches in town and ask for a description of their marriage preparation program. If you find nothing comparable to what Catholics are offering, by all means sign up for Engaged Encounter or Evenings for the Engaged at the Catholic church. You can still be married in the family's church.

WHY ARE SO MANY PROTESTANT PROGRAMS FOR THE ENGAGED SO MEDIOCRE?

There are three reasons why so many Protestant programs for the engaged are undemanding:

1. *Overloaded pastors*: The clergy of small churches are overworked. Although they find meeting with the engaged to be one of their more pleasant tasks, they simply do not have time to see an engaged couple more than two or three times. Why, then, don't they train lay couples in their congregations to be "mentor couples"?

2. *Pressure from parents*: The pastor who has a six-month marriage preparation program will quickly run into a deacon who says, "Pastor, great news! My daughter is getting married! Do you have a free Saturday in the next couple of months?" I can imagine a pastor with standards, replying "Sorry, Jim. I require the engaged couple to answer a questionnaire to help them assess their strengths and weaknesses, two counseling sessions to interpret the results with them, and attendance at eight classes on such issues as money and conflict resolution. At the minimum this takes four months, and six months is what I recommend."

Or, "Listen pastor, my daughter is living with this guy. It has taken them a year to even decide to get married. I don't want to tell them they have to jump through fourteen hoops if they want to get married here. Besides, she lives out of town and could not attend all your counseling sessions. We have been members here for fourteen years, and I have never asked for a favor."

3. *Pressure from couples*: A couple will make an appointment with the same pastor, hear about his marriage-preparation requirements, and say, "Pastor, we don't mind coming to several counseling sessions, but we've already reserved a reception hall in two months. Why *eight* counseling sessions? Meeting with an older couple? We are not even members of this

church. We don't know anyone here. And what's with this test? We know we love each other. We've been dating for a year."

The pastor might reply, "You should not have rented a hall until you had a date set for your wedding. Look at the fact that half of marriages are breaking up. We are trying to give you *divorce insurance* to increase the odds that your marriage will make it. It takes time to learn communication skills. How many years did you study to do the work you do?"

"Four years, pastor. We appreciate your concern. Frankly, we are moving here after our wedding, and we thought we might want to join your church. But we really can't change that date for our reception. We'd have to postpone for another six months. If you are going to insist we turn three dozen somersaults, we will have to find another Presbyterian church."

Since moving to the Washington area in 1987, my wife and I have attended Fourth Presbyterian Church (an Evangelical Presbyterian Church). It has a remarkable singles group of 300 people called "Ambassadors," which has its own worship service each Sunday, many small Bible studies, very substantial ministry to Washington's inner-city poor, and its own courses. In the spring of 1991, Ambassadors sponsored a Thursday night series with the zippy title of "Sexuality 101." Its subtitle: "A Biblical Perspective on Relationships, Dating, and Marriage." It continued for fourteen weeks and was largely taught by lay leader couples of Fourth.

Ambassadors distributed a twenty-eight-page outline of the course, with two pages per evening.[10]

WHAT ABOUT THE ISSUE OF COHABITATION?

I once asked a Catholic priest in Connecticut, who had designed an otherwise outstanding premarital program, "What do you do if a couple is cohabiting?" He replied, "Nothing. What they do sexually is their business, not mine. It is a private matter."

Most clergy would not be so openly blunt, but their position is much the same. They do not ask whether a couple is cohabiting, or say anything, if the couple lists the same address. I think that this is not only unbiblical but unethical. By removing God's rules on sexuality from their teaching, churches foster licentiousness, with grave consequences for everyone.

How can a church successfully confront cohabitants?

On the day of writing this section, I stood up at the beginning of a series of classes for the engaged and said, "I don't know if any of you are cohabiting with your fiancé(e), but I want to report the results of the *National Survey on Families and Households*. After interviewing 14,000 people—ten times the number interviewed by Gallup in a presidential poll, it concluded,

---

[10]For a copy of the syllabus for "Sexuality 101," contact Ambassadors, Fourth Presbyterian Church, 5500 River Road, Bethesda, MD 20816.

'Marriages that are preceded by living together have 50% higher disruption rates than marriages without premarital cohabitation.' With those odds, I would urge any of you who may be cohabiting, to separate and increase your odds of a life-long marriage."

Pastor Jim Talley, whose "Relationship Instruction" is described in chapter 5, is more blunt. He refuses to knowingly marry anyone living together. He tells them that they have to separate if they want to be married in the church. Some reply, "We can't afford to separate. Besides, it is only three months before our wedding." Talley replies: "If there is a financial burden, the church will help you with it." Few asked for help.

The result: Weeks after separating, they say, "The quality of our relationship has never been better. Our love continues to grow and amaze us."

The Lord blesses those who put on "the full armor of God."

MY GLOOM-AND-DOOM LECTURE

"As the pastor in charge of counseling, I have to deal with disappointment, disease, death, and divorce" began Dr. Willard Davis, 62, in the opening session of eight Sunday school classes required for couples getting married at Fourth Presbyterian Church in Bethesda. I fully expected him to then say what a joy it was to talk to engaged couples. But no. He shocked me as he continued. "I'm going to deliver my 'Doom-and-Gloom Lecture' on the pathology of divorce. There was a time when helping couples prepare for marriage was an enjoyable experience. But I have become more and more uneasy and more and more nervous about officiating at weddings, because of the rising statistics of divorce. Today I would rather perform a funeral service than a wedding.

"In the 1930s, one out of 6.8 marriages ended in divorce. In the 1960s, it was one out of four. Now it is one out of two. The decline in couples staying together is very, very alarming. That would be bad enough. But you have to add to that all the separations—both the physical and emotional separations, which happen when two married people live under the same roof, psychologically separated. One out of two does not tell the whole story.

"The odds are stacked against couples' finding happiness within a marriage. And it is not simply the future of the couple that is involved. The effect of an unhappy marriage can be devastating on their children." Clearly, this message was not what they had expected to hear.

"There is a new fad of books on adult survivors of parental divorce. What they have found is what could be predicted—that sick marriages make sick people. And with sick people, you get more sick marriages. Dysfunctional homes affect the lives of children," said Dr. Davis.

"But you are called to live in such a time. I am not trying to suggest that you should shrink back from marriage. But give yourself wholly to an adequate preparation for marriage . . . A friend of mine decided upon retirement that he wanted to run a Black Angus farm, and he spent five years studying everything about Black Angus cattle. Five years. The Sanitation Department of Los Angeles requires six weeks of preparation.

"Weddings are not the subject of this course. This is preparation, not for a wedding but for a marriage. There are very few things for which we have *less* preparation, than marriage and raising children."

It was an extraordinary talk, and I've only quoted the opening words. Dr. Davis explored the "pathology of divorce," and its many causes. "Many cited by people in divorce courts (sexual incompatibility, finances, differences over recreation, friends, in-laws, and religion) are merely symptoms," he said, "of deeper maladies: emotional maladjustment and poor communication. Marriage brings to the surface, emotional defects in a person's life. If you are not well-adjusted emotionally, talk to a counselor, take a test, and deal with the problem before the wedding day.

"Emotional immaturity becomes pronounced in marriage. Babies love things and use people. But there should be a time when as we mature emotionally, we learn to love people, and use things. But many husbands love their convertible but use their wives. They live in an ego-centered existence and have a lack of self-discipline. . . ."

As I listened, I thought, *Good. Perhaps some of those emotionally maladjusted people will seek counseling. And if they don't go on their own, perhaps their fiancées* will recognize symptoms in their partners and will persuade them to go.

SUMMARY

This chapter began by quoting Gallup Polls that found at least three-fifths of all divorces were caused by poor communication. I have, therefore, focused my suggestions on how an engaged couple can take "divorce insurance" by spotlighting a host of ways the couple might improve their communication skills:

- taking the Prepare premarital questionnaire
- reading *You Just Don't Understand* on male/female communication
- enrolling in a rigorous premarital course, possibly outside your own church
- working with a mentor couple as in "Evenings for the Engaged"
- attending "Engaged Encounter"
- studying Scripture related to marriage
- using a marriage preparation manual to spark deep thought and talk, especially *Before You Say "I Do"* by Wes Roberts and H. Norman Wright.

Chances are that to accomplish each and every one of these "Marriage Saving" opportunities, you will not have as much time as you would like. If time is limited, I urge you to consider three steps:

1. Take PREPARE to give an objective diagnosis of your relationship's strengths and the areas for needed growth and also to learn conflict-resolution skills.
2. Attend Engaged Encounter to deepen your love on a spiritual level and to develop superb communication skills.
3. Work with *Before You Say "I Do"* on weekends to add biblical depth and to strengthen your understanding of your partner.

Each of these steps can be taken by any couple, regardless of the quality (or lack of it) in your church's marriage preparation program. There are counselors and pastors in every community trained to administer PREPARE. Every Catholic diocese offers Engaged Encounter, as do many Protestant denominations. Engaged couples should not hesitate to ask parents to help with the costs of Engaged Encounter. If parents hesitate, have them read this chapter and suggest that *they* consider going on a Marriage Encounter! Tell them that its motto is "Helping make good marriages better." Finally, *Before You Say "I Do"* can be found in any Christian bookstore.

I also urge pastors and lay leaders of churches to compare how your church is presently helping engaged couples prepare, not for a wedding but for a marriage. Is your church helping accomplish or helping destroy God's plan for marriage, so beautifully summed up in Genesis:

The LORD God said, "It is not good for the man to be alone. I will make a helper suitable for him. . . ." Then the LORD God made a woman from the rib he had taken out of the man, and he brought her to the man.

The man said:

"This is now bone of my bones and flesh of my flesh; she shall be called 'woman,' for she was taken out of man." For this reason a man will leave his father and mother and be united to his wife, and they will become one flesh. The man and his wife were both naked and they felt no shame (Genesis 2:18, 22–25).

To be specific, does your church:

— teach that sex belongs only in marriage, and demonstrate a commitment to Scripture, which refuses to marry cohabitants?
— tolerate divorce by remarrying virtually anyone, or teach that God "hates" divorce, as expressed in Malachi 2?
— train engaged couples in communication and conflict-resolution skills that are essential to unite a man and woman for life?

— immerse engaged couples in the wisdom of Scripture on marriage and how to build relationships that are rock solid?

— inspire engaged couples by exposing them to mentor couples in your church?

— expose engaged couples to the best advice in such substantive areas as finances, sexual relations, children, male-female differences in communication?

Pastors, in the future, will the couples who married in your church in the 1990s call your church a blessing—or a blessing machine? It all depends on whether your church did its best to be a Marriage Saver.

It is one policy that costs no money—only *love*.

EIGHT

Newlyweds:
The Honeymoon Is Over

Better to live on a corner of the roof than to share a house with a quarrelsome wife.

—Proverbs 21:9

The biggest thing I have encountered is the lack of communication. No one says, "Expect the beginning to be rocky."

—Heather, a newlywed

In July 1992, we went to a wonderful wedding of Beth and John, whose relationship is described in chapter 6. It was held in the garden of a historic Maryland plantation. Few were happier about the day than Harriet and I, who had served as a mentor couple to them. We had seen their relationship deepen in a way that no one else had. The PREPARE questionnaire revealed a "wall" in their relationship—his "silent treatment" of her during disagreements. We taught them "Ten Steps of Conflict Resolution" and focused upon the "silent treatment" issue. John said that the Ten Steps were "like a ladder, which we used to climb over the wall." He told us that spring: "I will not be silent again. I will talk sooner about my feelings . . ."

Yet, only three weeks after they returned from their honeymoon, over dinner at our home, Beth disclosed: "He's giving me the silent treatment again. We really did not talk in two days. He left for work with me crying. I felt like I was hanging on his feet. I am a complete wreck."

Lamely, he explained, "She doesn't call me from work if she's late."

Then there was the matter of how she folded his shirts. John told us, "We fold shirts differently. She folds them down the middle, not squared, so I said, 'Let me fold my shirts. I enjoy folding shirts.'" But Beth gave a different version: "You said, '*I* will fold my shirts. You are not paying attention to how I want my shirts. I might as well do them myself.'"

They shared how they went to the beach with three of John's friends and her little sister, who was going off to college for the first time. While on the boardwalk, she walked with her sister. John was angry that she was not walking with him and also embarrassed that the sisters were holding hands. "John felt that I had rejected him. He was so upset that I went back to him, and he was ignoring me again. He was not talking. I am afraid to spend any time with any particular individual—that I will offend him—or make him feel that I love him less. I feel that I cannot be myself."

Problems like this, so early in a marriage, are shockingly frequent. How frequent? *Half* of all newlyweds "reported having significant marital problems," according to a study[1] by Miriam Arond (who worked for *Bride's* magazine) and her husband, Dr. Samuel Pauker, M.D. (a psychiatrist).

They conducted a survey among 455 newlyweds who had been married an average of only six months and 75 couples who had been married longer, looked back at their first year of marriage, answering questions.

The key reason that 49% of newlyweds had immediate problems in their marriages was unexpected change in their lives and relationships after merely saying, "I do"! Between 47% and 58% of the newlyweds reported dramatic increases in:

— the number of arguments they had after their wedding;
— their tendency to be critical of their mate;
— their feelings of self-confidence.

Of course, marriage involves a major change in anyone's life. The relationship before marriage is inherently different from afterward. Arond/ Pauker note that in biblical times, the special status of "bride and groom" lasted a full year: "If a man has recently married, he must not be sent to war or have any other duty laid on him. For one year he is to be free to stay at home and bring happiness to the wife he has married" (Deut. 24:5). *The First Year of Marriage* outlines three distinct phases for almost any couple:

1. Before the wedding, in the glow of romance is a *period of enchantment*. Most couples feel "on Cloud 9," that their mate is "perfect," and are delighted to be infatuated, charmed, and captivated by him or her. Obviously, such views are unrealistic.

2. After the wedding, often on the honeymoon itself, a *period of disenchantment* sets in. One feels upset, put down, irritated, hurt, wretched, and trapped by the relationship. Such views are equally unrealistic, given the love that sparked marriage.

3. Finally, couples move toward a period of *maturity*.

What was particularly baffling to the couples surveyed by Arond and Pauker was that 85% of them had had premarital sex before marrying, and 54% had cohabited before marriage. This intimacy led the couples to assume that they truly understood each other.

---

[1]Miriam Arond and Samuel L. Pauker, M.D., *The First Year of Marriage*, New York, Warner Books, Inc., 1987.

Sexual intimacy, however, can be deceiving. Mere physical closeness does not translate into emotional understanding or genuine commitment.

WHY IS MARRIAGE SO DIFFERENT FROM LIVING TOGETHER?

The assumption of most couples who live together is that it is wise to have a "trial" marriage—a test of whether the relationship "works."

Persons who, in childhood experienced the divorce of their parents are particularly likely to cohabit. They fear making a clear commitment to marriage because it might result in divorce, so they take a half-step, a "trial" marriage, to see "if the relationship will work out."

But the survey for *The First Year of Marriage* found *no* evidence that those who cohabited had an easier time with their sex life in marriage. Quite the opposite. The book cites a study,[2] which found that couples who lived together before marriage had significantly *lower* marital satisfaction than those who did "not cohabit." And the result can be disastrous. In chapter 2, I reported that the consequences revealed by the *National Survey of Families and Households*: "Unions begun by cohabitation are almost twice as likely to dissolve within 10 years compared to all first marriages: fifty-seven percent compared to thirty percent."

The Family in Cross-Cultural Perspective, by William Stevens, has a wonderful definition of wedded life:

> [Marriage is] a socially legitimate sexual union, begun with a public announcement and undertaken with some idea of permanence; it is assumed with a more or less explicit marriage contract, which spells out the reciprocal rights and obligations between spouses and between the spouses and their future children.

By contrast, Arond and Pauker, writing from a secular, not a religious perspective, say that cohabitation involves "no *public* commitment, no *pledge* for the future, no *official* pronouncement of love and responsibility. Theirs is essentially a private arrangement based on an emotional bond. Marriage, on the other hand, is much more than a love partnership. It is a public event that involves legal and societal responsibilities. It brings together not just two people but also two families and two communities. It is not just for the here and now; it is, most newlyweds hope, 'till death do us part.' Getting married changes what you expect from your mate and yourself" even if there has been prior cohabitation.

Cohabiting, however, was *not* Beth and John's problem (she was a virgin on their wedding night). Jealousy was the problem. When Beth saw a

---

[2]Alfred DeMaris and Gerald R. Leslie, "Cohabitation with the Future Spouse: Its Influence Upon Marital Satisfaction and Communication," *Journal of Marriage and the Family*, February 1984, 77–84.

girlfriend one Saturday, John said, "You could have spent those two-and-half hours with me." He made her feel suffocated. Harriet, my wife, told him: "You are threatened when she is not with you. You are trying to control her like your mother controlled your dad. Beth's trying to please you, but you're crushing her. She's a free spirit, a joy, who laughs a lot. If you crush that, she'll become a different person—crushed like your dad."

After the wedding vows, some people *do* change behind the security of marriage. Women often gain weight, thinking that they no longer have to keep trim once they have the ring. Men often spend many more hours at work during the week and at sports events on the weekend and take their wives for granted. Habits that were hardly noticed before the wedding, later become extremely annoying.

A CASE STUDY OF HELPING SAVE A NEWLYWEDS' MARRIAGE

As difficult as the problems of newlyweds may appear, there is more hope for saving a new marriage than a poor marriage of long duration, during which the bad habits of each partner attach to the other like barnacles on a boat. Why is there more hope? Unlike engaged couples, who think they know *everything* about their partner, newlyweds are truly baffled by a spouse and genuinely open to the help of a mature friend or relative.

They are even more open to an older couple with a solid marriage who take the time as a couple to meet with them together, to pass on the wisdom gained from decades of experience. Harriet and I have no training in psychology, but we did volunteer to be a mentor couple in a class for the engaged at our church. One couple, whom I'll call Peter and Heather Cole to protect their privacy, joined the class though they already had been married three months. Why? "We were committed to attending some sort of marital counseling, believing it's a wise thing for couples to do but did not have time for the classes before we were married," said Heather. "But we certainly find that we need them *now*." They had known each other four years before they were married. Like most couples in the courtship phase, their communication seemed wonderful. They did not think that they needed any help with their relationship . . . until they were married.

OUR ROLE AS A MENTOR COUPLE

I relate their story and our satisfying experience of helping them, to illustrate how couples with good marriages in any church can help newlyweds. The Coles are quite a bit older than average newlyweds. He was forty when he married and she was thirty-two, though neither had been married before. Each is sophisticated and well-educated. Peter has an important federal job as a fiscal manager. Heather stopped working when they married and she was attempting to brighten their seventy-year-old home that was run-down from years of being rented. Both had been very active Christian believers for some years.

Nevertheless, it was clear that their honeymoon was over. Peter seemed bored and aloof as he sat with our circle of younger engaged couples and was disdainful of the process that she had gotten him into, feeling that it was all quite unnecessary. Heather, however, was more vulnerable. She was obviously feeling pain and a quiet sadness that seemed out of place for a newlywed.

In the fall and spring, our church offers eight classes for the engaged, with lectures on such issues as money and sex, at which Harriet and I and other mentor couples lead discussions with four to five couples. Each couple seemed awkward and ill-at-ease sharing anything below a superficial level, so we shared stories about mistakes and problems that we had faced in our own marriage. Our vulnerability surprised, intrigued, and encouraged them. None wanted to acknowledge, especially in front of their peers from church, that they were having trouble. We needed privacy, working with each couple separately, and our mentoring had to target their specific struggles.

THE ENRICH MARITAL INVENTORY

Therefore, I suggested that we give each of the unmarried couples the PREPARE relational instrument (described in chapter 6) and that Heather and Peter take the companion ENRICH marital inventory, which is very similar to PREPARE in that 125 questions, asked separately of the male and female, are computer scored. The results are sent back to a counselor or mentor couple who meets privately with the couple to report and discuss an evaluation of their answers. ENRICH, unlike PREPARE, asks a number of questions that focus on a married couple's satisfaction with their relationship. Like PREPARE, it is not a "test" that one passes or fails. It is, however, an extremely penetrating X-ray of a relationship, which reveals both its strengths and its areas of conflict or misunderstanding—its flash points—where growth is needed. It is superbly designed for an older lay couple to use to probe beneath the surface to areas of difficulty in the newlyweds' marriage. We are not trained counselors, but we are willing to share our experience as "mentors" of young couples.

When Heather and Peter came to our home to take ENRICH, Heather said, "We appreciate your going the extra mile with us."[3] ENRICH took only

---

[3]It was no sacrifice from our point of view. Quite the opposite. Working with young couples has been the most exciting ministry we've ever been involved with in any church. What is truly odd and inexplicable is that so few churches create opportunities for mature married couples to counsel young couples. They are so eager to learn and so capable of grasping principles that older couples like us took decades to learn by hit-or-miss.

a half hour to complete. Afterward, I asked what they thought of it. "I like the fact that it takes one issue and works from different angles, three or four questions, which will give a more accurate coloration of our answers, with more valid results," she said.

We asked them to describe their relationship. "One of the biggest things I have encountered is a lack of communication about the problems that will inevitably be there for couples to resolve," Heather said. "Nobody talks about the problems. You begin to feel, 'I am a rotten Christian.' No one says, 'Expect the beginning to be rocky.' "

Peter said abstractedly: "I have an abiding faith in marriage," saying nothing about *this* marriage. He talked about caring long-distance for elderly relatives and about the new church they had joined. Like most men, he was more comfortable talking about anything other than a personal relationship.

As Heather curled up on our couch she said, "I'm glad we are doing this after we are married rather than before. I am much more aware of my needs than I could have been before my marriage. Once you are married, conflict that had not arisen before, surfaces. Before the wedding, the issues that you will have to deal with have not become clear."

Peter added, "During engagement there is the feeling that the conflict will go away after you are married. There is a tendency when you are engaged, not to confront things for fear of alienating the person. When you are engaged, you have limited time together."

Note here that they are *not* being clear about the nature of their conflict. As she said, "People don't like to admit areas of weakness in themselves or their relationships. Without the counsel of older couples and a forum like this to draw those things out, they don't get addressed." When Peter and Heather went home, we still knew nothing about their conflicts, but we were confident that the ENRICH questionnaire would bring to the surface, problem areas that our gentle prodding had not.[4]

Another feeling that I had afterward was a new appreciation for the difficulty pastors have in trying to have a meaningful premarital counseling session with couples they don't know. One could spend an hour as we did, attempting a meaningful conversation, and fail to penetrate their defenses. Everyone is skilled at fending off invasions of privacy. Despite having this couple in eight group premarital sessions at church and privately in our home, we had no idea what the nature of their conflict was.

---

[4]Some 20,000 pastors and counselors are trained to administer ENRICH. To learn who is equipped in your community, write to PREPARE/ENRICH, Box 190, Minneapolis, MN. 55440-0190.

WHAT WE LEARNED FROM ENRICH

ENRICH, however, a superb diagnostic tool, revealed their relationship to us better than if we had known them each for five years. It can give any older couple with a stable, satisfying marriage a clear idea of what qualities in a newlyweds' marriage should be praised—to encourage them—and where to ask hard questions.

Frankly, Harriet and I were quite dismayed by the ENRICH results of Peter and Heather. In the computer printout sent back to us we could compare the answers that they had individually given to each question. These answers were grouped in categories, such as "Communication" or "Children," and in six out of thirteen areas surveyed, Peter and Heather had only ten to twenty percent of positive-couple agreement. Their overall "Marital Satisfaction" was very low, as were scores on "Personality" issues, "Communication," "Conflict Resolution," "Financial Management," and "Children/ Parenting." No wonder they were feeling shell-shocked!

ENRICH suggests that the counselor or mentors begin by reporting three areas of "relationship strengths," where they agreed on ninety percent of the issues raised in order to be as supportive as possible. For example, Peter and Heather had a ninety percent agreement on religious issues.

I said, "One area of real strength in your marriage is your agreement on basic religious issues." Looking at their answers to specific questions, I added, "You both believe strongly that 'in sharing religious values, your relationship will grow.' Also, you both feel that your faith is an important part of the commitment you have made to your partner. This provides an important bridge for each of you to walk confidently over to the other person, a bridge that can span any problem that is dividing you. Another area of agreement is on 'Equalitarian Role.' You think you should 'jointly agree on all important decisions' and that 'if there are young children, the wife should not work outside the home.' Both are a cause of much friction in other marriages."

Then I turned to what ENRICH euphemistically calls "growth areas," saying, "As you know, you are having major problems in Communication and Conflict Resolution. For example, Heather, you say that you are 'sometimes afraid to ask' your partner for what you want. Peter, you wish that Heather were 'more willing to share her feelings' with you. You both agree that sometimes you have 'serious disputes over unimportant issues.' On financial management, you agree that 'deciding what is most important to spend money on is a problem.' Peter, you wish she were more thrifty. But Heather, what bothers you is that you 'cannot spend money without your partner's approval.' And apparently you disagree on whether your partner 'should smoke, drink, or use drugs less often.'

"Is there a substance abuse problem?" I asked. "No, but sometimes she smokes cigarettes," Peter said. I pressed on.

"Is the rest of my summary accurate of some of your relationship's strengths and weaknesses?" I asked. They nodded assent.

THE FIRST ENRICH-SPARKED DIALOGUE

Peter smoothly glided over the issues: "Yes. We consult a whole lot. We go smoothly about a division of labor. We do have differences on money and buying things. I encourage her to research before buying things."

Heather broke in. "That is a misunderstanding. I am as prone to research things as he is," she blurted out. Then she changed the subject. "Peter has been terrific about making my friends his friends. He's a good sport to go along with me, but every now and then there's a streak when he behaves so badly, putting me down in front of others. I tend to make matters worse. I say something I shouldn't because I am embarrassed and wounded."

ENRICH had quickly revealed real issues that had been disguised before, but there were so many! I shifted the subject slightly: "How do you resolve your conflicts?"

"We both get frustrated. It results in things we find displeasing," said Peter. He looked at her and snapped, "You get frustrated and are driven to smoke. It is less an enjoyment than an act of bitterness and lack of communication."

He continued. "I am terrible at remembering how we get into a fight. Then we argue about who said what. She tells me that 'You are just justifying yourself and not searching with the aim of getting to the bottom of it and resolving it.' It involves reconstructing how we got to that point . . . I am not surprised by the findings. They confirm my sense of it."

Clearly, they had no idea how to resolve conflicts. If they had a satisfactory process of settling arguments, every other issue would take care of itself. I asked, "Can you give an example of a disagreement and how you tried to resolve it without the satisfaction of either person?"

Peter responded: "Most of these conflicts have to do with money." Although Heather's family is affluent, and money is not an issue, Peter had struggled to save. He did own outright a charming old townhouse in an established neighborhood of Washington, but she kept proposing major renovations.[5] To illustrate a recent argument, Peter explained that "Heather bought a lamp on sale. To please me, she bought a less expensive one for eighty dollars, but it wasn't satisfactory. I did not like it and thought the price

---

[5]"In a marriage, one person is often a spender, and one is a saver," said Bill Boylan, the Roman Catholic Co-Executive Chair of Worldwide Marriage Encounter.

was a rip-off—that store charges high prices. I wouldn't mind if it were the ideal lamp—"

She added, "Here's a lamp that you are not happy with and I am not happy with—that made it more traumatic. Here we are having a major struggle over something not very fundamental. . . . We *can* communicate. We can articulate things, but we don't resolve our disputes. I sense a lack of desire to bring about a solution," she said, stating her gut fear. He is not just rejecting her choice of the lamp—but her as a person.

Heather continued, "One would assume that if you have two good communicators, that you communicate well. That's not necessarily the case. It is one thing to articulate your feelings and quite another for both people to be willing to listen and to change. Good communication should lead to resolution of issues. There was not a context of caring that makes the communication fruitful. We were arguing but not getting to solutions. After you have expressed your feelings a few times and felt shot down, you then tend not to want to share them again, out of a fear of being wounded, ending up hurt and frustrated again."

She looked at Harriet and me and asked, "What has worked for you? In conflict resolution, does one of you give in?"

HOW HARRIET AND I HANDLE CONFLICT

I replied, "Harriet is far more giving than I am."

Harriet said, at the same time, "No, Mike is more giving in conflict."

We laughed, and Harriet added, "When we are in a conflict, oftentimes one of us feels more adamant than the other. For instance, I could not care less about what kind of car we drive . . . if we can afford to buy it. Mike feels strongly about safety and thinks we should wait for our next car when airbags are available on both the driver and the passenger side. I will concede it. If we are unable to resolve the other issues, then we simply postpone making a final decision."

I added, "I feel that the relationship is more important than any issue. I want to be in consensus on any decision, especially those involving money, and will not argue over it. I will state my feelings and be open to hers. If we don't agree, we don't spend the money." They were listening intently.

I said that feelings often run high *when* in conflict, before there is a resolution. "Therefore, when we are angry, we stick to the issue and do not attack each other personally, or dredge up old history. A decade after we married, I heard that Paul, in writing to the Ephesians, said: 'Be angry, but do not sin. Do not let the sun go down on your anger.' In other words, it is not wrong to get angry, but it should not linger or it will corrode a relationship as rust does a ship. So even if I think I'm right on a particular matter, I will make peace with Harriet—even if all I do is hold her and apologize for having lost my temper. Our relationship is more important than any issue."

As we talked, their tension seemed to ebb. It was clearly helpful for them to hear how an older couple settled arguments without ridiculing.

As this first session on the ENRICH results drew to a close, absolutely nothing had been solved in Heather and Peter's relationship, but at least some of the issues had come out into the open. The couple was searingly honest, giving us a close look at the intimate details of their lives that very few people ever share with anyone else, let alone basic strangers. It was also a healthy beginning for them to speak openly yet gently—a skill of communication that is essential in conflict resolution.

In closing, I said to them: "Look, I just want you to know that I admire your willingness to share your pain with us. You did not have to do that. It shows a determination on both your parts to find solutions—to learn how to problem-solve. Conflict resolution is a skill that *can be learned*. It is not something that comes naturally, and it is not something that anyone ever taught you in school."

At bottom, Heather did not feel cherished. Nothing she did to fix up the house suited her husband. A longtime bachelor, he didn't care that much about the decor of his house. At home all day long, she felt unable to make even the smallest decisions in decorating. He was working under extreme pressure from very demanding politically appointed bosses who kept him at work until at least eight o'clock most evenings. When he came home, he simply wanted to relax and not have to face another round of battles over spending money on the house. Their minimal sexual activity was both a symptom of their failure to solve conflict and a cause of additional conflict because neither felt loved.

AN INTENSE EVENING OF CONSTRUCTIVE CONFLICT

A week later we met for the third time in our home. Our session began after dinner at 8:00 P.M., and it was a marathon session that did not end until 1:00 A.M. When it was over, we all had a great deal more hope for their marriage. It was an evening of constructive conflict, sparked by probing questions suggested by ENRICH, and by Peter and Heather's growing trust in us and a willingness to be utterly vulnerable in describing how they felt about different aspects of their relationship. (As a reporter, I took notes on my lap computer, with their knowledge, so that they might be quoted in this book.)

We asked them to describe in more detail the nature of their conflict, illustrating with examples. Peter responded first. "One thing we have disagreed about is that I go off and work and . . . get beat up at work, but Heather has nothing. She does not have a job, and we agree on that for spiritual purposes. All of her friends from school are breeding. She used to have affirmation from being in a Bible study two hours a day. . . . She has a book she wants to write. . . ."

Heather interrupted: "I have been hugely busy. I still have thank-you notes from our wedding to do, but he's right about the book. What I have in mind is a Christian book, a devotional book, drawing upon personal devotional material from a woman who is my mother's closest friend. She's become a godmother to me. The Lord called me to do this a number of years ago. It is very clearly an assignment from Him. It is a vast project. She has written 'conversations with Jesus' in notebooks filled with a gift of listening to the Lord. It is thousands of pages in longhand. The problem is that I am terribly busy with little things and am not moving forward on things that are weighty."

Peter, with a sense of exasperation, blurted out, "She doesn't know where the time goes, so she must be frustrated. I kill myself at work and lose respect for her at times when she uses all her time on errands and doesn't work on the good things. What's the point? I am working to free her to do work that we both believe to be creative. I am empathetic with her dream and want her to get on with it. Few people have that freedom." Here was the source of his anger that was erupting over little matters.

As he spoke, Heather watched him with wide, glistening eyes, perceptibly falling back in love with him. When he finished, she said, "He has never articulated that to me before." It was a special moment. At that point I *knew* that the process would be successful.

She said that the book "combines three loves of my life. I love working with things of God and with words and also with those dear to me. Three things. I have gotten to know this lady in many ways." She turned to Harriet and me, saying, "You have been a fruitful forum for us."

Peter was encouraged too: "Could you work on it an hour or two a day?" She nodded and said: "I have taken Peter's admonition to me as God giving me encouragement or goading. One reason I have fallen off is the wedding and having to finish the thank-you notes. And I have been struggling in this first year of marriage. It has taken energy. . . ." Her voice trailed off. Clearly, fights with Peter had drained her of energy, self-confidence, and security needed for such a big self-directed project as writing a book. "My bank of emotional equilibrium was low," she said.

I felt that enough progress had been made to return to an issue she had brought up in the last session: "Tell me about how he humiliated you in public."

After an evening out with another couple, Peter poured two glasses of wine for himself and their male houseguest. When Heather asked for a glass, he snapped, "You can't have any. It's for boys only." Thinking that he was teasing, she asked again for a glass of port. (Given to them by a friend, they had been rationing it to make it last longer.) Again he refused.

"I was hurt. He would serve a guest whom he hardly knew, but not his wife! Then he stomped off to bed. No one had drunk the port. One of the two guests said, 'We have seen this sort of behavior before.' He heard that comment and swore down the stairs. I nearly died. I excused myself and went to bed. That demonstration was not only embarrassing—I felt devalued as a person, as anyone he respected in any genuine way."

She turned to him and added, "I've hated you on a couple of occasions." I asked Peter for his side of the story.

"I find it difficult to remember, as far as the details or provocation, but I can think of other instances when Heather will be with friends of hers, girlfriends, and I become something she is displaying to her friends. What got me that evening was that I heard her talk about me to them, saying, 'He will never know. It will be okay.' What she says behind my back *does* matter to me. It caused a peculiar feeling in me."

Suddenly Heather's tone softened, "My genuine concern is out of my love for Peter. I feel that he takes on too many things as a burden, so tiny things become large issues." (How radically different each person's perception was! There could be no better illustration of the need to talk out such deep emotions as both Heather and Peter were doing, rather than to keep them bottled up.)

Harriet asked how they might handle such a situation differently. She replied, "We have a clear conviction that each of us is God's will for the other, His best for us. With that kind of certainty, you don't have to react to every perceived slight. You let it pass. We have been learning the delicate balance of the pattern, 'for better or worse.'"

Peter said, "I am very sorry that the event occurred. Regardless of the provocation, I am not going to try to defend myself."

Heather smiled broadly and said to us, "This has been a wonderful evening." Then she added, "I need to have some healing take place before I am able to talk without so much emotion."

Harriet, sensing that Heather was not being held by Peter during arguments, said, "Mike takes me in his arms at times like this, and he simply says, 'I love you. I'm sorry I was so angry.' In admitting that he regrets becoming angry, he is not necessarily apologizing for something he has said. However, it begins the healing process. It is impossible to stay mad at someone who is embracing you and apologizing."

Heather replied, "It is very rare that my anger's source is not due to hurt. Ninety-nine percent of my emotional response is due to hurt."

I asked, "What does he do that makes you hurt?"

"A lack of respect, a lack of cherishing," she replied.

It *was* a wonderful evening. They wanted to linger a bit longer, but we nudged them out the door at 1:00 A.M..

Harriet and I reflected on what had happened with "Heather and "Peter" and came to these conclusions: The ENRICH instrument had surfaced their problems—we had simply encouraged them to explain their feelings, or to illustrate a conflict. They then talked it out in front of us. We were there to encourage more dialogue, to keep it from getting off track, and to make sure that both sides were heard. And we prompted them to tell us how they might handle their relationship more effectively in the future. I should emphasize that we have no training as counselors and are no more expert in marriage than anyone else married for twenty-seven years. Any mature couple with a solid marriage could provide the same sort of help to a newly-wed couple. In doing so, your joy and satisfaction and your practical sugges-tions may well make you a Marriage Saver.

THREE WEEKS LATER

Three weeks later, when I was sharing the text of this chapter with Heather and Peter, I asked them separately how things were going.

"Better and better," said Peter. "We are more harmonious, instinctively. I make a bigger effort to cherish her. She has become more patient. She feels that all harmony cannot come overnight, but if you feel a trend, you are encouraged. We have had arguments but nothing severe. She has given up smoking. I don't give her a sense that I appreciate her as much as I should. I am learning to compliment her."

I asked, "On a scale of 0 to 10, where would you say you were the first night you were here, as you left the last night, and now?" He replied, "We were at a 6. On that last evening, we hit 8, and now it is a 9! What might have helped her was having people listen to her—talking to you and Harriet. If you find you are not the only one with difficulty, you feel less weird. You talked freely about your squabbles. This camaraderie helped. Having another couple to talk to was important."

I asked, "Weren't the ENRICH questions more important in surfacing the issues?" He replied, "It was fruitful, but talking with you is more important."

Heather's view was not quite as rosy, but she reported real progress: "We've had fewer arguments. A few things that were bones of contention. I've quit smoking. It is not a big deal, I wasn't smoking more than once every two weeks, but it was an issue with him. We have not had as many episodes of his behaving obstreperously. I have noticed deliberate verbal affection, and he's been kind and encouraging when I am struggling with something. I am trying to be more aware of my responses. I can keep things from escalating. In my devotional time, I came across the proverb, 'A gentle answer turneth away wrath.' That works better than making an attempt to respond to hurtful things so that they don't precipitate a heated exchange. I don't need to fan the flames. I know that he is under a lot of job-related stress."

"What has helped the most?" I asked.

"The greatest benefit of the process is making us concentrate on areas of our relationship that need working on—things the other person is unhappy with that should be addressed. ENRICH shined a light on the relationship, and gave us an objective forum. You can lose perspective when it is only the two of you banging around on these issues, but the test would be virtually useless unless there is follow-through. It is a rare couple that could take a test and use it by themselves."

The fact that these issues were surfaced with another couple, she said, "is important, as opposed to a marriage counselor or pastor. There are always two sides to an issue, and a couple can give you the full range of the two sides. The woman might say something that is supportive to the woman, that the man might not appreciate. There is the feeling, too, that this couple has had similar struggles. There is a place for the trained professionals on the heavy-duty things, but I firmly believe that God, more often than not, would prefer to put us in the intimate context of the life of the body. And working with another couple is such a natural arrangement."

It *is* natural, and it is exciting to feel, as Harriet and I do in this case, that the Lord has used us to help Heather and Peter to improve their marriage. It would overstate the issue to say that we were "Marriage Savers," because neither was considering divorce—but both were very dissatisfied and did learn how to communicate more constructively. Afterward they were clearly much happier than they had been before we took the time to meet with them. Peter and Heather might have been able to breathe new life into their marriage on their own, but if they had, it would probably have operated on a lower level of happiness.

SIX MONTHS LATER

How lasting was our intervention? To find out, I called Heather six months later. She said that her marriage was "a great deal more harmonious" though they have continued to have "real struggles," but she had a new understanding of the difficulties. "The Lord gives us what we need in terms of a spouse. Marriage is the most difficult training ground in life and, potentially, the most rewarding. I am more and more aware of the things God has given me for growth . . . Change has to start within me, and it can spread to the marriage from there. What are the changes God is after in me? Being long-suffering, patient, gentle, learning how to control the tongue, not letting emotions rule you or your relationship, learning how to practice real forgiveness, and to not expect your spouse to meet all your needs. I call it 'un-selfing'— death to self, having God deal with the ego so that you are not always putting your own agenda first, growing out of that into self-sacrificial love for the other person.

"God has been gracious to us. When we are Christians and find ourselves on a difficult path, we know that it is not an accident. He has purposed for our good and our growth," she said in conclusion.

Millions of couples who never actually divorce, suffer symptoms of what some call "spiritual divorce" as did Heather and Peter after only three months of marriage.

HOW CAN YOU BE A MARRIAGE SAVER WITH NEWLYWEDS?

If you and your spouse know newlyweds who seem to be floundering, what can *you* do? Most people feel helpless in such a situation—particularly parents or close friends of the newlyweds. You may be embarrassed to say anything directly to them. But the more important problem is that few people know *what* to say. Here are three quick suggestions:

1. *Assume you don't know what is wrong.* People are inherently private. You must be trained to administer the ENRICH marital survey, or see to it that the couple takes ENRICH with your pastor, another mentor couple or a trained counselor. It is a neutral tool that will reveal the painful issues that the couple must face. Remember how little of the picture Harriet and I had of the marriage of Heather and Peter until we had the ENRICH results in hand. ENRICH will reveal areas in their marriage where your mentoring can focus.
2. *Become trained with your spouse as a partner.* Mentoring a couple can best be done by another couple with a solid marriage. It is also a deeply joyful and exciting ministry to do as a couple.
3. *Urge the couple to go to a superb marriage counselor,* if your attempt to help fails. Frank Meier of the Minirth-Meier Clinics, now in 23 cities, says that if a husband and wife will meet with him four times, almost every marriage can be saved!

You are likely to feel embarrassed to invite a couple whose marriage seems to be floundering to your home to meet with you and your spouse, where you can ask, "Now tell us, how are things *really* going in your marriage?" But to a couple who feels its marriage is drowning, you'll look like someone on the deck, throwing out a life preserver. You will be more embarrassed than they and will be seen as someone who loves them.

If this ministry is appealing, ask your pastor to contact PREPARE/ENRICH (P.O. Box 190, Minneapolis, MN 55440) and arrange a time for you and other couples in your church to be trained as mentor couples.

Training is a simple two-step process. First, you and your spouse take the ENRICH questionnaire yourselves. This will give you a feel for what you are asking the newlyweds to do. Second, you will attend a six-hour training session some Saturday in which an expert will teach you how to interpret the PREPARE/ENRICH computer report for each couple you are working with. You would work under the supervision, of course, of a pastor from your church. If a problem arises that seems overwhelming, simply contact your pastor. This is rare. Of the ten couples we worked with as a mentor couple over a year, the issues that arose were ones that called for common sense, which any 25-year veteran of marriage can answer.

A WORD TO THE PASTOR

To any reader who is also a pastor, a brief comment: If you are like the pastors I've known, you are overworked. That is a major reason that you have not met six or eight times with each engaged couple you marry. The load could be lightened, however, if you took the time to train a core of mentor couples in your church. All of the work outlined in this book up to this point—with seriously dating couples, engaged couples, and newlyweds—could be handled by mentor couples that you could help train with relevant Scripture, along with a PREPARE/ENRICH instructor.

Chapter 9 points to another need for a different sort of mentor couple to work with couples whose marriages are in trouble. The chapter gives details on how seven couples who once nearly divorced, have helped save 28 deeply shaken marriages at St. David's Episcopal Church in Jacksonville, Florida. Indeed, there has *not been a divorce* among anyone that the church has involved in its "Marriage Ministry." Surely, your church also has couples whose marriages were once in deep trouble—who could assist you in working with those where separation and divorce appears imminent.

All of this will require extra work for you until your mentor couples begin helping you be "Marriage Savers" with others in your church. Then your work load will lighten. More important, you and your team of marriage savers will really be saving marriages.

You would be living up to Paul's letter to the Ephesians that the job of a pastor is "to prepare God's people for works of service" (4:12).

WHAT IF YOU ARE A NEWLYWED
WITHOUT A MENTOR COUPLE?

Of course, most of the newlyweds reading this book will not be in a church with trained mentor couples ready to help. Therefore, what can *you* newlyweds do to increase *your* odds of success?

In our mentoring, we were struck by how many young couples—like Beth and John and Heather and Peter—had 80%–100% agreement on religious questions, but only 10%–20% couple consensus on communication, conflict resolution, and financial management. These *are* three major cancers of marriage that can eat away even the most hopeful of newlywed relationships:

1. *Poor Financial Management:* Do you have a lot of arguments over money? Perhaps you need to make a "financial covenant" with one another.
2. *Poor Conflict Resolution:* Do you solve differences harmoniously or with bitterness and lashing out at each other?

3. *Poor Communication:* Do you find that you no longer talk for an extended period with your spouse as you did during courtship?

CRISIS: DANGER OR OPPORTUNITY

Let's look at the answer for each area, starting with communication. The word "crisis" in Chinese is written with two characters. One means "danger," and the other is "hidden opportunity." In a marriage, one choice is to allow lives to slip by in business, or to set aside daily time to communicate. That is the hidden opportunity. Newlyweds think they have plenty of time to talk, but if they don't reserve a special daily time, the talk will be hurried and focused on things outside their relationship, not on their deepest worries and highest dreams. Harriet and I get up early to take some daily time to chat, read some Scripture, and pray for one another. This keeps us tuned to one another, and makes the Lord a third, powerful partner or our marriage. Problems actually draw us closer together as "prayer partners" asking for the Lord's help.

In another sense, the marital choice is between selfishness and selflessness. Many couples drift into totally separate lives—as each pursues his or her own interests to the exclusion of the other. We have friends who are "married singles." He is always working in the yard or on the car or jogging—alone. They rarely have meals together. They attend church, but go in separate cars! She complains that he will not talk to her for days at a time, out of anger over some perceived insult.

Clearly, their marriage is far down the path of danger. They are living now in "spiritual divorce." What is that? Father Gabriel Calvo, the Spanish priest who created Marriage Encounter, writes in his book, *Face to Face*, that spiritual divorce "is marked by a progressive lack of intimacy between a husband and wife. It is a mental and emotional divorce. A man and woman are legally married, remain in the same house, but lead separate lives. They are strangers to one another. Their ideas and emotions no longer seem to connect. Instead of having concern and feelings for one another that stimulate the growth of the marriage, their lives are fixed on things outside of marriage."[6]

Some of the symptoms of spiritual divorce he cites applied to Heather and Peter: a deep feeling of isolation or loneliness, habitual sadness, disillusionment, dissatisfaction and frustration about the partner, indifference, coldness in the relationship, frequent tension and anger, distrust, feelings of fear or insecurity, avoiding sexual relations, substance abuse, and a lack of mutual respect—insults, ridicule, and so forth.

Look at your schedules. Increase time spent together, decrease time spent on solo activities. Dr. James Dobson says "Love is a four letter word

---

[6]Gabriel Calvo, *Face to Face: Becoming A Happier Married Couple*, International Marriage Encounter, 955 Lake Dr., St. Paul, MN 55120, 1988.

spelled T–I–M–E." The time Harriet spends with me has made her my best friend, and vice-versa. There's nothing wrong with a man playing golf with pals. But if it becomes a big time-consumer, if golf is a substitute to going to church with a wife on Sunday, a man is choosing selfishness over selflessness, and is imperceptibly moving down the path of danger.

The soul needs nurturing as well as the body. Harriet and I have found that church attendance has drawn us closer. Interestingly, the National Survey of Family Growth reports that the religious are *two-and-a-half* times as likely to remain married as the nonreligious.

"Couples who are religiously committed are protected against divorce," says Dr. David Larson, a former research psychiatrist at the National Institute of Mental Health for a decade. The religious also live longer. He jokes, "If you want to die early, don't go to church. Play golf on Sunday!"

Harriet and I turn all our problems and decisions over to God. His answers become clear in time, and are always better than our first thoughts as individuals or as a couple. We give newlyweds a gift of *Heirs of Life Together*, (The Banner of Truth Trust, Carlisle, PA, 17013), a daily devotional written by a pastor and his wife after four decades of marriage. As explained in chapter 2, each reading contains a Scripture on marriage or children, and a page-long commentary. It is a wonderful way to start the day and to learn to solve any communications problem.

ENTER A FINANCIAL COVENANT

Arguments over money destroy many marriages. How will you make money decisions? You might consider entering "into a financial covenant with one another," as suggested by the 1991 book, *Passages of Marriage*, written by staff of Christian psychiatric/counseling centers, The Minirth-Meier Clinics.[7] Harriet and I had operated on these principles, quite by accident. Result: we've had very few arguments over money. But a couple starting out might want to make a conscious agreement:

— "I agree that money will never be more important than our relationship."
— "I agree to let you know if I think either of us is becoming irresponsible about financial matters."
— "I agree to stay within the budget we plan together."
— "I agree that from our wedding on, money is ours and the problems and joys it brings are also ours to share."

---

[7]Dr. Frank and Mary Alice Minirth, Dr. Brian and Dr. Deborah Newman, Dr. Robert and Susan Hemfelt, *Passages of Marriage: Five Stages That Will Take Your Marriage to Greater Intimacy and Fulfillment*, Nashville, Thomas Nelson Publishers, 1991.

— "I agree that credit cards can be a major problem, and I'll always talk to you before making a purchase over $_____."

— "I agree to work with you until we agree on how to pay and who will pay the bills in our marriage."

BIBLICAL VALUES ON FINANCIAL MANAGEMENT

A more profound source of wisdom on money is the Bible. One of the best lectures given to engaged couples at my church, Fourth Presbyterian in Bethesda, Maryland, was by Beth Gordon, a long-time member, and a certified financial planner. She notes there are more Scriptures about money than almost any subject. She urges couples to learn and follow:

TEN COMMANDMENTS OF FINANCIAL MANAGEMENT

1. *Acknowledge biblical principles of money management.*
   — *God owns it all.* "The earth belongs to God. Everything in the world is His." (Ps. 24:1) (Living Bible version used for Scripture references).
   — *Faith requires action:* An example is the parable of the servants who invested their master's money. (Matt. 25:14–30)
2. *Establish priorities.*
   — *Our tithe.* "Honor the Lord by giving Him the first part of all your income, and He will fill your barns with wheat and overflow your wine vats with your finest wines." (Prov. 3:9–10)
   — *Our taxes.* "Give the emperor (government) all that is his and give to God all that is His." (Luke 20:25)
   — *Our savings.* "The wise man saves for the future, but the foolish man spends whatever he gets." (Prov. 21:20)
   — *Our families.* "But anyone who won't care for his own relatives when they need help, especially those living in his own family, has no right to say he is a Christian." (1 Tim. 5:8)
   — *Our giving.* "It's possible to give away and become richer! It's also possible to hold on too tightly and lose everything. Yes, the liberal man shall be rich. By watering others, he waters himself." (Prov. 11:24, 25)
3. *Know your basic money personality type.*
   — Are you a hoarder, spender, money monk, money avoider, money worrier, money amasser, risk-taker or risk-avoider?
4. *Establish goals.* Typical goals include:
   — giving   — children's education
   — saving   — financial independence
   — standard of living — retirement
Put these goals in dollar terms; have a timetable to accomplish them.

5. *Know your financial position.*
   — What you own and what you owe (your balance sheet)
   — What you earn and what you spend (your income statement)
   — ". . . watch your business interests closely. Know the state of your flocks and herds." (Prov. 27:24)
6. *Control your spending.* Budget wisely; avoid debt.
   — "Any enterprise is built by wise planning, becomes strong through common sense, and profits wonderfully by keeping abreast of the facts." (Prov. 24:3–4)
7. *Protect yourself against all insurable risks.* (loss of income, health, property). Do not risk what you cannot afford to lose.
8. *Get good advice and shop around.*
   — "Plans go wrong with too few counselors. Many counselors bring success." (Prov. 15:22)
   — "Get the facts at any price and hold on tightly to all the good sense you can get." (Prov. 23:23)
9. *Be alert and patient.*
   — "Steady plodding brings prosperity. Hasty speculation brings poverty." (Prov. 21:5)
10. *Count on God's faithfulness, direction and love.*
   — "I have created you and cared for you since you were born. I will be your God through all your lifetime, yes, even when your hair is white with age. I made you, and I will care for you. I will carry you along and be your Savior." (Isaiah 46:3–4)

IMPROVING CONFLICT RESOLUTION

Conflict is inevitable. What matters is how it is handled. Is it handled constructively, or destructively? Dave, one of the young men in the premarital class where Harriet and I were a mentor couple, said, "I brag how we never have an argument. But we avoid areas of disagreement."

I replied, "A whole book had been written about how excessive agreement can *break up* a marriage." All four couples sighed and their eyes rolled upward. Harriet added, "I grew up in a family where anger was not supposed to be expressed, a belief that it was socially unacceptable to express such an emotion."

We learned when we went on Marriage Encounter, that all emotions—anger, hurt, fear—should be expressed, but considerately. "Emotions are neither right nor wrong," says Marriage Encounter. "They simply *are*."

Newlyweds have a natural instinct to walk on eggshells around each other. They seem to fear begin open, thinking that is the path to conflict. What they have not discovered is that the more open and honest a couple is, the greater becomes their opportunity for deeper intimacy. Dr. Kathy Arveson, a former counselor at our church, outlined five mistakes often made in conflict between husbands and wives:

1. *First Mistake: perceiving conflict as "winning" or "losing."*

Kathy noted that "most disagreements deal with subjective issues on which there is no right or wrong." Others do involve right and wrong. She gave the example of leaving their daughter with friends, rather than using a baby-sitter, which meant having to drive a long way to pick her up and not getting home before midnight. "This was *your* idea," her husband grumbled. Kathy was still mad two days later. He was right, and he "won" the argument. But her anger proved her point: "No one ever wins an argument in a marriage. When one partner loses, both lose."

2. *Second Mistake: excessive accommodation.* To avoid argument and prevent conflict, some spouses give in too easily, which is unhealthy. The moral: Some disagreements are healthy and necessary!

3. *Third Mistake: assigning blame.* "Creating guilt is not helpful," said Kathy. "If you get lost while driving, it is no use to say, 'It's *your* fault, because you were not watching, or '*your* fault, because you were not looking at the map.' The main thing is to get where you are going."

4. *Fourth Mistake: bickering.* Pick, pick, pick is what some spouses do. One person puts the other down and is attacked in return. The issue is often trivial. The alternative is to state an opinion briefly on an objective issue, while avoiding attacking the other person's character.

5. *Fifth Mistake: unhealthy conflict which leads to abuse.* There is *never* an excuse for physical abuse. If it happens, seek outside help. A problem of physical assault will only grow worse with time. Many women are too forgiving when they are physically beaten, perhaps by a drunk husband. Kathy told of a wife of 25 years who was beaten once during courtship, again after 12 years of marriage, 6 months ago, and just recently by her Marine sharpshooter husband. Kathy put the woman in a shelter for abused parents and convinced her to get a court order to have him evicted for 30 days. He said he was provoked to hit her, but that he was sorry. His wife's leaving the house, and Kathy's intervention, finally persuaded him that *he* needed counseling for his temper. He joined a men's group to learn how to cope with anger, ways to break through the "I don't have a problem" syndrome. And his wife is in counseling. Their marriage is being salvaged, but they should have sought help earlier. "Both parties were at fault," said Kathy. "By continuously accommodating him, she gave him the impression that he was always right."

A GUIDE TO KEEPING CONFLICTS CIVIL

USA Today published a quiz that each person can take to measure whether he or she "fights dirty." The July 23, 1991, article quoted psychiatrist Mary Ann Bartusis, author of *Off To A Good Start*, as saying "Fighting dirty is often a way to avoid emotional intimacy, or keeping your distance. Or it can be a power play, a way to trying to 'win.' Or it can be a way of just dumping your emotions on somebody."

To learn whether you keep within the bounds of fair play, take this quiz, designed by Dr. Bartusis. Do you:

1. Refuse to stick to rules you made for handling fights? _____
2. Bring up old problems instead of sticking to the current issues? _____
3. Drag in references to in-laws, parents, children, etc.? _____
4. Call your partner names, such as "stupid"? _____
5. Yell at your partner? _____
6. Give your mate the silent treatment? _____
7. Leave the room to avoid conflict? _____
8. Use obscene language, knowing it offends your mate? _____
9. Quarrel under the influence of drugs or alcohol? _____
10. Try to physically intimidate your partner? _____
11. Deliberately push your partner's "buttons"? _____
12. Lie about facts or withhold information? _____
13. Refuse to listen attentively while preparing your own rebuttal? _____
14. Refuse to accept responsibility for your share of what went wrong? _____
15. Encourage friends and/or relatives to take sides? _____
16. Fight in public? _____
17. Refuse to make a sincere apology? _____
18. Hold a grudge? Seek revenge? _____
19. Confide in others about fights when you know your partner would not approve? _____
20. Keep fighting about the same problems over and over without seeking a true solution? _____

To score this test on how fair your fight, total the number of "No" answers. Dr. Bartusis is very generous in her scoring:

— 16–20. Your fights help clear the air and come to a better understanding. Still, work on becoming a "20".

— 11–15. You're on your way to solving problems amicably. But you have work to do.

— 5–10. You are struggling to handle conflict. Try honing relationship skills through a course in communication.

— 0–4. You might use fighting to avoid emotional intimacy. Take a relationships course or consider a counselor.

CONFLICT CAN LEAD TO INTIMACY

Conflict can be an opportunity to grow in intimacy. Few newlyweds discern it. Of course, conflict handled poorly (such as the 20 steps listed above), does not produce intimacy but rather pain and alienation. . . . And separation. However, there are two strategies couples find effective when the disagreements are profound. One is to compromise. Another is to turn the matter over to the Lord and wait on His response.

COMPROMISE

Bill and Ann Latimer are friends of ours. They have had to move several times in their marriage. Since Bill is the wage-earner, he "takes the lead" in deciding where he will seek a job. "Ann takes the lead in looking for houses, since she is the person who will spend most of her time there," Bill says. But each has a veto on the "lead" of the other. "She picks the house, subject to my going down and looking at it," he explains. Harriet and I have usually operated on the same principle except for one time when I insisted on choosing both the job and the community we would live in. Harriet was not happy, however. And I learned that hard way a lesson that came naturally for Bill and Ann.

WAIT UPON THE LORD

Frankly, Harriet and I don't compromise very much. We would rather wait until we can agree. I asked Harriet to explain: "We usually wait until we find unity. I call it 'waiting upon the Lord.' When we disagree on a major matter, we often simply pray about it, postpone a decision, and wait until the Lord makes it clear how we are to proceed. He can shine a light on our path and bring us to one mind." I think of Isaiah 40:31:

> . . . they who wait for the Lord shall renew their strength,
> they shall mount up with wings like eagles,
> they shall run and not be weary,
> they shall walk and not faint." (RSV)

For example, in 1987 I felt we should move from Connecticut, where we had lived since 1971, back to Washington, where we had spent our first five years of marriage. I had begun writing two syndicated columns in Stamford—one, political, which I called "Solutions"; the other was "Ethics and Religion." I could have continued to write them in Connecticut, but Washington is a more strategically located city for a nationally syndicated columnist. Also Harriet's parents were in their 80s, and I felt we should move down to be close to them in their final years. Harriet was torn. She wanted to be near her parents, but she loved our home, which she had totally redecorated. More important, she worried about yanking our son Tim out of school where he knew everyone and was thriving.

It was spring, 1987, and Tim was in the 9th grade. I said, "Let's put our house on the market at a big price, If we sell it, we can use the money to help pay for college for Adam, John, and Tim. And if we find a buyer by June or July, we can move in August, before Tim begins the 10th grade. He will have three complete years in high school in Maryland. But if we don't sell the house at a good price before July, we will stay here for his three high school years. We will leave it up to the Lord." That seemed fair to Harriet. More important, it relieved us of any anxiety. Both of us would have been content with either outcome.

Then we waited on the Lord. As it turned out, He provided a buyer in July! We signed a contract in August and moved in September. It was good that we did. Harriet's mother lived only another two years. We saw both of them regularly, a source of joy for all of us. And when she died, her father became part of our family. He was able to remain in his own house and join us regularly for dinner in our home only five miles away.

DON'T ISOLATE YOURSELVES: JOIN A NEWLYWEDS GROUP

A very important way to gain perspective on conflict within a new marriage is to join a church fellowship group for newly married couples. If your church doesn't have one, go to a bigger church that does. First, such groups tend to examine Scripture or books that can be helpful. Second, both men and women need to meet same sex peers who are in the initial phase of marriage—people one can talk with confidentially for perspective and support. Finally, young couples need to make new couple friends, people with whom they will enjoy socializing—but people who also recognize the Lord as a third partner in their marriage.

BE A MARRIAGE SAVER

I'd like to close this chapter with a word to our peers: middle-aged couples. You probably did not learn anything new in reading these twenty-five pages directed at newlyweds. What you read was common sense about communication, money, and conflict resolution that you have learned through two or three decades of married life. To young couples in your church, however, this is wisdom to which they do not have easy access. My question to you is: What is your responsibility to the new generation —to keep silent out of fear of invading the privacy of young couples, or to share what you have learned as a mentoring couple with those who yearn for a life-long marriage?

My dream is that you and your spouse will aspire to be marriage savers. If you are in a strong marriage and are willing to be trained to work with seriously dating couples, engaged couples, or newlyweds, you can be a Marriage Saver. You would have to learn to use PREPARE and ENRICH, but you don't need a Ph.D. in counseling to help. There are only two requirements: first, that you be willing to share your life—its shortfalls and its joys—with couples seeking help. That is a very rewarding task.

What's tougher is that you must also have the courage to stick your nose into what is normally considered the private affairs of others and ask hard questions and sometimes offer trenchant opinions about inappropriate behavior of one or both partners.

As I reported at the beginning of this chapter, when Harriet and I met with Beth and John three weeks after their honeymoon and found out that he had given her the silent treatment a number of times (once for two days), Harriet boldly challenged John: "You are smothering Beth. What you love about her is that she is a free spirit, but in your attempt to control her, you will keep that flower from blossoming." I added, "Your problem is jealousy. You don't want her to spend any time with anyone but you, even her little sister. This is irrational. You may need to seek help from the Minirth-Meyer Clinic, Christian counselors who can help you deal with this problem."

For two months we did not hear from either of them., so early one morning, after John had gone to work but before Beth left, I called and asked, "How are things going?" She replied, "Much better. When we were driving home from your house, he said that he felt a little ganged-up on, but that night in bed, he rolled over and said, 'I don't want to smother you. I don't want to keep you from blossoming. I *have* been too insecure. I really am sorry for how I've treated you the last few days. I want you to feel free.' And he has made more of an effort to continue talking. There have been no silent treatments. We still have some problems. A habit like his is not easy to break. He is struggling with pride. It was hard for him to be confronted like that. But we are both so grateful that you were willing to see us. He got some perspective."

Mentoring, however, is best undertaken under the supervision of a church. A mentor is not a solo counselor but a part of the body of Christ. In our case, we were trained to use PREPARE/ENRICH before our clergy at Fourth Presbyterian, though we worked with their knowledge. The results were so encouraging that Dr. Willard Davis, Pastor of Congregational Care and Counseling, and ten other mentor couples were trained by PREPARE/ENRICH in October 1992 so that we could reach every couple getting married in the church and thus be connected to all newlyweds.

Chances are, your pastor and other solidly married couples would be just as willing to strengthen what your church offers to engaged couples and newlyweds. For too long, pastors have tried to save marriages on their own—and usually at too late a stage. Our church now has many "Marriage Savers" working when we can be most effective—early in the life of each couple.

To couples who feel as though their marriage is drowning, a Marriage Saver is a *life* saver.

NINE

Marriage Encounter:
The Best Marriage Saver

"Submit to one another out of reverence for Christ."

—Ephesians 5:21

"We have this to say: Every couple should make a Marriage Encounter. . . . It's like coming home with a new bride!"

—Husband, age eighty plus, interviewed
by the National Institute for the Family

In spring 1976, Harriet and I experienced a weekend retreat that literally changed our lives. After a decade of marriage, we fell back in love with one another but at a far more profound level than anything we had experienced before. When the retreat ended, we felt as if we had been on a honeymoon, but one designed by God to bond us together in a transcendental marriage. The impact of the weekend has been permanent because we learned a new form of soul-to-soul communication that has deepened and enriched each day of our marriage in the seventeen years since. There is no question that I never would have considered writing a book on how to save marriages if our own marriage had not been irrevocably uplifted and transformed.

The weekend is called: *Marriage Encounter.*

Our experience is not unique. Some 1.5 million couples have made a Marriage Encounter weekend since the movement was founded twenty-five years ago in 1968, and objective, scientific research on Marriage Encounter is unanimous: Eight or nine of every ten couples who attend an ME weekend *fall back in love with their spouse*—the same experience that Harriet and I had. That's an astonishing track record.

If you can't take my word, or that of the academicians on this, take the word of Dr. James C. Dobson, the Christian psychologist, whose radio program, "Focus on the Family," is the most widely aired show (more than 1,700 radio stations) in America. He confesses that he attended Marriage Encounter "for professional reasons, "not expecting to get anything relevant to my wife and me. If there is anything I felt that Shirley and I didn't need, it was help in communicating. I rarely have been more wrong:"[1]

> Marriage Encounter gave Shirley and me the opportunity to occasion the deepest, most intimate exchange of feelings we had known in 20 years . . . It proved to be one of the highlights of my life.
>
> I just wish that everyone who trusts my opinion would now accept this advice: Attend a Marriage Encounter weekend at the earliest opportunity.

THE SINGLE STEP THAT COULD DO THE MOST TO SAVE MARRIAGES

I am convinced that the single step that could do more than any other to slash America's divorce rate is for every married couple to attend a Marriage Encounter weekend. If you are married and have not gone on a Marriage Encounter, put this book down and sign up for the next one. To learn more, call 1-800-795-LOVE. Your call will be tape recorded by Worldwide Marriage Encounter, which organizes weekends for 15,000 couples a year. You will be called personally by an ME volunteer in your area who can tell you when you may attend a local ME weekend with people from eleven different denominations.[2]

Assuming that exhortation alone moves no one, this chapter provides evidence that the best Marriage Saver is Marriage Encounter.

There are other weekends designed to refresh a marriage, such as "Marriage Enrichment" (1-800-634-8325), which is growing and now involves 10,000 couples a year, and "Family Life Conferences," which is also growing and is run by Campus Crusade for Christ (501-223-8663). Some 22,300 couples attended Family Life in 1992.

This chapter focuses on Marriage Encounter because ME has already involved about five times as many people as the two above major options combined.

RESEARCH EVIDENCE OF *ME'S* IMPACT

A recent study conducted by the National Institute of the Family (the most comprehensive ever made of Marriage Encounter, involving couples who attended between 1965 and 1989) concludes:

---

[1]Dr. James Dobson, *Love Must Be Tough*, 1983, Word Books, Waco, Texas, p. 198.

[2]There are two other, smaller national organizations coordinating ME weekends: National Marriage Encounter (405-672-0177), which involves 2,100 Catholic and Protestant couples together, and United Marriage Encounter (1-800-334-8920), which reaches 1000 mainline Protestant couples a year.

> The Marriage Encounter Weekend/Program stands as the central positive experience of most couples. Over half of the couples participating in the weekend program consider their experience of it as "excellent." Another third of all couples reported it as "rather good." *Together, these two categories verify that the Marriage Encounter experience is a positive marriage enrichment experience for nine out of ten couples.*

The National Institute for the Family sent questionnaires to 4000 couples who had attended ME weekends over twenty-five years, 325 of which were returned from "a total spectrum of couples involved in Worldwide Marriage Encounter," writes NIF's Dr. Donald Conroy, author of the report.[3] Seven couples attended ME within a year of their wedding day: two-thirds within the first fifteen years of marriage, and one couple who had been married fifty years.

Who are the people who have made a Marriage Encounter weekend?

In seven out of ten couples, the husband was the main wage-earner, but in 23% the incomes were equal. Only a tenth had no children at the time of their Encounter; half had kids up to age twelve; another 30% were parents of teenagers, and a tenth had grown children.

More important, only 55% came from good marriages, and 45% said that their marriages were "average" or "unhappy."

With nearly half having only fair-to-poor marriages, it is impressive that nine out of ten attendees give Marriage Encounter such high marks. Only one out of twenty couples said that their marriage relationship "is much the same" or "poorer" after attending ME, according to the NIF study.[4]

More important is the "vastly preponderant positive impact" measured by thirty academic studies cited by the Reverend George McIlrath, a Presbyterian pastor and a leader of United Marriage Encounter.[5] They reveal a surprisingly wide consensus that "Marriage Encounter programs have often received affirmations of 80% to 90% in post-weekend surveys and that the program demonstrates clear effectiveness when its participants are involved in rigorous and controlled pre/post-weekend research."

McIlrath notes one complication in evaluating ME: "It is an experience.

---

[3]The 1990 study, called "Worldwide Marriage Encounter: National Survey and Assessment," was conducted by the National Institute for the Family (3019 Fourth St., N.E., Washington D.C. 20017) and initiated in collaboration with The Center for Applied Research in the Apostolate.

[4]But this understates those with negative experiences, since a very small percentage of couples do divorce after having attended an ME weekend.

[5]George McIlrath, "Assessing Marriage Encounter," chapter 3 of a Doctor of Ministry thesis for the University of Dubuque Theological Seminary.

If one has not participated in a Marriage Encounter, it is very difficult for one to appreciate what is being discussed . . . It is like attempting to discuss swimming with people who have not been swimming."

The NIF study, however, has the strength of being conducted on participants for years, even decades, after they attended. People were asked to compare the initial impact of the weekend with its residual effects. Of 325 respondents, 160 said that it had had a "very good" impact. Years later, 200 still said that its long-term impact on "intimacy and closeness" was high or very good. In terms of improving "communications," 150 said that the immediate impact was high, and another 120 said that it was very good. *That's 83% giving it high marks.* Today, 200 still say that their communication is excellent as a result of ME—nearly *two-thirds*.

More than 200 said that ME had a high or very good impact on their sexual relationship at the time, and 155 say that their sexual relations are much better today due to a long-ago weekend. The residual impact is strong.

Here's the bottom line: Only forty-eight attendees out of 325 said that they had an excellent marriage before the weekend, but nearly 200 felt that way immediately afterward, *an astonishing fourfold jump.* Today, 100 couples say that their marriage is "excellent" and 145 call theirs "very good," while 60 say that is "pretty good." Only ten say that their marriage is "the same" and another ten call it "rather poor." Those are extraordinarily good odds!

MARRIAGE ENCOUNTER'S BIRTH
AND REMARKABLE GROWTH

In 1962 Father Gabriel Calvo, a Catholic priest in Spain who created the first Marriage Encounter weekend with a few couples, began with a firm conviction: "There is within each couple a divine energy of love, and if it can be brought alive, it can loose a true revolution of love over the whole earth. But in order for this energy to be produced, it has to be released by a deep sharing between husband and wife, through the communication of their feelings and of their whole life together. It cannot be done in just one moment. It is done rather through the sharing and dialogues of many hours and many days. This is where the true revolution of love begins!"

To speak about that deep sharing, Father Calvo and two other couples with strong marriages designed a weekend with lead couples sharing intimate details of their marriages with guest couples in a setting away from their homes. After a period of listening, couples were asked to write each other a "love letter" on a particular theme. Each husband and wife then exchanged the letter and talked about it—privately. They returned to hear more talks on various issues within marriage and went back to their rooms for further writing and dialogue. This routine repeated itself over a two-day ME weekend.

The first Marriage Encounter conducted in the United States was in 1965. It took off under the leadership of a Jesuit priest, Father Chuck Gallagher, S.J., who conducted his first weekend as a spiritual leader in 1968 with Ed and Harriet Garzero and Janie and Arlen Whalen in Port Washington, Long Island, New York. He helped organize Worldwide Marriage Encounter in 1968, which celebrates its twenty-fifth anniversary in 1993.

"The movement grew like Topsy," Father Gallagher told me. "We tried to recruit everybody we knew. My aim was to get us up to one Encounter a week. We accomplished that by January 1970. We grew to six a month by March. Some 281 couples attended in 1969 and 1,806 in 1970. Before long, 25,000 couples had attended on Long Island alone. It was more than an accomplishment. It was a phenomenon. There were seventeen per weekend by 1973!

"At the beginning of 1970, we made plans to take it to the ten metro areas with the highest Catholic populations in the United States: Boston, New York, Philadelphia, Chicago, Los Angeles, New Orleans, San Francisco, and so on. We made a list of the people we knew in each area and contacted them. We had a goal to establish a beachhead in all those places, and by 1973 we had established a presence in all those cities."

"By 1970 we were reserving a quarter of spaces for non-Catholic couples, believing it was the ecumenical thing to do. We did not think it should be restricted to Catholics. But this experience is not just about marriage. It is a whole faith-experience. People deepen their faith." Therefore, they helped Methodists, Lutherans, Jews, and other denominations to develop their *own* "expressions" of Marriage Encounter. In non-Catholic ME, a clergy couple assumed the spiritual role of a priest on Catholic ME weekends. A few words change. "The Lord's Supper" was used instead of "Holy Communion" or "the Eucharist." The essence of Marriage Encounter, however, moved smoothly across denominations. By 1974, 100,000 couples had made an ME weekend—an astonishing mushrooming after a half dozen years. Today *ten other denominations conduct ME weekends*: United Methodist, Baptist, United Church of Christ, Episcopal, Presbyterian, Reformed, Seventh Day Adventists, Orthodox, Mennonite, and United Church of Canada.

WHAT IS MARRIAGE ENCOUNTER?

Father Calvo asks this question[6]: "Would you and your spouse enjoy a special weekend alone in a quiet atmosphere, taking the time to share deeply the joy of marriage? If your answer is 'yes,' then you deserve a Marriage Encounter Weekend."

---

[6]Gabriel Calvo, *Face to Face: Becoming a Happier Married Couple*, International Marriage Encounter, 955 Lake Dr., St. Paul, MN 55120, 1988.

He describes it as:

A unique opportunity for you to pause and sincerely consider the most important area of your lives . . . your marriage.

A challenge for you to develop more fully your potential for growth in love, wholeness, holiness and happiness, as you live out God's vision and plan for your marriage each day of your lives.

A series of presentations and informal talks, given by one of three team couples and a clergy person (or couple). Presentations are intensely personal and testimonial. Their purpose is to inspire the couples making the Encounter to become aware of their own lived experiences about their marriage. The second step is exchanging their personal living experience with each other, primarily through conjugal dialogue. The team's purpose is to set the atmosphere. Actually, the husband and wife give the Encounter to each other.

Unfortunately, the number of couples making a Marriage Encounter has fallen from a high of 105,000 couples in 1975 to only 15,000 in 1992, according to Bill and Mary Anne Boylan, the National Executive Couple of Worldwide Marriage Encounter. That is a tragic outlook for the most hopeful force to save marriages in America. However, I am convinced the trend is reversible.

"HOW TO MAKE A GOOD MARRIAGE BETTER"

As I related in chapter 1, by late 1975, Harriet and I began to hear about Marriage Encounter from friends at church. During that time, I had a temporary job in Washington, D.C.—a nightmarish weekly commute by train from Stamford, Connecticut. I only saw my wife and children on weekends. Some couples from our church, St. Paul's Episcopal in Darien, had attended and were enthusiastic about what a "wonderful weekend" it was.

"Give yourself and Harriet a wonderful gift of a Marriage Encounter weekend," said parishioner Al Scribner.

"What is it?" I asked.

"It's the best weekend ever. And it will strengthen your marriage."

"I already have a good marriage," I said defensively.

"But Marriage Encounter is designed to make a good marriage better. It is not aimed at the troubled couple," Al replied.

I asked, "What is the weekend like?"

"I can't reveal the details. We are sworn to secrecy. But you'll love it. It was the best thing my wife and I ever did together."

I found the mystery a little annoying. But I knew our marriage had been under strain during the months I worked in Washington. A weekend alone with Harriet, rebuilding our relationship sounded wonderful to me. But when I suggested to Harriet that we go, she was cold and firm: "No."

"Why not? I think we need a weekend away."

"We can't just leave. We have three small children."

One Sunday, Gordon and Alta Jelliffe were talking to us over coffee after church. "The two of you ought to go on Marriage Encounter," Gordon said.

I saw Harriet wince, so I spoke up. "We have three boys at home."

"Oh, that's no problem. Some of us who have gone would be glad to take care of them for you," Alta said.

Harriet replied: "But we can't afford a weekend at a motel."

Gordon smiled and shook his head: "You don't understand. Your way has already been paid. People here love you enough to have made it possible for you to go."

Wow! That impressed me. "Come on, Harriet, let's go." She relented.

As I shared in chapter 1, little did I suspect that that weekend in spring, 1976, would surface an unverbalized tension and unhappiness that Harriet had repressed about aspects of our marriage, and forever transform my perception of how to communicate with my wife.

FEELINGS ARE THE FOUNDATION OF THE WEEKEND

Though our Marriage Encounter was sixteen years ago, we saved our notebooks on the talks, as well as the "love letters" we wrote each other. In the first talk, the husband of one of two "lead couples" introduced the central idea of Marriage Encounter. The word "encounter" means to meet on a feeling level. He said most couples think they communicate, but usually their communication is on a reporting level. There is a better way, to focus on your feelings, because your real communication takes place in your gut, your emotions, not your head.

"Feelings are the foundation of the weekend. At times we feel joyful, tense, drained, frightened." Often people are ashamed of their feelings and do not share them. The leader said, "Our feelings are neither right nor wrong. They just are. I am what I feel. Feelings are the real me. They *must* be shared. The way to know me is to know my feelings.

"Judgment is reserved for explicit behavior, and does not apply to feelings. Thoughts may appear to be the same as feelings. They are not. The difference is between reading a good book and experiencing it. Thoughts involve a moral judgment. Often we use the same words, 'I feel that,' when we mean 'I think that.' Try to get below a thought to feelings, which are waiting to be explored. When he gives you a gift, you may comment on the color. But what he cares about is whether the gift makes you happy. How do you *feel*?" said one of the leaders.

"In describing feelings, use the five senses to describe the emotion. Use words that make the feeling vivid and alive. Let go of complacency. Let your feelings come loose. Don't be afraid to be discovered.

"If you are tired, say, 'I feel like a bee crushed under a wheel.'

177

"Beneath a feeling are more underlying feelings. There are different layers. For each, we can go deeper. You will run into feelings of hurt, rejection, despair. Fear is a barrier we all have. Don't worry about that. *Trust each other.*

"Trust the weekend and trust us. Don't analyze what is happening. Never cover up your emotions." We were told that women tend to be more comfortable in talking about feelings than many men: "Asked how they feel about something, many men will say, 'I don't feel anything about it.' That's not true. There is no such thing as having no feelings."

"Feelings are neither right nor wrong. They simply are.*"*

Then we were given an exercise: to write each other a "reflection" answering these questions:

1. What do I like best about you? How does this make me feel?
2. What do I like best about us? How does this make me feel?
3. What do I like best about myself? How does this make me feel?

EXCERPTS FROM OUR FIRST "REFLECTIONS"

We never planned on sharing what we wrote. Our reflections were written for each other alone. As you will see, I was happier in our marriage than was Harriet. Why would we share such intimacy? We want you to see how Marriage Encounter enables couples to fall back in love.

There is no more important message of this chapter.

By having to write down our feelings, we expressed them at a deeper level than we would in mere conversation. As we wrote and then read each other's letters, we realized how much each of us felt for the other. I discovered I had been taking Harriet for granted.

FROM MIKE TO HARRIET

What Do I Like About You?

"What I like best about you, Harriet, is your character, your high moral standards. You make me want to be the best person I can be. This has always been the case. I remember when we were dating, I found you inspirational. You were always so absolutely confident about what was right and wrong and never had any trouble picking the correct path . . . ."

What Do I Like About Myself?

"What I like best about myself is my vision and dedication toward building a better world—one in which people's frustrations and dreams can be articulated in a way that government has to respond." I have always sensed a seed of an important mission within me, an inner drive to serve others. I soon found that this is far more rare than I had imagined.

"... Having an inner direction rather than an institutional commitment or loyalty has made day-to-day living difficult at times. But I like this sense of vision. It makes me feel that the Lord has put me here for a purpose which is particularly important. ... My current work (researching Northeast economic woes) reinforces my sense of mission with an important dimension. I feel I will be able to see tangible results very quickly. The mass media process I have worked with has been so attenuated from actual results that I only now realize how frustrated I have felt.

"I have not had the sense of satisfaction in my work that I now feel since I worked for the *Middletown Record* (a small paper in upstate New York). There I could not only take pride in being a good reporter—I could also see the results of my work—something that I did not see at *TIME* and something only glimpsed after years of work on Town Meetings."

What I Like Best About Us

"You have always understood and supported me as I have pursued my dream. When other wives would have insisted that their husbands simply 'get a job,' you have been willing to sacrifice comforts and stability of finances for my pursuing this inner vision. I would never have left *TIME* had you not been supportive. ...

"I have liked the sharing of our growing spiritual life together. I really feel a great sense of power and strength in the Lord's promises. And I do think our experience clearly proves that he listens and responds. I had never really thought of God as an active force, something that can actually intervene in our lives. Had you not sensed that power, too, I would not have grown in this spiritual dimension.

"The strength of our marriage rests on several strong foundations:

- We have high ideals that we work at daily.
- We have a trust in the Lord that he will recognize our best efforts and reward them in time.
- We respect each other's internal drives and do our best to nurture them and to be a place of refuge for each other.
- We reject the temptation to be petty, to denigrate each other, as some do.

"Yet I do think this weekend can be of help in strengthening our marriage. We have, perhaps, taken too much for granted. We need to say these things to each other. And I do like the idea of writing them down. I like the focus on feelings. I think I have tended to focus on thoughts, rather than feelings, causing some of the spark to diminish from our marriage. You always want to talk more than I seem inclined to do. But I think that by putting my focus on feelings I will have more to say and thus we will have a stronger, broader grounds for communication."[7]

I concluded my first "Love letter" to Harriet: "I came here with hope but with skepticism. The hope was grounded on the uniformly high opinion people have who have gone through the experience. But none of them communicated what is exciting about the process—which at this stage looks like a rediscovery of the world of feelings within ourselves and in each other. I can see how the weekend can strengthen our marriage."

HARRIET'S LOVE LETTER TO MIKE

(Harriet's love letter was being written to me at the same time I was writing my letter to her. She did not see what I had written until she was finished and we exchanged notebooks.)

What do I like best about you? How does it make me feel?

"You give me a peace of mind. Isn't it a relief to know precisely just where one stands, and how one is thinking—as unvarnished as it may appear? So often people say only what will not cause any waves or muddy the water. But underneath that seemingly placid unrippled pond are layers of unseen eddies, rough currents, and hidden whirlpools. I feel relieved at knowing what you think and feel. I don't have to second-guess you. Or feel that you are hiding something—perhaps to spare me worry or hurt. And I never fear not knowing who the real you is. You allow me to grow by sharing your work, your hopes, your successes. Your openness permits me to see *you* as a whole person—as a human being, not a lopsided superman who wins every battle and is ever successful. Or a saint who is only lightness with no darkness. It makes me feel that you trust me."

---

[7]Father Chuck Gallagher, who did more than anyone to make Marriage Encounter a national movement, said in an interview with me, that a major reason that Marriage Encounter "raises the level of happiness and joy in marriage is that it gets the husband in touch with his feelings. You know how men have been trained not to be much into feelings. Little boys don't cry. . . . This experience gives a man permission to have feelings, which, when he revealed them to his wife, was such a relief to her. She believed that she was the only one who had them. It means so much to both of them. The prime function of Marriage Encounter is to change the man. The average man saw himself as a provider, saw his wife as the one with the most invested in the marriage. She was the one most capable of determining what was a good marriage. As a result of Marriage Encounter, he saw that *he* could be as much involved as she. That was such a relief for her. And it had an effect on parenting. Up until that time, she was the prime parent. Once he got fully involved in marriage, he got fully involved in the parenting."

What do I like best about myself?

"My desire for quality, I suppose, is in attempting to live up to the highest standards I can set in every way. You knew when I met you my feeling regarding never accepting 'second best' (like marrying you—first best). How does it make me feel?

"Worthwhile. Living life with a higher purpose. It is a goal I can strive for, but, of course, can never fully achieve.

"When I speak of a desire for quality you know I am referring to internal qualities—honesty, completing a job responsibly, using my energies to form offspring who will also have high standards. The most tangible aspect for quality that I can quickly point to is a high quality of education for the boys. Their Christian education too is obviously important. Searching for the right church—knowing it existed, but where? Gladly making the twenty-minute drive (to the church)—an investment, not a sacrifice.

What do I like best about us?

"That every 'tragedy' makes us closer. I suppose some problems or failures weaken relationships. Perhaps that's good in that it exposes the relationship for what it was—weak and not very substantial. With us, our little problems have *always* made us more closely attuned to one another. More sharing, more deeply enmeshed in each other's lives. I always feel like we've just gone through an exam when we've had a heavy burdensome problem, but inevitably I come out of it feeling refreshed and clean, knowing I have been tested but always knowing we're going to pass. This special 'gift' we have of sharing our woes and failures, or experiencing an outside buffeting at our door, does not lead me into complacency, or a numb plateau mentality existence. It does not make me feel safe. Our lives have never been safe.

"I believe in you, Mike, even if I don't fully comprehend your work. A bird can be beautiful only if its allowed to be free.[8] Have you ever seen that golden eagle at the Stamford Nature Museum? He's magnificently formed, but he never spreads his wings. He looks like the result of an expert taxidermist—each feather in place. All of his majesty, his strength, his power, his God-given gracefulness are imprisoned in that cage with him. That is how I feel about you. Our tests of strength and love as individuals and as spouses are reassuring. How nice to discover when our marriage is so young yet that *we* can endure the test of time, like a glass enduring the fire's heat to become an exquisite vase," Harriet concluded in her first love letter to me.

After writing those long letters Friday night in our room, Harriet and I talked and talked and held each other, happily losing total track of time, until we fell asleep. A pound on our door the next morning woke us with a start.

---

[8]I cherish this in Harriet. She has always given me freedom to be me.

We ate breakfast with others but talked only with each other, as requested. Then we assembled for the next talk.

ENCOUNTER WITH SELF

ME leaders talked about the "mask" that each of us wears, the behavior pattern we use to be accepted by others. And the leaders shared some of their own masks with us. "Be honest with yourself," said Father Bob, an Episcopal priest who was one of the weekend leaders. "What you are going to write this time is to be a totally private encounter with oneself. There will be no exchange of notebooks. We all have images that we project of ourselves."

We were asked to write down how we would describe ourselves—both what we project to others, our mask, and what we feel inside. "Do I really like myself? How does my answer make me feel?" We were asked to differentiate how we project ourselves to others at work, for example. And how do we try to appear to our spouse? We were asked to write for ten minutes and then to list our "good points" and our "bad points."

The pastor pointed to a poster on the wall made by a ten-year-old in Newark, which read: GOD DON'T MAKE NO JUNK. Too many people, he said, have too low a sense of self-worth. We are more aware of our shortcomings than our strengths. He asked, "Why would God create anything that was worthless? You are more important to God than you think."

Christians tend to forget that self-love is an important part of our capacity to love others. Jesus said, "Love your neighbors *as* yourself" (Matt. 19:19).

MARRIAGE IN THE MODERN WORLD—"WE" PHASE

"We aren't trained for marriage," said the speaker at the beginning of the third talk. "The child sees how parents interact, and the influence of parents is indelibly imprinted—in living color, as to what is expected of us as husbands and wives, mothers and fathers.

"We also gain a sense of marriage from TV, movies, and friends. One of the messages our modern world communicates is that 'Marriage is a 50-50 proposition.' That seems reasonable. Each of us has half the burden. This is a seductive lie. It is very easy to begin to think: 'I am doing my fifty percent for this marriage but he (or she) isn't. So if he isn't going to do his share, I'll cut back on what I do for him.' Thus, they quickly slip into a negative spiral. Both partners do less and less for each other while rationalizing the whole time." (Jesus suggested an absolutely opposite model: "Love each other as I have loved you. Greater love has no one than this, that he lay down his life for his friends. . . . This is my command: Love each other" (John 15:12–13, 17).

The leaders warned that another danger in marriage is that of slipping into being "married singles." Father Bob explained, "I was married to my job." I gulped and winced as he spoke because that sounded like me! "There are many ways to be married singles—in the way you communicate and where you spend your time. I gave little time to Susan. I put up a 'No Trespassing' sign from 8:00 A.M. until 11:00 P.M. The parish became my world. A funeral or emergency could always intrude. . . . In relation to Susan, I felt wise, convinced that I was always doing right. . . . I was super-reliable."

He rationalized, "We used to go out to dinner every Friday. I knew I was a better husband than our friends . . . But the world's standards are low. And we settled for a so-so marriage instead of striving for a great marriage. We were becoming independent of each other. I'd mow the lawn, fix my car, or descend to my workshop. Due to this, for a great part of our marriage, we had separate lives. And yet I would complain about my wife! I could not have asked for a better wife. Yet, we accepted the world's plan of being married singles."

Then his wife, Susan, shared with us, but as she spoke, she began sobbing. She had been so hurt by Father Bob's emotional abandonment that his raw words brought the feelings back. She could hardly speak. "I had a friend who said, 'I would like to be a minister's wife.' 'You're crazy,' I said. 'All day we are public property. . . . It's as if he were born with a two-way radio, responding to everyone but his wife," she wept as she sat in misery, trying to tell us her hell of being a married single.

Susan, between sobs, admitted that she felt that "a conspiracy kept me separated from my husband. No one could touch me. Our conspiracy made it impossible to show the effect this had on me in public. It reinforced our singleness. I was totally ignored. I was left alone, a wife without a husband. I lacked the social graces. I held other clergy wives in awe. I was singled out as being different. . . ."

THE VULNERABILITY OF LEAD COUPLES

There were many deeply moving moments like this. The Reverend George McIlrath researched ME weekends for his doctoral thesis, to identify what makes the weekends so life-changing. His conclusion: "The most powerful element was vulnerable, intimate personal sharing. The power unleashed in such sharing is like the high voltage on an electric grid that is then processed through transformers, which is reduced to electric current in your home. Consequently, programs that only discuss ideas, generate less 'power' voltage than even the most halting and inarticulate personal sharing."

The lead couples modeled deep, often painful sharing—which inspired each of us to be equally vulnerable with our spouses.

"Marriage Encounter encourages couples to drop their masks and postures of self-protection, becoming vulnerable to their humiliation, and then discover the truth of Jesus' admonition that before a seed can be raised to new life, it must go into the ground and die," writes McIlrath.

THE CYCLES OF MARRIAGE

Vera, another member of the leadership team of three lay couples explained that all marriage relationships go through three cycles:

1. Romance
2. Disillusionment
3. Joy: Love Is a Decision

Romance

Vera talked of their whirlwind courtship: how they never tired of talking; how much fun they found each other to be, how they felt they were the only two people in the world on their two-week honeymoon.

Disillusionment

When they came back to earth, little things, unnoticed before, became increasingly annoying. Sam—a big, rough gas station attendant and motorcycle fan—during his courtship took off his shoes and threw soiled socks at Vera. They both had laughed. It became a kind of ritual. "The socks thing became old-hat" after the wedding, she said. He couldn't understand why his smelly socks no longer got a rise out of her. He became taciturn, hardly ever sharing anything that happened at the gas station. *He's not the man I fell in love with*, she thought. Romance seemed eaten up by boring day-to-day activities. Then they began to fight over things like socks. But she learned some principles about fighting that helped her to limit the extent of the disillusionment she felt with Sam.

Vera called them "Fighting Fair: Marriage Encounter Guidelines."

"Fighting is a means of communication," Vera said. "Too often, however, we focus on our spouse, rather than the issue. We eventually learned some guidelines for fighting fair:

1. *Be Fair*: Don't hit below the belt.

2. *Stick to the subject.* Fight about one thing at a time.

3. *Don't repeat past history.* If it is more than two days old, forget it. Have a statute of limitations of forty-eight hours.

4. *No name-calling.* That is character assassination.

5. *Finish the fight.* Don't walk away.

6. *Don't go to bed mad.* ("This is when I first heard Ephesians 5:26: 'Be angry, but do not sin. Do not let the sun set on your anger.'")

Joy: Love Is a Decision

Vera's husband, Sam, said "Joy is not a product of big events, but usually comes from little things that foster closeness. I can think of precise moments together that were full of peace and joy."

Next, he surprised me by saying the clearest path to joy is to recognize that "Love is a decision." That seemed contrary to all logic. How can one "decide" to have a feeling? Sam explained: "If you perceive that love is not a feeling but a choice, you have a greater range of ways to tell her, 'I love you.' Actions speak louder than words. I can decide to love her by not screaming, in spite of feelings I may have. By putting the other person first, I am acting out my love. If I am more open and honest with her, letting her know how I feel—that decision to share wholeheartedly involves risk and is an act of the will. I felt relieved when I heard that 'Love is a decision.' It gives me more freedom to show my love in spite of feelings. My act of love is freely chosen."[9]

THE LOVE LETTER

We were then told how to write a "love letter" to our spouse (the most innovative part of the weekend) for ten minutes and then dialogue for ten minutes. These "10-and-10s" opened us up to each other as we focused on different subjects. Guidelines on how to write:

1. Keep your spouse in mind at all times.
2. Begin and end the letter with endearment so that your spouse knows it.
3. Use your spouse's name throughout the letter. This is not "to whom it may concern." Make it personal.
4. Let caring for your spouse come through.
5. Be yourself a gift to your spouse.
6. Use the five senses in describing your feelings (what an experience looked like, smelled like, sounded like, appeared like, felt like).

Several of the speakers acknowledged that they had never written a love letter to their spouse. Harriet and I smiled because we had written many love letters and poems during our courtship. However, I had written her only one since our wedding, while on an extended trip. Here are excerpts of our letters after talks that "focused on feelings, not symptoms:"

---

[9]With 17 years of experience in regarding love as a decision, I now know that actions of love make me *feel* more love. Why? If I do something special for my wife, I love her more. She, then, is more loving toward me. So the feeling of love—a deep joy—grows. Jesus said, "Give, and you shall receive." It is not the economics of this world, but it is a truth of the spiritual world, of how a marriage can be built that endures.

Dearest Harriet:

. . . I did not realize that by regarding love as a feeling, not a decision, I was putting gloves on my hands, earmuffs on my ears, blinders over my eyes, and a sock on my tongue.

You have always criticized me for loving my work more than my family. I think you were partly right but only partly. What really happened was that I took you for granted, did not realize that you needed watering like a garden, and that by deciding to shower my rains of love on you, I would myself be refreshed. The burden of my work—I now see has been too much for me. It wasn't that I loved my work more. I often hated it. I look back now and wonder how I forced myself to work. I was pursuing some vision of glory that was beyond them, beyond you, beyond the children. . . .

The coolness which you have felt for me—which, in turn, made me feel cool—will be replaced by a warmth that characterized our early years together. I have rediscovered your warmth here and hope I am learning to cherish you now and in our years ahead. . . .

With a love of a new life in the Lord and in you,

Mike

Dear Mike:

. . . I am a strong, independent spirit . . . and perhaps seemed so all sufficient that I lost my womanliness. I love and miss gentleness, or quick tender moments, an intimate smile in a crowd, your checking on me at a cocktail party, opening the door for me. . . . Helping me feel more like a love-mate. Only you can make me feel like a lady. Caring about me in the teeny-tiny ways a woman cherishes. . . .

Your conversation is never mechanical. It makes me feel as if I'm on an adventure—not knowing what I'll visit next. It always reveals your innermost desires but invariably concerns your work. I treasure that conversation but also like to talk about the things that I suppose other people find mundane. . . . I suppose all I'm asking is for us to round out your subject matter again, the important with the unimportant, the gossipy with world-shaking events, the children with your career aspirations. . . .

I love you for your communication gift. Communicate more of your feelings and impressions along with your very articulate thoughts and cerebral conclusions.

Love, Harriet

MISCELLANEOUS TALKS AND LOVE LETTERS

There were many more talks and "10-and-10s" that Saturday, sixteen years ago. I won't go into most of them. Men may appreciate one point I wrote: "I feel suddenly rather exhausted about all this communication we need to do. It was exhilarating this morning, but I feel like going outside and walking in the breeze. I want you there with me, silent, just sharing the breeze and being with nature and God without having to communicate." Those words were written honestly, but underneath I simply did *not* want to face one writing assignment of describing our atmosphere at home. Why? I had to acknowledge my failure to take the time we once took naturally to simply talk together: "I feel responsible to 'get to work,' " I wrote. "Chatting somehow seems a waste of time to me. Perhaps it is because we have created our independent worlds. . . . We have ceased to talk about feelings. . . . I have tended to think the reason I don't sit down is that I don't "have time."

"But if there is not time for life, for love, what is there time for?" It was painful, but I was learning.

Bill Latimer, a leader, offered a penetrating insight: "We, in order to believe in our own goodness and beauty, need to be loved. We all have the need to be changed by the kiss of our beloved from a frog into a handsome prince, or princess, to be transformed by love."

His wife, Ann, added, "To *be* loved and transformed, we have to share ourselves openly in love, but also we have to allow ourselves to *believe* in the goodness and lovability our spouse sees in us. I reach out to Bill in love, and he responds by returning that love. I accept the love he has for me and am transformed by it, and I, in turn, reflect it back to him, like an image reflected infinitely back and forth by two mirrors that stand facing one another."

This is not easy. It involves risk-taking, being vulnerable, and not knowing the outcome in advance. For that reason, to share a deep feeling takes confidence in one's spouse.

To help us learn this lesson, we were given our next assignment—the toughest of the weekend: to write a love letter to our spouse on "What feeling do I have that I find most difficult to share with you."

For Harriet and me, it was the turning point of the weekend and of our marriage. We were inspired by the honesty of our lead couples.

WHAT FEELING DO I HAVE THAT I FIND
MOST DIFFICULT TO SHARE WITH YOU?

Dearest Harriet,

Upon reflection, I believe that the feeling I have found most difficult to share with you is my fear of professional failure. . . . I guess what I have never shared with you is the sense of panic and fear of failure that has been my constant companion in these struggles . . .

As I wrote issue papers, I began with a sense of overwhelming ignorance and desperately tried to read newspapers and interview up to the last minute before the deadlines. Insight always came very late—3:00 A.M. before a paper was due the next morning. Compounding these fears is my difficulty in getting along with some of the people I have had to work with . . . I was right in most of my clashes and got 85% of my view accepted, but not without horrendous, hair-raising, fear. Naked fear.

Finally, after all these fears were fought and largely overcome, I fear that what I've done professionally has not been really all that significant. I have lived, particularly since June, 1973, when the project failed to live up to my hopes—with the feeling I was a Don Quixote tilting at windmills in the night and falling flat on my face. . . .

And then, when the Washington work ended, I looked into the mirror, saw hair turning grey and falling out, our bank savings non-existent, and without a job, and all the feelings of incompetence rushed over me again.

But oddly, when I came home, I felt no more panic. For I had really developed a trust in the Lord. I knew He had a purpose, and my task was simply to find it. These past months have been sledding downhill. Only now can I look back and describe the sheer, unholy horror I have lived with for the vast majority of days over these past eight years.

I'm so glad I can share this burden with you now and wonder that it has taken me so long.

Love, Mike

I had never been so vulnerable with Harriet. Nor she with me in her love letter written at the same time:

Dear Mike,

The feeling I have most difficulty sharing with you is a feeling of being needed as your beloved, your love. Not Harriet, the housekeeper, the chauffeur, the barber, the mother of your children, you wife, but the soft inner me. The Harriet who rests inside the clam shell so still and quiet. And soft and unprotected too if you care to lift the lid. The shell—you may find is not locked shut, but closed awaiting only your gentle entrance. If you but approach and enter, you will find me raw and vulnerable—quite naked and exposed with a pearl for you to treasure.

Often I have tried to broach this subject. . . . I want to be held and cherished, snuggled and nipped, chatted to and cried with. I want to be loved as your beloved. You recall how much the boys treasure being hugged, tickled, plumped and bumped, prayed with, ear-nipped and kissed tenfold when they are tucked in bed? Adam once said, "You don't kiss me as much, Mommy. Am I too old?" We are never too old. . . . We all need affection, reassurance, tenderness, and caressing. It's an opportunity to be close, share and sit in the middle of a moment. Will you please sit in more of my moments with me?

Love, Harriet

Harriet's next entry in her notebook is to a slightly different question: "What feelings did I have today that I wanted to share with you that I either couldn't or didn't share?" In it, she probes a feeling beneath her sense that she wanted to "be held and cherished" more. She explores the probable cause of not feeling cherished, a sense of being "deserted" while I worked in Washington all those months:

YOU LEFT ME FOR A YEAR AND A HALF!

Dear, dear Mike,

Isn't it peculiar that our dual dialogues showed how much we each needed one another—you to bare yourself to me, releasing your worries and fears, and I wanting and waiting to be told I was needed. I have not actively told you that I love you. I love you as you are—vulnerable, not a superstar. I loved you so much when I married you—almost so much, it was painful—an exquisite, sweet pain. Now I love you in a sore way. Somewhat bruised—not wounded but definitely sore.

You left me to pursue your career for a year and a half. I mentally understood, agreed, endorsed, and encouraged. But you left me. Quite voluntarily. That is how I felt, not what I thought. And how could you leave me for something that made you unhappy? I felt deserted. Now you are home again. I am your home—not our house, not our future, but me, here right now.

Love, Harriet

This letter stunned me. I was profoundly shaken. I had no idea Harriet felt so abandoned by me. She had buried that feeling deep within and could unearth it only when she felt a new confidence in our love as a result of Marriage Encounter. In our dialogue I asked her to tell me more of what she felt. She replied: "During that time of your working all week in Washington, I kept feeling, *'This is no marriage!'* I never saw you during the week. You moved me to Connecticut where I did not know anyone. All week long I only had the children to talk to. None of our neighbors would have anything to do with us. Remember when Tim was to be born? My water broke and you ran from one neighbor to another to get someone to take care of Adam and John while you took me to the hospital? And *not one* neighbor would help! When you came home on Friday nights, I fixed a nice dinner, but you fell asleep. Then you worked all weekend! I'd ask you to 'Take the boys for a swim.' You'd say, 'I don't have time.' This is not why I married you! You are a workaholic. You love you career more than me!"

Suddenly, I broke down and cried. Tears flowed, as I said, "I was so absorbed by the difficulty of my life that I was utterly unaware of the impact of my life on you! Please, please forgive me!" I held her as I wept, shaking with a grief I had never experienced before.

When I came under control, I added, "I do *not* love my work more than you and the boys. But, as I told you in my last letter, I felt an utter sense of panic that I was failing. I felt as if I were a man in the middle of the Atlantic, trying to get to shore, but unable to swim. I told you, I often *hated* my work. I put up with that horrible commute, getting on the train at 2:00 A.M. and barely sleeping on the way to Washington.

"The main thing I want you to know is that I will never abandon you. I am so sorry for having caused you to feel that kind of pain. I never felt such feelings myself. I have only felt love for you. But I understand how you came to feel this way."

We hugged each other tightly. That evening we had clearly fallen back in love with one another, discovering at a new and far more profound level what it was about each other that had led us to exchange wedding vows "to have and to hold till death us do part" on October 16, 1965.

THE GIFT OF DAILY DIALOGUE

On Sunday morning we heard our leaders strongly urge us to continue our "10-and-10s," ten minutes of writing a love letter and ten minutes of dialogue on a *daily* basis. When I first heard that, I wrote in my notebook margin: "Oh, no, not every day!" but then I started listening.

Rod and Diana, two of the group leaders, said to those of us being "encountered," something that sounded strange, at first: "We love you." But they did not even know us! However, they had traveled across a state line and given up an entire weekend for people they had never met. Surely, that *is* Christian love. They continued: "As the weekend has progressed, you have seen us share our hearts and souls because we care very much for you and your marriages.

"For that reason, we yearn for your 'dialogues.' Our love requires us to say we wish to pass on our joy and peace with you. Therefore, we offer you an opportunity to continue growing, the gift of daily dialogue, to renew the beauty and love built deep within each of you.

"Unless we can pass this on to you, we will have failed."

We tried doing "10-and-10s" when we got home but found that writing was unnecessary. But we did make a major change in our lives as a result of ME: We began getting up earlier every morning for a private time of chat, Bible reading, and prayer as a couple. We still do this.

MARRIAGE AS A SACRAMENT (WE AND GOD PHASE)

One theme of the weekend was the relationship of each couple to God. We looked at Genesis 2:24 —God's purpose in creating marriage:

> For this reason a man will leave his father and mother and be united to his wife, and they will become one flesh.

We were told that each couple had to discover what God's plan is for their marriage. "There are several elements to the plan of God:

1. It is simple—a blueprint of what to do every day.
2. It is knowable. You can figure it out for yourselves.
3. It is unique. . . . You are to become one flesh—united, a new creation. Therefore, whatever unites you, spiritually, emotionally, physically, and intellectually is part of God's plan for you. Whatever attacks the unity or erodes is not part of God's plan."

Later our leaders talked about marriage as a sacrament, "a visible sign of invisible grace, instituted by God to elevate and sanctify us." Sam, one of our leaders, confessed, "We thought we needed the church and a priest only to make our marriage legal. Now I see that there is a daily 'I will,' a commitment to love her, or not. 'I will' keeps it active.

"It took a long time to encounter God in our marriage. Now we see that we belong to the universal church. Our love is a seed to be germinated in others." His wife, Vera, added, "I now see we have a stake in the entire body, the entire church. We can't be alone. Rather, we must give ourselves totally. *We are the church.*

"Our love is like a little church within a great church.

"Our marriage is 'catholic' (universal). It is not private but is meant for all people of love and hope. We have been asked to reach out and share our love. Love must be used to be fed. We must be used. That growth will return many times, though we have to reach out even when we face rejection," said Vera.

"Our marriage is also 'apostolic.' We want to heal the hurts of others. We rejoice in serving others. We are a vine of the branch of God in Christ. We must belong to and grow with a community of believers."

This was not mere rhetoric. These Marriage Encounter leaders were sharing their private marital pain, their growth, their hopes, and their joy in many communities on many weekends—with other members of the body of Christ. Each time they had to give up forty-eight hours of their life to give fifteen major talks. Though split between three couples, they were exhausting.

ENCOUNTERED COUPLES CAN BECOME MARRIAGE SAVERS

These lead couples are true *Marriage Savers.*

There is no one else like them in the United States. Everyone works as a volunteer, yet no one has been more successful in helping already married couples fall back in love with each other. The more than thirty studies previously cited above show Marriage Encounter has a positive impact on eighty to ninety percent of participants.

So Marriage Savers like Bill and Ann Latimer have every reason to feel that something sacred happened, as the Lord used the witness of their walk as a married couple to strengthen the marital unions of dozens of couples who attended weekends when they were "presenting couples."

Yet six out of ten new marriages are failing. No nation has a higher divorce rate. And it is so unnecessary. *Marriage Encounter* suggests that *nine out of ten marriages can be saved*. In late 1991, political liberals and conservatives drafted a "Communitarian Platform" that contained this sentence: "Though divorces are necessary in some situations, many are avoidable and are *not in the interest of the children*, the community, and probably not of most adults either."

Surely, there must be a way to expand the availability of Marriage Encounter to save millions of marriages now heading for the divorce court.

There is a way.

At present, it is only a dream, but it is simple: The 1.5 million couples who have been on Marriage Encounter weekends are people who could be trained to reach out to enrich America's fifty-two million presently married couples. *All of them.*

It might even be possible for Marriage Encounter to strengthen most marriages in America by the year 2000.

Certainly, America's divorce rate would plummet if many more couples, whose marriages were saved or strengthened by Marriage Encounter, caught a vision of seeing their marriage as not merely a private source of joy but a treasure to be shared with others. There is no question that those 1.5 million encountered couples are an untapped national resource to save marriage in America.

But there are three major obstacles. For each, there is an answer.

First, far less than one percent of couples who attend recent Marriage Encounter Weekends are being trained as ME team leaders. Most are young couples with children, who feel stretched meeting day-to-day obligations.

However, most of the already encountered couples attended between 1973–1980. And they are now aged forty-five to sixty-five. Most of their children are grown, and their marriages have thrived for a quarter century or more. And they have more time available to serve. What's needed is a way to recruit them and persuade them to give something back for what they received.

Second, there are relatively few priests or clergy couples now active in the movement. The lack of Protestant clergy is a real bottleneck among Presbyterians and other denominations. Most pastors feel that they have to be in the pulpit every Sunday, and many are not aware of Marriage Encounter's success in saving and revitalizing marriages.

The marriages of many clergy themselves are in trouble; all are under strain and would benefit from attending an ME weekend. Protestant couples who know the value of Marriage Encounter might offer an ME weekend as a gift to pastors who have not had the experience. Catholic couples might take a similar initiative and help their priest attend by finding a substitute priest to say Mass for a weekend.

A third impediment is that Marriage Encounter has been in decline. People have heard of it but don't know what it is. And the current activists are a bit weary of trying to recruit new people.

Therefore, a bold strategy is needed. Here is my suggestion.

Readers who know the value of Marriage Encounter might have their pastor or priest ask during announcements at their regular services: "How many couples in church today have been on a Marriage Encounter weekend?" He should give a quick count of the hands in the air, report the results, and say, "After the service, I'd like to meet with these people who have experienced Marriage Encounter. Six out of ten marriages are failing in the United States, but Marriage Encounter was a positive experience for nine out of ten couples. Couples who have experienced Marriage Encounter can help. That is what the meeting is about."

Bill and Mary Anne Boylan, leaders of Worldwide Marriage Encounter, think that such an appeal might persuade half of encountered couples to attend such a meeting after the service.

Marriage Encounter activists would run the meeting. I suggest they begin by asking: "For how many of you was Marriage Encounter a positive experience?" Most hands will go up. Ask a few to summarize the significance of ME in their marriage. If no one volunteers, the activists can summarize their personal experience. More important, the National Institute of the Family data could be presented on slides. This will provide the hard evidence of the movement's importance.

The ME leaders could then make a case for couples who have experienced Marriage Encounter to attend a special refresher weekend, with two goals:

• to strengthen their own marriage.
• to be trained to recruit other couples to attend Marriage Encounter.

The leaders might say: "You all see marriages around you that have grown stale or strained or that you know would benefit from Marriage Encounter. We want to equip you to reach out to those couples and help them. Who knows, for many of them you might be a Marriage Saver! You may remember that at the end of the ME weekend, you were asked to live your marriage apostolically, in service to others. We need you to help us reach out to every couple in this church, to offer them the same blessing that you have enjoyed. Remember, some other couple loved you enough to tell you about Marriage Encounter. You have a responsibility to do the same.

"Let us tell you about our national goal. Some 1.5 million couples have been on a Marriage Encounter weekend. Our dream is that they be mobilized to reach out to the fifty-two million U.S. couples who have not had the experience, and offer it to them. Each encountered couple would only need to recruit twenty-five other couples to reach the entire nation!

"Okay, I'll concede that it is unrealistic to think that all 1.5 million already encountered couples would be willing to reach out to couples who have never gone on a Marriage Encounter weekend," the ME leaders might say to those gathered after a church service. "A few of those couples have died or divorced, for example! And some people may feel uncomfortable talking about their own Marriage Encounter experience with others. But if 80% to 90% of couples actually fall back in love with one another on these weekends, as the studies indicate, surely a good percentage of them would be willing to encourage other couples to attend an ME weekend. At present, only 2,000 couples out of the 1.5 million, have assumed responsibility to reach out to others. Surely, we can do better than that. What is a reasonable goal? In this church we'd like to see at least a third of encountered couples become "Marriage Savers." The need is clear, and no one can do more to help couples refresh their marriage than those of us who have been blessed by Marriage Encounter.

"But if only a tenth of those who have attended a weekend—150,000 couples—signed up to help other couples in their church, it would be possible to reach an astonishing percentage of the nation's married couples by the year 2000—30 million couples or more than half of America's marriages by the 2000th anniversary of Our Lord's birth! Here's the math," they might say as they write these numbers on a chart:

150,000 ME couples, two per weekend, organize 75,000 weekends
x 20 couples per weekend, reaching 1.5 million couples

1.5 million couples reached per weekend
x 3 weekends/year = 4.5 million a year

4.5 million couples reached per year
x 7 years (1993–2000) = 30 million couples by 2000!

Of course, there would have to be a build-up of couples who caught a vision of being Marriage Savers. It would probably take at least three years to recruit 150,000 couples to serve.

Even so, in seven years, by the year 2000, Marriage Encounter leaders could reach *a majority of* married couples in America.

Of course, it is quite likely that we will fall short. But my dream is to see little platoons of Marriage Savers working in each of America's 300,000 churches, with the goal of "encountering" every couple in the church. An alternative approach worked for the Reverend Paul Martin, pastor of the Faith Christian Center, an Assembly of God Church near Peoria, Illinois. His church spent four thousand dollars of the church budget to give any interested couple a twenty-four hour "Valentine's weekend Getaway" that enabled any couple who wanted to strengthen their marriage to do so. The technique used was not Marriage Encounter but videos prepared by Campus

Crusade For Christ, Family Life Conferences referred to on page 172. Some thirty-eight couples attended, and the experience was so positive that it will be repeated in 1993, with couples outside the church invited to attend.

Furthermore, the pastors of dozens of churches from sixteen denominations in Peoria, Quincy, and Moline-Rock Island, Illinois, signed a "Community Marriage Policy, one plank of which was "Encouragement for all married couples to attend a couple's retreat such as Marriage Encounter or Marriage Enrichment" (see chapter 2 for details).

Pastors recognize the need to do more to strengthen marriages. What they have lacked is a plan. Enthusiasts have an answer, and I am convinced many of them have a heart to be Marriage Savers. They know, more than anyone else, one clear, stark, positive fact: that a Marriage Saver can be a *life* saver!

I asked Bill and Mary Anne Boylan of National Executive Couples for Worldwide Marriage Encounter, to react to my dream of trying to give most married couples in America the opportunity to fall back in love by the two thousandth anniversary of the Lord's birth. I asked, "How realistic is it?"

"May the Lord bless the dream!"

TEN

Saving Troubled Marriages: Marriage Ministry, Retrouvaille, Solution-Oriented Therapy

If you have any encouragement from being united with Christ, if any comfort from his love, if any fellowship with the Spirit, if any tenderness and compassion, then make my joy complete by being like-minded, having the same love, being one in spirit and purpose. Do nothing out of selfish ambition or vain conceit, but in humility consider others better than yourselves. Each of you should look not only to your own interests but also to the interests of others.

—Philippians 2:1–4

We found that our marriage got better, and we had a desire to help others. . . . Marriages are worth saving. Our own experience is transferable.

—Howard and Jackie,
Jacksonville leaders of Marriage Ministry

Marriage Encounter saved our marriage, but Retrouvaille healed our marriage.

—Marie Pate, International Executive
Coordinator of Retrouvaille

This chapter will explore three alternatives for saving deeply troubled marriages. Two options involve couples whose marriages were once in deep trouble, reaching out to help their marriages in current difficulty:

1. "Marriage Ministry" that can be initiated by any local church.
2. "Retrouvaille" ('Rĕt-troo-vī = French, for *rediscovery*), a ministry patterned on Marriage Encounter, that is now in fifty-eight Catholic dioceses.
3. "Solution-Oriented Brief Therapy" is a nonreligious means to save a marriage. Its strength is that it can be initiated by one partner who

wants to save a marriage even if the other partner appears uninterested.

Any one of these strategies can save eight or nine marriages out of ten. A skeptic might ask, "Why bother? If there are years of conflict and apparent irreconcilable differences, isn't it better for the couple to separate to achieve both peace and new opportunity?"

DIVORCE IS NOT THE ANSWER

"Few adults anticipate accurately what lies ahead when they decide to divorce," wrote Judith Wallerstein and Sandra Blakeslee in their landmark 1989 book, *Second Chances.* "Life is almost always more arduous and more complicated than they expect. It is often more depleting and more lonely for at least one partner in the marriage. At the time of divorce, people are intent on getting rid of their unhappiness, and they find it difficult to conjure up understanding for something they have never experienced. It is hard for them to imagine the multiple changes that divorce will bring."

A more recent and superb book, *Divorce Busting,*[1] by Michele Weiner-Davis, outlines why her therapy with troubled couples convinces her that "divorce is not the answer":

> People can and should stay together and work out their differences. . . .
> Over the past several years I have witnessed the suffering and disillusionment that are the predictable by-products of divorce. I have seen people who have been divorced for five years or longer who have wounds that won't heal. These people failed to anticipate the pain and upheaval divorce leaves in its wake. I have heard countless divorced couples battle tenaciously over the very same issues they believed they were leaving behind when they walked out the door. . . . I have heard too many disillusioned individuals express regrets about their belief that their ex-spouse was the problem only to discover similar problems in their second marriages, or, even more surprising, in their new single lives.

> Diagnosing one's spouse as the source of the problem, a common antecedent to divorce, doesn't take into account the roles both partners play in the deterioration of the relationship. The habits that spouses developed over the years go with them when they end the marriage. This may partly account for the saddening statistic that 60% of second marriages also end in divorce.

> And then there are the children, who are also victims in a divorce. Research shows that except in extreme cases of abuse, children want their parents together. Children have no say in a decision that profoundly affects them for the rest of their lives. When parents decide to end their

---

[1]Copyright 1992. Reprinted by permission of Summit Books, a division of Simon & Schuster, Inc.

marriage, it means the death of the family. As the family disintegrates, a child's sense of comfort and security becomes shaken.

Equally important, Michele Weiner-Davis has developed a revolutionary and rapid program for couples to heal their marriage: "Solution-Oriented Brief Therapy," described at the end of this chapter.

A Call for "People Whose Marriages Were on the Rocks, But Have Healed"

During a service in the fall of 1987, Father Dick McGinnis, then fifty-eight and Associate Rector of St. David's Episcopal Church in Jacksonville, Florida, made an announcement that led to the creation in his church of a "Marriage Ministry" that has helped save thirty-three troubled marriages. In fact, there have been no divorces in the church since 1987 among those who asked for help! *Marriage Ministry could be transplanted to any of America's 300,000 churches.*

Father Dick said, "I want to meet after the service in the chapel with those people whose marriages have been on the rocks but who have successfully come off of them—people who have been in extreme difficulty and have threatened divorce but are now in recovery."

Ten couples showed up! Father Dick "was astounded, overwhelmed, and overjoyed," he said later. He told them, "I've been wondering if God has a way of restoring marriages. There are so many marriages in trouble. I have more work than I can handle in marriage counseling. There is no way to keep up with it. I could do it one hundred percent of my time, not do anything else, and still not meet the need. So I prayed about it.

"What came into my mind after I prayed, was that I should not be looking at the problem but the solution. That triggered in my mind how Alcoholics Anonymous got started. It began with "Bill" and "Doctor Bob" helping each other to stay sober. Then they began trying to help other alcoholics stay sober. Two clergy—a Roman Catholic and an Episcopalian—helped them, and from that assistance they were able to develop the twelve Steps of AA that have helped millions stay sober.[2]

"If God has a plan for restoring marriages, *you* are the people who would know. I want to meet with you over a period of time to hear what you had to do for your marriages to be restored. You will have to expose an awful

---

[2]What Father Dick didn't divulge that Sunday was that he used to attend Calvary Church in New York where AA began. It was there that Father Dick first developed his idea of lay leadership. As he told me recently, "Essentially the church is made up of lay people. There is the whole idea that Martin Luther recognized in Scripture, of the 'priesthood of all believers.' God calls every person to some kind of ministry. One of the big jobs of the clergy is to 'equip the saints for the work of ministry.' . . . AA has saved millions with lay people helping each other."

lot of yourselves and what's going on in your lives. It will take a while. I'd like to meet with you weekly. I also want to see if there is anything of a common nature you had to do for your marriages to be restored. You'll have to share openly and deeply. It may be embarrassing."

What he dared not divulge at the time was his dream of using these couples in recovered marriages to reach out and help others now in deeply troubled marriages. For the moment, however, he simply asked them to meet and share their stories of healing. Seven couples agreed to the process. Feeling that the group was too large for intimate sharing, he broke it up into two groups; one met on Friday night, the other, on Sunday morning. Father Dick's wife, Phyllis, joined him "as my process observer, to keep us on track and on time, and she picked up what I missed."[3]

His question to each couple was the same: "What was it that you and your spouse had to do for your marriage to be restored?" As each couple spoke, Father Dick took large sheets of newsprint, tacked them to the wall, and wrote down the steps each couple went through. "My job," he said, was to stay as objective as possible, put aside my preconceptions of what had to be done, let the ideas come from the couples, and simply record them. Over three to four months, we came up with two lists, one from each group. They were remarkably the same."

VERY DIFFERENT MARITAL PROBLEMS

That there was any similarity is remarkable, because the couples are so different. Consider four couples (with pseudonyms to protect their privacy):

— Bob and Betsy went deeply into debt as he set up a dental office before he had any patients. He was so financially stretched that he did his own lab work after hours, working until midnight. Pressures on the marriage were compounded by "my use of alcohol," Bob acknowledges.

— Sam and Faith had a stormy marriage that included his drug abuse, her repeat visits to a mental institution as a manic-depressive who attempted suicide, his losing a job, and a resulting bankruptcy. In addition, Sam was a bisexual who sought out male liaisons, resulting in his contracting the HIV virus. He now has AIDS, but he and Faith are still together and now closer than ever.

— Ray loved his work in telephone maintenance and worked long hours to support his family. "It nearly cost me everything," he now

---

[3]Father Dick's use of his wife as a partner was a wise step. She added a female perspective—someone whom many of the women in troubled marriages felt that they could approach more easily than the associate rector. More pastors and counselors should try involving their spouse with couples.

says. He would come home late, lie down on the couch to watch TV, and fall asleep at an early hour. So Dora found other interests. She worked as a paramedic by day and as an emergency policewoman at evening rock concerts. There she met an EMT, with whom she had an affair for eight years. Ray never knew about her adultery until she told him years later.

— Howard and Jackie "loved each other but hated each other." She wore the pants in the family, but he didn't care, immersing himself in TV sports to escape her. Also, he had trouble holding a job. They seemed to have irreconcilable differences and a lack of mutual respect.

MARRIAGE MINISTRY GUIDING ACTIONS (M&Ms)

The couples quickly discovered they had much in common. Six of the seven had been on Marriage Encounter, where most had improved their communication skills.[4] The majority had also gone through dramatic role reversals. Shrewish, domineering women had become more feminine and gladly conceded leadership roles to men who had been self-centered couch potatoes. The element of faith played an important part of each of their lives and was one of the cements of their marriages.

Interestingly, each couple had experienced the identical spiritual steps that enabled them to rebuild their relationships as men and women and as husband and wife. These same Marriage Ministry principles surfaced in both of the groups led by Father Dick. So after a few months of separate storytelling and principle-defining, he brought both groups together to refine the Marriage Ministry action steps or M&Ms. They spent months thrashing out a consensus on the exact wording of what emerged as M&Ms. They are analogous to the Twelve Steps for Alcoholics Anonymous, such as:

- We admitted that we were powerless over alcohol—that our lives had become unmanageable;
- We came to believe that a Power greater than ourselves could restore us to sanity;
- We made a decision to turn our will and our lives over to the care of God as we understood him;
- We made a searching and fearless inventory of ourselves.

The following are the seventeen M&M action statements of the Marriage Ministry couples that have been the guiding actions in the restoration of their marriages.

---

[4]Two of the six couples had a bad experience at Marriage Encounter. Couples with deeply troubled marriages should not go on Marriage Encounter but on Retrouvaille Weekends, described in this chapter.

A. Christian Example
   1. Through other Christians' testimony and example we/I found hope for our marriage.

B. Commitment to God
   2. I experienced God's love and forgiveness.
   3. I made a decision/*commitment* to *love*: Christ, mate, self. (This wording indicates that this kind of love comes only after commitment is made. Known as *agape*, it is the form of love that is self-giving rather than self-receiving.)
   4. I made a decision and commitment to follow Jesus as my Savior and Lord.
   5. Once obedient to God, we were able to begin to love by his standards, not ours.
   6. I became accountable to God for my behavior, thoughts, and actions and became aware of my accountability to others.

C. Commitment to Partner
   7. We/I made a decision to stay together.
   8. We/I made a decision to forgive mate and myself.
   9. I accepted my mate as he/she is.

D. Changed Myself
   10. I realized that the problem was with *myself*.
   11. I began to look at myself as needing change to be able to love, no matter what. I became aware that I needed to change, became willing to change, learned *what* and *how* to change, and began to change with God's help.
   12. I made an examination of my *role* in our marriage according to God's Word and changed accordingly with God's help.
   13. I accepted change in my mate.

E. Trust
   14. Through Christ, I began trusting enough to increasingly put my whole self in the care of my mate.
   15. I learned to communicate honestly, truthfully, and openly, in love.
   16. I learned to put God and mate ahead of myself (became humble before the Lord).

F. The Process
   17. We are still in the process and realize that we must share what we have found with others.

COMMITMENT TO GOD

I asked each of the Jacksonville couples to tell me their stories, illustrating the Marriage Ministry steps. Here are several condensed stories, each focused on their particular areas of spiritual growth.

I asked Howard and Jackie, "What do you mean by saying you 'made a commitment to follow Jesus as Savior and Lord.' "?

"I was out of work," replied Howard. "I had spent six years in the Army, was gung-ho, succeeded, got rank quickly. When I got out of the service, things began to change. We were having problems with our children. We were non-Christians and were having enormous communication problems. We felt, 'I love you . . . but can't stand you.' We had tried books like *I'm OK. You're OK*. We had non-Christian counselors. Nothing was working."

Jackie added, "I was at work, and I said, 'I am looking for something, but I don't know what I'm looking for!' A co-worker replied, 'Why not try God?' And he dropped it. He didn't say anything else. (I later learned he had become a born-again believer.)" She came home and repeated his sentence, "Why not try God?"

Howard replied, "Why not? What have we got to lose?"

The following Sunday, they attended St. David's Episcopal Church. Howard did not like it—at all. He did not know when to sit, or kneel, or stand. The sermon was on humility. For a man out of work, with his wife threatening to leave him, the message of being humble seemed stupid. But Jackie was touched by something and persuaded him to return "one more time." This visit was much more moving for Howard. The first thing he noticed in talking to parishioners afterward was that "They have a joy we did not have. We did not know why. We could not put our finger on it. It took us a while to grab a hold of it. We were so numb," he said.

"We did not know how to relate to each other. She had been married before and had certain expectations in the marriage. I did not know what I wanted in the marriage. I had a concept of what a husband is—that the world had taught me. I did not know how to express my love to her except physically.

"But the people we saw at church had something, I thought. *It must be the Jesus they are talking about.* Their lives were different and they were happy. And they cared about us. They didn't care what our background was. Through their lives, we saw there was hope for our marriage," Howard told me.

For Jackie, "The first step was to learn that God loved me enough to send Jesus Christ to die for me. I did not use to like myself, and I did not like anybody else either. I thought I was garbage. I grew up in a home in which my mother was an alcoholic and my father had mental problems. I got married at eighteen to get out of the house. My first husband left me for another woman. That compelled me to think, 'I am not worth very much.' I had two children. As a Catholic I could not receive Communion or get married again. I thought, *'I am garbage. I can't keep a husband. My father killed himself and left everything to the two sons.'* "

At St. David's, the pastor cared enough to visit them. "In contrast," Jackie said, "The God I knew while growing up was a mean God. When I heard that Christ had died for us, he was not the God I knew, but I thought that if Christ died for us, we *have* to be worth something."

Jackie began to change and remembers, "It was not easy. At church they said I was supposed to be submissive. But Howard was not the head of the house, or the spiritual head. I was head of the house. I ran everything. He just followed. He did football games and took out the garbage. I would do everything else, and he let me. It was not his job to help around the house. He left his laundry on the floor. He did not help discipline the kids. It was hard for me to let Howard be the head."

Then she realized that part of the problem was her sharp tongue. "I had always let him know what his failures were. So I prayed to the Lord to send angels down to clamp shut my jaws. I had been the nag before I made a commitment to Christ. But I did change with the Lord's help."

The next time she saw his clothes scattered about, she did not scream "Pick up your clothes!" as usual.

Howard noticed the change right away: "It became obvious. She stopped complaining!" So he was motivated to start picking up after himself. That made her feel affectionate, a welcome change! Thus, Jackie realized three important points that some couples never learn: She could not *change her mate,* but she could *change herself. Her* change had prompted *him* to change! What had been a downward spiral, reversed itself.

Two other factors were very important. "Marriage Encounter was the greatest thing since sliced bread," said Howard. "If I had to say a specific time when I met God, it was on that weekend. . . . On Saturday afternoon we were asked to share our innermost feelings. We had never shared our feelings with each other. It was life-changing for our married life. It was the first time we ever experienced real love."

Also, adds Jackie, "We were discipled by another couple—allowed to see their marriage in action, in the best of times and the worst of times. From that we learned how a marriage can work."

DRUGS, BANKRUPTCY, MENTAL ILLNESS, AIDS

"We have gone through many storms," Sam told a group who came to St. David's to hear about Marriage Ministry. A big man, he spoke plainly, sharing intimate details. "I had a ten-year drug history. I bought drugs and sold them and wanted more. The church confronted me with my addiction. I was playing music in a folk Mass, but because I was selling dope, they would not allow me to take Communion. They said, 'We love you.' My wife, Faith, kept praying for me. In 1976 I had a drug overdose, but it was not until the church confrontation in 1978 that I made a decision to quit one night. I have been in recovery since. . . . I got straightened out through AA and the church.

"Humanly, none of us are supposed to be together. We are already supposed to be divorced, according to man's law. Faith has been in a mental hospital four times in our marriage, but it was not her fault. They were not giving her the right drugs. I was ready to leave her the last time she was in a psychiatric hospital. I asked her sister to pick her up. I had filed for bankruptcy, and an assessor came to look at our things. He said, 'You don't have enough to sell.' I sat down on the kitchen floor and cried, 'What do I do now? Dear God, you have to help me through this.' I called Father Dick, and he was very, very helpful.

"I went to the hospital and brought her home. She was my only asset.

"She had been misdiagnosed. She has a chemical imbalance. With lithium she has been able to function normally and is back to her old self when we first got married. For many years I held her responsible for her behavior. I knew we are supposed to be together through sickness and health. The world teaches us that if it doesn't work out, to dissolve it and get on with your life.

"Then on June 1, 1988, I received a call from my doctor. I was HIV positive, due to (homosexual) lust. How could I deal with that? I told Faith: 'I have the HIV virus.' When I told her, she scooted over next to me and hugged me. She said 'We will get through this, too.'"

Faith said, "I was hurt many times by things Sam did. He would go out and not come home for hours. I had to forgive him. At St. David's I learned it is an act of the will. I could ask God to help me forgive."

Sam's condition has deteriorated since I heard him speak in 1991. He was diagnosed in 1992 as having full-blown AIDS, and he quit his work as a drug counselor.

However, Sam and his wife have counseled other couples in trouble. He tells them, "My wife and I are both believers in the vows of marriage. Anything you go through can hurt, but we have come out on the other end. We know many who have divorced over trivial matters." He stuck by his wife when she was sick, and now she stays by his side as he suffers.

But all is not smooth. The last Marriage Ministry step is to recognize that "We are still in the process." One night as they were going to counsel a young couple, Pete and Sue, who had also been through bankruptcy, they got in a fight and argued "all the way over." Sam turned to his wife and said, "The way we are going at each other, how can we help anyone?" They walked in and Sam announced, "I did not want to see any of you people."

That sparked laughter from Pete and Sue. "Have you been reading our mail?" said Sue. "That sounds like us!" She had said exactly the same thing to Pete on the way over—that she did not want to see any of those people. Both couples relaxed immediately. Pete said later, "We found that we were not alone. There is no substitute for knowing that the person helping you has been through it."

As I write in June 1992, Sam is on disability but is studying for the diaconate despite the fact he tires easily. He is following some of the suggestions for Dr. Bernie Siegel[5] on how five to six percent of those with AIDS are living successfully with it. He and his wife are a couple with inspirational faith.

EIGHT YEARS OF ADULTERY

The natural feeling of most husbands and wives is that their partner needs to change—not themselves. Ray and Dora are a classic case. They have now been married nearly forty years. He is bald and a bit overweight; she is a vivacious blond. They have taken mission trips together to help build churches and seem to enjoy each other.

It was not always so. Ray looks back and says, "I figured I had to work harder and longer than others. I enjoyed my work in telephone maintenance and took every opportunity to be at work. I devoted my time, thinking that I was providing for my family. Even on weekends I was away from my family, who needed me. It nearly turned out to be a disaster. One day Dora told me that she wanted a divorce." They had been married over twenty years.

Dora says, "I planned on leaving. His work was his idol, but I was gone as much as he. I'd rather be at work than at home. After the kids were older, I went to work for a drug-abuse program. I inherited a job doing first-aid at rock concerts and was gone most evenings. Ray did not have many communication skills. . . . I met a guy at the Coliseum. I thought I had fallen in love with him and got real involved. I wanted to be free, free to do what I wanted to do. One night I told Ray that I was moving out the next weekend. The next day, he said, 'Let's have lunch.' He said that if I would stay, he would give 100%. That was in February 1980."

What changed things was an initiative taken by her daughter, Lee, who had been "born again." On Dora's pillow she would leave tracts for her mother to read. Dora resented it at first. "Lee gently encouraged me but never pushed," she recalls. "One night coming home from the Coliseum, I said to the Lord, 'If you can do anything with this life, you can have it.' " She knew that this meant the eight-year adulterous affair was over, and thought: *If Ray is asleep, I will ask Lee to pray with me*. I woke him up, but he started snoring. So I prayed with Lee. It was the day before Mother's Day.

---

[5]Bernie Siegel, M.D., *Love, Medicine, & Miracles*, HarperCollins, 1990.

Dora recalls, "I started to change. . . ." She became more loving, Ray said, began cooking him wonderful meals, and suggested that they take a long vacation together. Ray was astounded. "I saw the change in Dora, the drastic change. I could not get over it. I knew what had brought about the transformation—had never experienced such a 180-degree change.

"I used to think that Dora needed to change, but I began to look at myself. For years, I did not think I needed to change. Then I found things wrong with me. I tried *not* to make a commitment to Christ. But I began to see changes and became willing to change. Trust hadn't been there. I found out that what I trusted was my job. It had nothing to do with the security of my family. They did not need the income. They needed *me*. You have to get a balance in your life with your family. When you are gone, they will get someone else." Eventually, he did make a commitment to Christ.

"We've got a new marriage. Our relationship changed, and everything seemed to blossom," said Dora. She did tell Ray about her affair, after a period of time. He had been totally unaware of it.

What was it like to tell him? "When you tell your husband you had been involved with another man for eight years, it was like a big burden had been lifted off.

"Now we do everything together. Ray has retired. Last summer we went to Jamaica and built a church. We have been to Africa once and are going back this summer for a praise-and-worship conference."

THE IMPORTANCE OF COUPLES' SHARING

None of these couples knew each other's stories. Each had felt isolated and had struggled alone. When they met each other in church, they simply saw other smiling faces. We all know how to wear public masks that can hide the anguish we feel. "It was good to have a place where the small stuff could be expressed and talked about and not be ridiculed," said Father McGinnis. "It was good to have a place where you could trust that what you were saying would not be misunderstood." The first Marriage Ministry principle is: "Through other Christian testimony and example we/I found hope for our marriage."

Bob is a dentist whose marriage suffered while he was trying to launch his practice under the burden of $200,000 of debt for equipment. His wife, Betsy, told me: "One of the main things that I have taken from the group is the fellowship. A big key in this is sharing what is going on in your life with people who have been there and can understand. It makes you feel less like a freak. A big part of the problem is the loneliness that people go through when their marriages are in trouble. If we had had this support group a decade ago, it would have helped us and made it possible for us to go contrary to what the secular world throws at us."

Bob says, "The conflict we had was mainly my being selfish and immature. In the past I had just been very demanding and very perfectionistic. . . .
We have always tried to find solutions to the problem. We have sought out
counseling through our twenty-two years of marriage."

Betsy adds: "A lot of the problem was communication. We could not
say things in a way the other could hear. He would say something. I would
take it one way that he had not meant. So many of our problems could have
been avoided if he really knew I love him." She looked at Bob and said, "I
really doubted your love."

It was enormously therapeutic for each of the couples to tell their stories
to Father Dick and begin the collaborative process of thrashing out a consensus on the Marriage Ministry action statements. In time, they gained his
vision of reaching out to help other couples in trouble, using the developing
M&Ms as an outline of the testimony to be shared with others.

I asked each of them to rank the quality of their happiness as a married
couple, from 0 to 10, with 10 being supreme happiness. Each said that before
Father Dick began working with them, they were at a 3, 4, or 5. But after some
time of hearing each other's stories and seeing that the Lord could use them
as couples to reach out to others in trouble, their happiness moved on average to 8 or 9!

Thus, the process of describing their healing actually accelerated it!

Why? Betsy said, "We had a lot of different angles on the same problem.
We brought a lot of information, and couples were open to hearing. Most of
us were still pretty raw. We had open wounds. As we have shared with other
couples, it has helped heal our own wounds. Some did this for us when we
needed it. When you can be used, when you are needed, when someone
needs to hear your testimony, you love to give your support. You are blessed
by that."

SIGNIFICANCE OF THE MARRIAGE MINISTRY STEPS

"The Marriage Ministry statements are not in sequential order," says
Father Dick McGinnis, unlike the Twelve Steps of Alcoholics Anonymous,
which must be taken in order because each builds on previous steps. In Marriage Ministry, he says, "One does not have one done after another, nor are
they in order of importance. We all had to do all of them, but there was no
order or priority. Some might have decided to stay together first, and then
later made a commitment to the Lord. Others made a commitment to God
and then decided to stay together."

Betsy summarized all of the M&Ms in a quote she has on a plaque:

Success in marriage is more than finding the right person. It is a matter of
being the right person.

At one point, Betsy was at her wits' end and was ready to leave Bob. "I did not know what to do. I started praying, 'I can't handle this any more.' I gave God a deadline. I said, 'If things are not better by Wednesday, I am out of here on a plane. But in the meantime, I will do everything I can for three days.' We needed $3000 by Saturday. To help him out, I went into Bob's dentist office to work for three days.

"On Wednesday, a lady came to his office for an examination. He told her that she needed to have periodontal work done (which would have to be done elsewhere), then restorative treatment that would cost three thousand dollars, and that it would take three months for the tissue to heal prior to his work. She said, 'If I gave you a check now for three thousand dollars, would that make you happy?' I took it as an answer to my prayers. We were new Christians, and the whole thing of relying on anybody but ourselves was foreign to us. Yet, the only time we were delivered from a crisis, it was through a miracle!"

Another hard-to-measure variable was the influence of Father Dick and his wife, Phyllis. One step he took with each couple was to administer the relational instrument described in chapter 8. It provided each couple with an objective X-ray of their relationship—its strengths and weaknesses. And it enabled Father Dick to see where his counseling should be focused.

For example, he nudged Bob to "get beyond the denial of my alcoholism," Bob told me. "He impressed on us that if you have liquor involved as an escape, it is a problem even if you don't lose control. People may not drink much at all, but it may be a big part of their relationship problem. When my drinking stopped, a lot of communication was available that had not been available before." Three of the seven couples had had someone come to the same conclusion and join AA for help.

MARRIAGE MINISTRY WITH HURTING COUPLES

At the time I visited Jacksonville in April 1991, the seven couples had already worked with twenty-four other troubled marriages. Most were members of St. David's, but many were not. Father Dick did the pairing up. Mostly, he assigned a troubled couple to an M&M couple on a one-to-one basis. They might meet four to thirty times, depending on need. Sometimes he organized a "cluster" of two M&M couples with two hurting couples. In 1990–91, several M&M couples organized and took turns leading a support group during Sunday school time. Also, there have been three "Evenings of Hope" when the Ministry couples tell condensed summaries of their stories, pegged to the seventeen M&Ms to couples who might need help.

I attended one in 1991. It was a deeply moving experience. One image sticks in my mind. Bob was sharing his problem with alcohol: "I have used alcohol, and was not so far advanced. So I could deny it. Father Dick said, 'There is no place for mind-altering substances in a relationship with problems.' I had to admit that its effects hurt me. There is no place for drinking, even on an occasional level, because it can distract you from the relationship."

As he spoke, I noticed one man's head sank down to between his knees! He remained in that position for twenty minutes, while his wife rubbed his back. Clearly, he, too, had a drinking problem and identified with Bob.

As Father Dick said later, "If I were doing counseling with twenty-eight couples, it would not have been nearly as effective as having couples with healed relationships sharing their pain and recovery with others now in turmoil." The seven original couples meet monthly as a support to one another and to compare notes. One woman with a troubled marriage has been to every couple in the group, seeking easy answers. They all told her the same thing: "*You* have to change." She is beginning to do so, and to the surprise of some, her marriage is still intact.

More typically, a mentor couple sticks with a couple in need until they feel that their help is no longer needed. The original seven Marriage Ministry couples have worked now with thirty-three couples. None have gotten divorced. Bob emphasized the value of the M&Ms in guiding their testimony and giving direction to other couples. He told of a Catholic couple who, ironically, were being driven apart by the fact that the man had experienced the "born again" experience of "speaking in tongues." When he tried to share this with his wife, a woman very active in her church, she was threatened and offended. Their teenagers took every advantage of their divisiveness, playing one parent off against another.

"The Marriage Ministry principles were made to order," said Bob. "It gave them a place to plug into, to see that they both have a commitment to God and to each other. He could say to her: 'We have already gone through this many steps.' " Betsy added, "But he had to demonstrate love to his wife by showing her that the Bible doesn't work if you don't love your wife. They needed to be together as a couple. In doing so, they were able to deal with the disturbance of the kids."

Bob said: "Before they had started to work on their relationship, the wife had settled into a humdrum existence. The kids were left to take care of themselves. The dad was never home. That created turmoil and anarchy."

The father had to be persuaded that the problem was not with his wife but with himself. When he changed his routine to spend more time with her and with the children, they began to change, too. It is the upside-down economics of Jesus: "Give, and it shall be given unto you."

THE SECOND GENERATION: ED AND JOAN

One couple was so powerfully influenced by Marriage Ministry that they have volunteered to be in a second generation of M&M mentor couples, reaching out to others. It is interesting that they heard about Marriage Ministry by reading my column about it in the *Florida Times Union*.[6] At the outset, their situation seemed hopeless.

Ed and Joan, both forty-five, have been married twenty-one years and have four adopted children at home. "Our marriage has been one struggle after another," Ed told me. "In the first fifteen years, I was changing jobs every two to three years. I had a real problem with authority, was a people-pleaser (at work), a workaholic, and a perfectionist. When I came home, I would expect peace and harmony, my needs met, and I gave very little. That made our relationship less and less intimate. Five years ago we started sleeping in different rooms. In my job move here I was the low man on the totem pole. Because I disagreed with my boss, I was under severe stress. Due to anger, I went to a psychologist, and I was hitting my pillow. It was a dysfunction, and drinking was a problem from time to time."

Joan found each of their job moves very trying. On top of that she said, "Ed would criticize me for taking the kids to sports activities. He'd say 'You're running around too much and are not here for me.' Yet when I stayed at home, he just watched TV. There was no interaction. Ed never emotionally separated from his family." He left to visit them three times and was gone "a total of three months" in the year his mother died. During those absences, "I felt better without him. There was less turmoil." She started going to "codependency classes," where she found that *she* had aggravated his irresponsibility by not standing up to him.

When he came back from his third long trip home, she demanded that he leave the house. "I realized she meant it," Ed sighed. "She had never said *that* before. I couldn't accept it. We started seeing a marriage counselor. She didn't get much out of it, though I did."

That's when they began attending Marriage Ministry, meeting at Sunday school with three of the original couples. "It was great. Bob and Betsy were very helpful. And they *cared*," said Ed. "Their purpose was to be concerned about us. They asked questions to find out more about us. That amazed me."

Joan said the M&Ms "helped pinpoint problems. I was having a problem with trust." One of the M&Ms is "Through Christ, begin trusting enough to increasingly put my whole self in the care of my mate." She said, "While he showed a new interest in the marriage, would he change tomorrow?"

For Ed, the key principle was that "I realized the problem was with myself and began to change with the Lord's help." Ed recalls, "I had too

---

[6]I wrote two columns about Marriage Ministry in January 1990 and put the address of St. David's Episcopal Church in my column (12355 Fort Caroline Road, Jacksonville, FL 32225). The story sparked 1,600 letters of inquiry—the largest outpouring for any of my columns written in fifteen years. Fourteen months later, a follow-up piece generated 500 more inquiries.

much pride to change before, but I knew that I had to change because I did not want to lose my wife and family."

What inspired him was that the M&M team was "so empathetic and caring, and they revealed themselves to us." The first change he made, sparked by Marriage Ministry, was "to make a commitment to the Lord." Ray, the telephone maintenance man, asked the banker if he was "ready to accept the Lord." Ed said, "Yes." Ray then said a prayer of commitment, repeated by Ed. "I was on cloud nine for a month," Ed recalls. In time, some commitment began to wear off. To deal with that, Ed and Joan met three more times with the M&M couples personally—after eight weeks of Sunday school.

More important, they "sought to deepen my contact with God, in a daily spiritual program of getting up twenty minutes earlier than usual for prayer and meditation. Almost immediately, my life did begin to change. It is amazing how all the ups and downs settled down. I am much closer to straight-line behavior now; I've always had fluctuations, a wavering behavior, but that left as the spiritual side grew."

For Joan, the most important Marriage Ministry principle was that "I made a decision to forgive my mate and myself." She said, "What I learned from Marriage Ministry was that you have to say that you forgive and want to forgive even though the feelings don't go along. You want to forgive, and you pray to the Lord to help you do that."

HOW RETROUVAILLE HELPED

At about that point, in the fall of 1991, Ed and Joan attended a "Retrouvaille"[7] weekend arranged through their Catholic church.

Joan said afterward: "Now I do feel freer to express my feelings. He is more accepting of them. He is helping a whole lot more with the children. It makes a difference in their lives to have interaction with their father. He is taking our boys to basketball games. He's willing to discipline them but jokes with them and lets them express themselves."

Ed added a final word, "The bottom line is that giving ourselves over to God was what saved our marriage. The last five months have been the best months of our twenty-one years of marriage."

Much of the rest of this chapter deals in-depth with Retrouvaille. First, however, I want to give some thoughts on transplanting Marriage Ministry.

---

[7]A reminder: *Retrouvaille* is a French word, pronounced "'rĕ troo vī," for *rediscovery*. As Ed described the weekend, "It is like Marriage Encounter except that it is for couples having trouble. One of the couples making presentations had had one or two affairs. My feeling after the first Friday night was, 'At least we haven't had some of their difficulties!' We learned that our problem was poor communication."

TRANSPLANTING MARRIAGE MINISTRY

I noted earlier that 2,100 people who read about Marriage Ministry in my column, "Ethics and Religion," wrote St. David's Episcopal Church to learn more about it. About 500 of those inquiries came from church pastors or counselors—yet Father Dick McGinnis does not know of a *single* church that has adopted the Marriage Ministry approach. Nor do I. I called a sample of those who wrote in, and the best that anyone could say was, "Oh, yes, I use that in counseling."

That misses the whole point of Marriage Ministry. It is a *lay ministry* in which the clergy's function is simply to get it launched and step back to allow God's people with the experience of saving and restoring their own poor marriages to turn and "share what we have found with others," as the seventeenth step puts it. Few alcoholics ever heard of the Reverend Sam Shoemaker, the Episcopal priest who helped "Doctor Bob" and "Bill" develop the twelve steps of Alcoholics Anonymous, but within AA, millions know about Doctor Bob and Bill.

Marriage Ministry is a self-help program that could take root in any of America's 300,000 churches. In my column of February 3, 1990, I concluded:

> Dick McGinnis says, "I started this off looking to see if God had a way for marriages to be restored. What we see is that He does. It is summed up in the seventeen Marriage Ministry principles. Any pastor could use them to equip recovering couples to help others. The experienced couple's personal experience breathes life into the principles.'"

> The twelve steps of Alcoholics Anonymous have saved millions of people. I predict the seventeen M&Ms will save millions of marriages. Write for them. . . . In my view, Marriage Ministry is a discovery of far greater importance than the discovery of AA's twelve steps. Only a tenth of people become alcoholic, while half of America's marriages fail."

See the complete list of Marriage Ministry steps listed earlier in this chapter. What should you do with them? I'd like to make two concrete suggestions to test the transplantability of Marriage Ministry:

1. The Pastor's Initiative

Any pastor could stand in his church and use Father Dick McGinnis's words: "I want to meet after the service with those people whose marriages have been on the rocks but who have successfully come off of them—people who have been in extreme difficulty and have threatened divorce but are in recovery."

He could then share the St. David's story and take one of two steps:

(1) He could ask couples to meet with him over a period of months so that he might hear their stories and see if they have taken any common steps to save their marriages. This sharing of stories is enormously therapeutic

both to those speaking and to those listening. The pastor can then compare any consensus that may emerge with the M&Ms.

(2) Alternatively, he could share the M&Ms at the outset and ask if any of the couples went through similar steps to save their marriages. Odds are that there will be some differences and much similarity. The M&Ms could be revised for your church to use with other couples in need.

Either way, the church will end up with a group of people who really can be Marriage Savers for others in need in their congregations.

2. The Recovered Couples' Initiative

Undoubtedly, many of you reading this book will see that the M&Ms are an outline of the steps *you and your spouse* took to save your marriage. You may know of other couples who underwent a rocky time but who now have healed marriages. You could invite them to meet with you for a period of weeks to hear each other's story in-depth.

Then your cluster (who may or may not belong to the same church) could take the initiative to revise the M&Ms if necessary.

This experience will equip *you* to become Marriage Savers. Undoubtedly, you know couples who are in deep distress at present. You could organize your own "Evenings of Hope" as St. David's did in which each of you share some aspect of your recovery to illustrate several of the M&Ms. You might then offer to meet privately on a couple-to-couple basis, or together as a cluster group.

Another option, of course, is to make Marriage Ministry a conscious outreach of your church to any couple who needs help. You could offer this service to assist the pastor and could announce an "Evening of Hope" to explain it to those who might be interested. You could write about it in church bulletins and make your names known as couples with saved marriages who are willing to help others in need.[8]

If you have any doubts about the value of Marriage Ministry, consider what Bob, the dentist, says the experience has meant to him and Betsy:

> Of the seventeen steps, the first one, the sharing of other resurrected relationships has been a positive experience and influence on our lives. It has been a very gratifying and personally healing experience. It has definitely enhanced our marriage.
>
> We have had the opportunity to work with six or eight couples. But it has gone beyond the formal relationship with Marriage Ministry to affect our

---

[8] If you form a Marriage Ministry group, please write to Father McGinnis at St. David's Episcopal Church, 12355 Fort Caroline Road, Jacksonville, FL 32225) and drop a photocopy to me at 9500 Michael's Ct., Bethesda, MD 20817. I'm convinced that Marriage Ministry will grow into an important movement and want to report what you are doing to save marriages.

lives as we informally counsel employees or friends or neighbors. We (all seven M&M couples) would as a person agree that we are more open because , without having had the experience of Marriage Ministry and without a formal education in counseling, we would not be as prepared or as open to share, to help people cope with their problems. We find people opening up to us. . . .

Recently a repairman was in my office to work on the sprinkler. He had been separated for a year and was talking about his need to start dating again. During the afternoon, I shared our experience, strength and hope. That next week he had the inspiration to call his wife, and say, 'Why don't we get together?' Their marriage has been restored! We have no way of knowing the extent of this kind of influence.

To the knowledge of Father Dick and the seven core M&M couples, however, none of those whom they have counseled have gotten divorced even though many had been on the verge of doing so. Therefore, if you have been able to rebuild a marriage that was once on the rocks, the chances are that the creation of a Marriage Ministry would give *you* the opportunity and satisfaction to be a real Marriage Saver.

WHAT HAPPENS IN RETROUVAILLE?

Retrouvaille is an outgrowth of Marriage Encounter and is quite similar. Husband and wife experience a new technique of communication over a weekend and in follow-up sessions. The communication takes place in three steps, repeated many times.

— First, there are presentations by a pastor and three lead couples who share stories on the near-failure of their marriages. This focus on pain is quite different from the Marriage Encounter content, which is aimed at stable but boring or unrewarding marriages. (For details about ME, see chapter 9 of this book.)

— Second, couples are asked to write their answers to questions framed by the lead couples, as personal letters to their spouses.

— Third, couples then read each other's letters and dialogue about the feelings in total privacy, at no time ever asked to share their problems with anyone else.

"The weekend is not a 'miracle cure,'" says a Retrouvaille brochure. "Therefore, follow-up sessions have been designed to continue the marriage renewal begun on the weekend." It adds, "Although Retrouvaille is a Catholic program, we welcome couples of other faiths. (In fact, in Texas and Florida, up to half of those who attend Retrouvaille are Protestant.) However, as it is designed to help marriages, we do not recommend it to those living common-law."

THE GROWING IMPACT OF RETROUVAILLE

The growth of Marriage Ministry into a movement is only a dream as I write, but Retrouvaille is *already* a rapidly growing movement that began in 1977 in Quebec as an outgrowth of Marriage Encounter (thus, its French name, for *rediscovery*). "Marriage Encounter leaders, increasingly concerned with the number of troubled marriages they saw, tried to adapt the Marriage Encounter weekend for hurting couples," wrote the Reverend Gerald K. Foley, then the international coordinating priest of Retrouvaille, in an article for the February 1989 issue of *St. Anthony's Messenger*. "Minor changes, however, in the Marriage Encounter program could not effectively meet the vastly different needs of couples in troubled marriages."

Therefore, it was overhauled to include a three-month follow-up program that was as carefully scripted as the Retrouvaille weekend itself and is felt to be "more important than the weekend," says Marie Pate, who serves with her husband, Bob, as International Executive Coordinators.

The Catholic Archdioceses of Chicago and Los Angeles introduced Retrouvaille to the United States in 1982. "In 1984, it burst loose in a number of states," says Bob Pate, the coordinator of Retrouvaille. Since then, the number of dioceses involved has nearly doubled each year.[9] Today the movement is in fifty-eight dioceses in the United States and eleven in Canada. It is in such diverse areas as Baltimore, Cleveland, Fresno, Kansas City, Washington, D.C., Detroit, Buffalo, Atlanta, Boston, Little Rock, Houston, Dallas, Denver, Columbus, Long Island, and Sacramento. In 1992 it was picked up by SanDiego, Albuquerque, Tucson, Shreveport, Albany, and others.[10]

The exact number of participants is not known because the volunteer leaders often fail to report the number of participants to the Pates. They know of 2,400 couples who participated between September 1991 and August 1992.

BOLD CLAIMS—SUBSTANTIATED BY EVIDENCE

In a pamphlet on Retrouvaille, some bold claims are made:

> Our program offers you the chance to rediscover yourself, your spouse, and a loving relationship in your marriage.

> If your marriage has become unloving and uncaring or if your relationship has grown cold and distant, if there is little or no meaningful communication, or if you feel disappointment, even despair—then we believe that Retrouvaille can help your marriage.

> If you are thinking of separation or divorce or you are already separated but want to try again—then we believe that Retrouvaille can help.

---

[9]The first Protestant-run Retrouvaille was conducted in Fresno, California, in the summer of 1992. Protestants are two-fifths of attenders at Catholic Retrouvaille weekends and are welcome at any weekend anywhere.

[10]To learn if Retrouvaille is in your area, call Bob or Marie Pate, 817-284-7078.

Those are bold claims, but what evidence backs them up? Of the 600 couples who have made a Retrouvaille in the Fort Worth area, nearly half were *already separated*, and one to two couples per weekend were already divorced! Yet informal studies in Jacksonville and Buffalo, for example, show that four out of five of the marriages were intact a year or more afterward! As Retrouvaille leaders say, "If you and your spouse want your marriage and are willing to put in your best effort—then we invite you, even urge you to come."

RETROUVAILLE REQUIREMENTS

Not everyone who asks to go on a Retrouvaille Weekend can attend. The organizers ask four questions that both husband and wife must answer:

1. "We want a commitment out of both people that they *do* want to make their marriage work," said Bob Pate. "It does no good for one to work at the marriage, and only one person.
2. "If a third party is involved in the relationship, that must be terminated. You can't come on the weekend if someone is waiting.
3. "If either is under professional care, we have to have permission to contact that professional and explain the weekend and get their blessing. Are they sound enough to go through an intense, emotional experience?
4. "Are they willing to attend twelve follow-up sessions spread out over three months—with two sessions normally scheduled every other weekend?"

The weekend begins the improvement of communication, of conflict-resolution skills, and the creation of forgiveness and trust. But secular conventional wisdom is mistaken that one can "forgive and forget it." It takes time, months of demonstrated goodwill, and genuine change before trust can be fully restored. Time is an important ingredient, but so is practice in the process of presentation, question, reflection, and dialogue—which continues in the Retrouvaille follow-up sessions, usually held every other Saturday afternoon for three months.

THE SHARING OF PAIN

Marie and Bob Pate, the International Executive Coordinators of Retrouvaille, "let it all hang out" when they lead a weekend. Like some of those who attend, they first found hope for their marriage on a Marriage Encounter weekend. "*Marriage Encounter saved our marriage, but Retrouvaille healed our marriage*," says Marie. "Marriage Encounter saved our marriage by putting God in our lives. As a result of the weekend, we got baptized and joined the Catholic Church. I had not been in church in thirty years. We also learned communication skills—how to talk. (Our communication was little more than 'How are you?' We'd turn on the TV and that was the end of it.)

"And we both discovered that we both cared for each other. I discovered that the man I married really cared about me. We had been separated twice over the years, and once I filed for divorce," she said. "We had a normal marriage; we did not know it could be different."

Bob said, "I found out that she did not care what we had. To me, that was the mark of success—how big a house, how many cars. As long as you had that, the woman had no gripes."

But beneath the improved communication and rediscovered feelings Bob and Marie felt for each other as a result of Marriage Encounter, there were black, gathering clouds, a cancer long ignored that ate away at the marriage: his infidelity. "Retrouvaille gave us the opportunity to be honest about our relationship," Marie told me. "It was very painful to dig it up and lay it on the table—Bob's affairs. We had never talked about what each of us felt. And I never faced *my* responsibility for his unfaithfulness. No one partner is responsible for the breakdown of a marriage. Both have a part in that. My part in Bob's unfaithfulness was that I quit paying attention to him when we had kids. My total focus was my kids—their activities. They took precedence in our relationship. So he went looking for other relationships." Bob adds: "When I saw you packing the kids off endlessly, I felt irritated and frustrated. After a while, I did not have any feelings left."

No one can be unmoved by such intimate sharing, such compassion—not only for each other but for the strangers sitting in front of them. In telling such stories, Retrouvaille leaders model the exchange of feelings and the dialogue process that inspires attending couples who can see themselves in the stories they hear. The fact that the lead couples overcame massive problems gives most couples hope for renewal and the willingness to write the letters and begin the dialogue to rebuild their marriages. Troubled couples will usually perceive the presenting team as the "shepherds who will lead them out of their particular wilderness."

A SAMPLE OF RETROUVAILLE CONTENT

The first two talks on "Communication" and "Dialogue" are relatively easy and unthreatening. Presentations on "Marriage" and "Forgiveness" are more difficult, because past hurt is recalled. Leaders say that one has to learn to deal directly with the pain in a marriage in order to give it another chance. Usually, the talks are written out and read with voices that are full of emotion. Getting choked up and even weeping is commonplace for both presenters and attendees.

For example, couples are told that anger can often mask other emotions that need to be surfaced: hurt, rejection, fear, disappointment: "Often it's like peeling an onion. Below the first layer of skin is another layer. To get to the second layer, you have to take off the first layer."

At one point participants are asked to "recall a mistake that you have made," something that hurt another person or themselves, a mistake that is still unresolved. They are asked to write an answer to these questions about the incident—an answer that will *not* be shared with their spouse:

1. In what ways do I punish myself because of this mistake?
2. Can I begin to love myself enough to forgive this fault?
3. If so, what precisely am I going to do to accomplish this forgiveness?

A MARRIAGE DISINTEGRATES

That is followed by a description of the masks one uses to manipulate or control others—particularly a husband or wife—in decision making, finances, problem-solving, use of leisure time, handling of children, or one's sex life. Going deeper, presenting couples describe the pattern common to almost every marriage in which both people, slowly, innocently, unconsciously become more focused on personal interests than on couple interests. This gradual trend toward being "married singles" is not taken to spite the spouse but in a desire to pursue individual goals that seem harmless to the marriage at the outset—but the frequent result is that one partner feels neglected and far more unhappy in the marriage than is the other. What happens, in time, is that one escapes into television or gardening or car repair— to avoid the spouse.

Before the marriage really deteriorates, we tend to say, "Well, I am not as bad as so-and-so who is an adulterer, who spends more money, or drinks more heavily or gambles more." This attempt at reassuring ourselves that we are not such a bad husband or wife is a prelude to hitting bottom, where the rationalizations continue: "Well, no one expects marriages to last these days." "At least we had good years." Instead of holding up a high ideal for our marriage, we use society's standards and even settle for separation or divorce because that seems *more common nowadays than good marriages*, say the leaders.

THE MARRIAGE CYCLE:
ROMANCE, DISILLUSIONMENT, MISERY, JOY

The pastor will describe the romance he/she sees in couples in courtship, and a couple will tell their own love story of how they fell in love, what was so attractive about their partner, and what being a newlywed was like.

Lead couples give examples of grating annoyances that transform romance into disillusionment and the growing feeling that we are no longer special to our husband or wife. Presenters describe their realizations that I am not who I thought I was; she's not who I thought she was; our marriage is not what I thought it would be: "He was not the helpful husband. He never seemed to have time to make needed repairs. I always seemed to be nagging about something. We really never talked anymore. All we seemed to do was fight or be silent." That period is contrasted with the romantic time when there were deep conversations, good listening, laughter.

The misery phase is described by the person who was *most guilty*—the adulterer, the heavy drinker, for example. The other spouse then shares the impact of the negative behavior and how it made things worse. Bitterness, distrust, anger, hopelessness come out from husband and wife.

The priest describes couples who lash out at each other, wounding one another. He shares his anguish at the bitterness that separates couples and his longing that couples learn how to be free of the misery and pain.

Obviously, however, the presenting couples learned to restore the joy— and, indeed, at much deeper levels. How?

A DECISION TO LOVE

Presenting couples explain that their breakthrough came when they realized that "*love is a decision*," not a feeling. "This concept frees us to act beyond our feelings, not allowing ourselves to be controlled by them," they say. "We are talking about more than just being nice to one another when we don't feel like it. A decision to love is a decision to respond to the other person. It's a decision to not react to our feelings but to love in spite of our feelings. Deciding to love frees us from basing our relationship on our feelings only. Feelings are flighty. They come and go. Love, as a decision, gives us the control over ourselves we need in order to have a solid relationship," a presenter might say.

This view of love is in profound contrast with that of our modern culture, the leaders note. The Hollywood solution presents the easy way out as the attractive alternative. It rarely shows the pain of divorce for the couple, much less a divorce's impact on children. Movie and TV characters *never* make a case for the value of lifelong commitment, or for the value of hard suffering and sacrificial love. They argue that loneliness or unfulfillment are signs that the relationship is dead. Marriage is seen only as a path to self-fulfillment, not as a way of self-giving to spouse and children. Love is *always* presented as a feeling, not a decision.

The couples tell stories from their own lives, illustrating how they bought into conventional wisdom but found that spiritual principles were key to saving their marriages. The priest adds that there is nothing evil about disillusionment, but that the error comes in thinking that one is stuck at that stage—which leads to the misery stage. But even at that point, the resurrection of love is possible, to those with a biblical view:

— Jesus' love for his people is a pattern for us: sacrificial, selfless, and even suffering for others.
— Love is a decision (1 Cor. 13:4–6).

— Recall your vows to love the other in good times and bad, "in sickness and health, until death us do part."

— Resurrection of marriages is possible with God's help. How?

— Ephesians 5:21–33 to "submit to one another out of reverence for Christ."

A restored marriage can best be demonstrated by telling the story of a couple named Mike and Brenda, of Fort Worth. Before telling the story of their restored marriage and the role that Retrouvaille played in its recovery, you must first know about the near-destruction of their marriage.

MIKE AND BRENDA'S MARRIAGE DISINTEGRATES

Mike, forty, met Brenda, now thirty-nine, in middle school. She was in a strict family that would not allow her to date in high school. Her first date with Mike was to the senior prom. He went into the Air Force and married her on his first leave. During his seven years of service he learned to repair computers. He gave her a new sense of freedom in her first years of marriage, freedom to live in a new community and to work. However, she suffered a miscarriage in their third year and in the fifth year had a still-born baby. "We did not want to be with each other," Brenda recalls. "At the first sign of trouble, we began drifting apart. We did not know how to talk with each other."[11]

Mike used his training to teach computer maintenance all over the nation for a private firm, but that meant a lot of travel. Mike says, "I started sitting in bars, drinking instead of going to the hotel room. Episodes led to one-night stands and drifting further and further from Brenda." And it led to role-playing—he, the husband and provider when he was home—and she, the perfect wife and mother. "We were each doing a very good job but did not know how to talk to each other," she recalls.

Sex on the road almost became an obsession. Why? "From my perspective, all my friends talked about sex. It was macho; okay to have affairs." Although he had been an altar boy in his youth, he had not been to church for years, except to get married.[12] A job promotion brought them to Texas near Fort Worth in 1986. By this time, Brenda had given birth to two sons. She

---

[11]This is such a common problem, one wonders why schools don't teach communication skills between male and female students. Deborah Tannen's book, *You Just Don't Understand*, would be an excellent textbook. More important, *every* couple who marries should be required by the state that issues the license, to take a course in communication skills and conflict resolution. See chapter 12 for more detailed suggestions.

[12]People who are not religiously active are much more likely to divorce. Mike's story illustrates why. Selfishness reigns over selflessness. The carnal man cannot see that the Commandments, such as "Thou shalt not commit adultery," are given for our protection.

did not know about his affairs. ("I trusted him so much that had he died and someone told me what he had been doing, I never in my life would have believed it," Brenda said.)

Mike's sexual antics became more daring. He had sex in their condominium complex with his secretary and with a neighbor who was one of Brenda's best friends! Why would he take such a chance? "Perhaps I wanted to get caught," he says now. Sex with the neighbor happened only once, but "her husband found out and approached me before Thanksgiving, 1987, and said he knew everything but would not tell Brenda because of the kids," Mike recalls.

His fear of exposure now became acute. "It was eating me up so bad that I began having anxiety attacks marked by 'hyperventilation,' shortness of breath, and perspiring. These attacks could happen anytime—on a plane, in a business meeting."[13] Brenda knew something was wrong but thought it was just business pressure. Then in February 1988, the neighboring husband told Mike that he did not think he could keep from telling Brenda. Mike said he himself would tell her the truth.

"I tried to sit down and tell her, but she blew up, went straight to their house to confirm it," Mike relates. She came back enraged. Brenda recalls, "I wanted to kill. If I had had a gun in my hand, he would not be alive. It was horrible. I tried to beat him." And the worst part of it is, this screaming confrontation took place in front of the two boys, ages nine and six. The horrified boys had never seen them argue about anything before, let alone about infidelity. "I regret that my children saw it," she said. It was the low point of their marriage, but for Mike, things got worse.

Early the next morning, she got up and said, "There is no way I can lie here beside you. GET OUT!" The boys screamed that he should stay. He was uncertain what to do, so she grabbed them and left. "That is what woke me up," Mike says. "I had a gun. I pointed it at my head and stared down the barrel for a while . . . God would not let me do it."

The next day he was on a trip. Brenda called him at his motel to tell him she was leaving permanently. Then she heard a ghastly sound on the other end of the line—a gasping, hyperventilating, anxiety attack that sounded as if he was having a heart attack. She changed her mind and said that she would be home when he came back.

---

[13]Two Scriptures come to mind: Proverbs 6:27–29: "Can a man scoop fire into his lap without his clothes being burned? Can a man walk on hot coals without his feet being scorched? So is he who sleeps with another man's wife; no one who touches her will go unpunished."

And 1 Corinthians 6:18: "Flee from sexual immorality. All other sins a man commits are outside his body, but he who sins sexually sins against his own body."

Brenda had already started going to Catholic church in a small Texas town to help her oldest son make his First Communion. When Mike came home, she suggested that they visit "Father B" (as Father Baltasar Szarka is known). Mike thought it was useless to talk to a celibate priest, but Father B "opened his arms to us and made us feel good as persons," Mike says. "He was there when I needed it." He was the first person to give them hope that their marriage could be restored and that Mike's tremendous guilt and feelings of worthlessness could be overcome. Everyone else, her friends and family, for example, told her to leave Mike. Father B suggested that they go on a Retrouvaille weekend, saying that he knew how much it had helped a number of couples. However, since the next one was some months off, Father B urged that they see a Christian counselor, who was of some help to Mike but not to Brenda.

IMPACT OF RETROUVAILLE ON MIKE AND BRENDA

"There is no way to explain what a Retrouvaille weekend is like," said Mike. "They teach a technique of communication—dialogue where you learn to express feelings. They do it in small steps. You write an answer to a question, exchange papers, and gradually the process helps get you in touch with your feelings. Lead couples share their own experiences through different phases of their lives. One couple we could really identify with took us through their romance stage, how happy they were at first, the disillusionment, and the misery stage. Their sharing was so powerful that it broke them up. Your heart goes out to them, though you are in misery.

"It was all so applicable. You go back to your room and tell each other that you both want the relationship to work. You share your feelings and basically rediscover—*retrouvaille*—each other. I found out things I had long forgotten—that we were still friends who still loved each other. After being married so many years, we found that our conversation had become so superficial. We had become self-centered," Mike said. "I was trying to get ahead and lost sight of the relationship. We were not as giving to each other. We were leading married singles' lives.

"I found out that I was not a bad person. I could be lovable and could be all things I wanted to be. I could learn to forgive myself and have new hope. We saw couples who had been through so much misery in their lives—adultery, drugs, the loss of children—to see them in their misery, and how they came out of it and are now shining examples of happy people *really is* motivating. It really makes you want that happiness in your marriage and to realize that 'God does not make junk.'

"I had never looked upon marriage as a sacrament, or its underlying principles. I said the vows, but they were just words. I had not internalized them. It was really moving. It gave me a different view.

"Saturday was a day when we were asked if anyone wants to share openly on how much this was doing for us. I said, 'When I learned that love is a decision, it gave me hope.' " Brenda added, "My parents did not back me up. My friends did not. They'd say, 'How can you say you want to stay with him? Why not leave him? Divorce him!' Only one girlfriend and Father B did not condemn me (for trying to save her marriage). People are more accepting if you divorce than if you stay with someone who cheated on you."

Both came away realizing that they had never been trained in how to be married. The weekend gave them hope for their marriage. However, they needed the follow-up sessions to learn "more tools, reinforced dialogues, values, and ideals," said Mike. "We learned the need to work at it to make it work, and learned through forgiveness, the trust and conflict management to understand that marriage *can* work."

Basically, Retrouvaille gave them both the vision of a healed marriage, the tools to work for it, and the heart to make essential personal changes. For example, Mike, who had started smoking as a way to avoid being with his wife (who couldn't stand the smoke), stopped smoking. He quit drinking when they were apart and now takes only a rare glass of wine at dinner with her. He spends much more time with Brenda and the boys. Mike and Brenda have continued to meet with their Retrouvaille follow-up group and have become leaders in the movement both in sharing on weekends and in scheduling four new weekends during 1992.

They both call the change "a miracle." As soon as they began genuine reconciliation at Retrouvaille, Mike's anxiety attacks *disappeared*. Home-life improved so dramatically that the boys blossomed. In the summer of 1991 when he was eight, their youngest son, Jacob, asked if he could take a pamphlet on Retrouvaille to a friend's house where the mom and dad "argue all the time." And on their anniversary, Jason, thirteen, wrote them a moving letter:

Dear Mom and Dad,

Thank you for being mine and Jacob's parents, and all that you do for me—helping me when needed, driving out of the way for me, taking me places, playing sports and board games, standing up for us, encouraging me to do whatever you think is good, and disciplining me when I have done wrong so I won't do it again. These are some of the things you parents do for us kids. You did it together, which really counts.

You stayed together mostly because you did not want to lose us or hurt us, and we respect you for making that decision. You don't know that if we listed all the things you do for me we would be talking or writing for the rest of our lives.

Happy Anniversary,
Jason

THE DIVORCE BUSTER

Michele Weiner-Davis is a family therapist in Milwaukee whom some call "the divorce buster" because she has developed a nonreligious strategy that has helped 85% of her patients save their marriages. She attracted enough attention to be asked by the American Association for Marriage and Family Therapy to give the keynote address to 5000 therapists attending their annual meeting in 1990. Using a form of short-term therapy usually only four to six sessions, she has helped people in troubled marriages find immediate solutions for their marital discord. Equally important, she has written a powerful book about her approach.[14] It is *must* reading for anyone who wants to transform a troubled marriage into a happy one.

She believes that

> ... divorce is not immoral or bad. In fact, in extreme cases, certain relationships are better off terminated for the health and well-being of everyone involved.... However, most people considering divorce do not fall into this extreme category. For example, research shows that the primary complaints leading to divorce are not physical abuse or addiction but, rather, lack of communication, lack of affection, and nagging. I've grown increasingly convinced that most marriages are worth saving simply because most problems are solvable. Or to put it another way, most unhappy marriages can be changed and therefore are worth changing.

Mrs. Weiner-Davis does *not* emphasize psychotherapy or delving into childhood trauma, which is of questionable relevance to marital discord. As she puts it, "Farewell, Freud!" And she is angered by the therapists with few solutions, who seem more interested in expensive, open-ended therapy. By contrast, she has developed a "Solution-Oriented Brief Therapy" that puts an emphasis on "finding solutions to marital problems rather than exploring the problem." It is based on what she calls a "fairly simple formula: doing more of what works and less of what doesn't. Couples learn to identify what they do differently when they get along, so that they can do more of it—and to identify unproductive patterns of interactions so that they can eliminate or do less of that."

What's most hopeful about her approach is that the effort of only *one* of the marriage partners can save the marriage. "Relationships are such that if one person makes significant changes, the relationship must change," she says. "Too many marriages go down the drain because each spouse is waiting for the other to change first."

"The purpose of this book is to tell you it is *not* too late to mend your

---

[14]Michele Weiner-Davis, *Divorce Busting*, Summit Books, New York, 1992.

broken marriage. If you have even the slightest interest in working things out, change is possible."[15]

Most people in unhappy marriages blame their spouse: "If she didn't nag so much, I would enjoy my life!" "He's gone so much, of course I'm miserable." But Ms. Weiner-Davis argues, "Diagnosing your spouse as the problem means that your microscope lens may be too narrowly focused. You are failing to notice how the habits you *both* have developed and the roles you've *both* played have contributed to your unworkable marriage. . . . If getting rid of one's problematic spouse was a solution, why would 60% of second marriages end in divorce?[16] If divorce were truly an answer, people would learn from the mistakes they made in their first marriage."

Space constraints do not allow me to illustrate with her case studies. But, some additional descriptions of her approach may be helpful. Instead of dissecting their relationship *problems*, she asks those seeking help to recall what they had done in the past *that had worked* before. Typically, couples talk about things they did that were *fun*. Why aren't they doing that now? One woman said, "Lately I've been feeling so bad, I haven't felt like spending time with Steve." But in not doing things that were fun with him, she acknowledged contributing to her bad feelings about the marriage.

One answer of *Divorce Busting* is novelty. If in response to Sue's complaining, the man starts sobbing, she's not likely to respond in the same old way (defending herself). Or George surprised his wife, Paula, by kissing her in the morning, instead of picking a fight. She then made him coffee, which she had not done in months . . .

There are striking parallels in the principles of "solution-oriented therapy" and Marriage Ministry. Quick examples.

1. *Divorce Busting* says, "People can and should stay together." One of the M&Ms: "We made a decision to stay together."

2. "If *you* want your marriage to change, *you* can change it," writes Ms. Weiner-Davis. And M&M: "I became aware that I needed to change, found how to change, and began to change."

3. "Blaming your spouse for your unhappiness is easy to do . . . but not helpful. [That puts] the solution out of your control." M&M: "I accepted my mate as she/he is."

---

[15]Ibid.

[16]This sixty-percent failure rate of second marriages is confirmed by demographers Arthur J. Norton and Paul Glick in "One-Parent Families: A Social and Economic Profile," published in *Family Relations*, January 1986.

4. "If *you* change *your* actions, *your* marriage will change," she writes. M&M: "I made an examination of my role in our marriage according to God's Word and changed accordingly with God's help."

This chapter has outlined three different strategies for saving the most deeply troubled marriages. Two are religious and one is secular in approach, but all have parallel requirements that the individual in a bad marriage must first change himself or herself. Then 80–90% of marriages can be saved. However, religiously oriented people can learn from *Divorce Busting*. And certainly, secular people can gain by involving the Lord.

ELEVEN

No-Fault Divorce:
The Need for Legal Reform

"Why then," they asked, "did Moses command that a man give his wife a certificate of divorce and send her away?"

Jesus replied: "Moses permitted you to divorce your wives because your hearts were hard. . . . I tell you that anyone who divorces his wife, except for marital unfaithfulness, and marries another woman commits adultery."

The disciples said to him, "If this is the situation between a husband and a wife, it is better not to marry."

—Matthew 19:7–10

When any state legislature shall pass an act annulling all marriage contracts, or allowing either party to annul it, without the consent of the other, it will be time enough to inquire, whether such an act be constitutional.

—Chief Justice John Marshall *The Trustees of Dartmouth College Versus Woodward,* 1819

"IF ELECTED, WHAT WILL YOU DO TO CUT THE DIVORCE RATE?"

During the 1992 Democratic Convention it seemed that every politician with a microphone trumpeted how "pro-family" he or she was. Of course, so did the Republicans at their convention. It prompted me to write a column suggesting a pro-family question to ask any candidate running for office— particularly those seeking an office in state government:

"If you are elected, what will you do to cut the divorce rate?"

"Expect a blank stare in response," I wrote. "It is the one pro-family question, I suspect, that has never been asked of a political candidate.

"Admittedly, divorce is rarely thought of as a political issue," I acknowledged. "But consider the impact of California's 1969 Family Law Act. It allowed a marriage to be dissolved when either the man or the woman simply declared that there are 'irreconcilable differences which have caused the irremediable breakdown of the marriage.' "[1]

This "reform" is popularly know as "no-fault divorce." It was a drastic change in the law. Before no-fault, marriage was considered a contract that could not be dissolved unless one party could prove the other was at "fault" for destroying the contract by adultery, desertion, and so forth. No-fault allows either partner to walk out of the marriage, even if the other spouse wants to save the marriage. A faithless husband or wife can run away with a lover and demand that the family home be sold to give them half its value! Thus, the innocent have to *subsidize* the guilty!

Yet California's no-fault swept through forty-seven other state legislatures almost without debate. The result has been devastating to marriage and families. No-fault is largely responsible for adding a half million divorces a year in America as can be seen in this table:[2]

Year	Number of Divorces
1970	708,000
1980	1,182,000

NO-FAULT CAN BE REFORMED BY STATE LEGISLATURES

California, the state that invented no-fault divorce, has found fault with it. In 1988 the legislature passed laws increasing the likelihood, duration, and amount of spousal support especially in marriages of long duration. And judges were asked to defer the sale of a family home if it were deleterious to the children. The result: Divorces have dropped by 5% in California as the population has increased by 7%.

Illinois Representative Bernie Pedersen offered a bill to allow couples to apply for one of two types of marriage license: either a *Marriage of Commitment*, expected to be lifelong, which can be dissolved only with proof that one's spouse was at fault due to adultery, etc.—or a *Marriage of Compatibility* that either can walk out of—today's no-fault law.

This bill would give couples a unique option to choose a traditional marriage license with legal teeth to their wedding vows. Similar bills were introduced in Florida and Washington State. None passed by July 1992.

Another reform would be to allow courts to consider "fault" in making decisions on the awarding of property, alimony, and child custody.

---

[1] Invoking "irreconcilable differences" in court is now tantamount to one spouse handing the other an Old Testament "certificate of divorce."

[2] By 1970 divorces had nearly doubled from 393,000 in 1960 to 708,000. One factor in the divorce explosion of the '60s was the "Sexual Revolution" spurred by the pill, and the willingness by women to become more sexually active. Also, as the number of divorces grew so did its public acceptance.

MARRIAGE AS A SACRAMENT

Why was no-fault's impact so sweeping? It "destroyed the religious roots, the moral structure of marriage," writes Dr. Lenora Weitzman in *The Divorce Revolution*,[3] the nation's most cogent indictment of no-fault.

First, she outlines America's religious foundation of marital law: "Traditional legal marriage was grounded in the Christian conception of marriage as a sacrament, a holy union between a man and a woman, a commitment to join together for life: 'to take each other to love and to cherish, in sickness and in health, for better, for worse, until death do us part.' [Before 1969] divorce laws reinforced those responsibilities, rewarding spouses who fulfilled their marital obligations and punishing those who did not. The radical innovations of contemporary no-fault laws are highlighted by this historical context," she writes.

Another element of the sacramental marriage was its lifelong commitment. Marriage was permanent, a joining of people "till death do us part." Therefore, when divorce did occur, the man was expected to be financially responsible for a former wife until she remarried or died. Thus, the traditional marriage had different expectations for men and women. "The courts say that the husband has a duty to support his wife, that she has a duty to render services in the home, and that these duties are reciprocal," wrote Professor Homer Clark[4] in his book, *Domestic Relations*.

WHY WAS NO-FAULT CONSIDERED A REFORM?

Feminists chafed at this division of labor. Weitzman wrote, "By promising housewives lifelong support, the law created disincentives for women to develop their economic capacity. Legal marriage designated the husband as head of the family, with his wife and children subordinate to him." Therefore, feminists were among those pressing for no-fault, to "eliminate the anachronistic legal assumptions about women's subordinate roles and recognizing wives as full equals in the marital partnership." How? No-fault awarded property equally to husband and wife, assuming that both would work to support themselves. Women also thought reduced strife would "facilitate the parties' ability to cooperate in postdivorce parenting."

Another force for reform came from conservatives wanting to reduce divorce rates! When California Assemblyman Pearce Young held hearings on divorce in 1963, conservatives expressed alarm at the high breakup rate in California compared to other states. (In 1960 the ratio of divorces to marriages was 47% in California compared to 26% elsewhere in the U.S.) Weitzman notes that Judge Roger Pfaff, who had pioneered in the work of the Los

---

[3]Lenora J. Weitzman, *The Divorce Revolution*, The Free Press, 1985, xi.
[4]Professor Homer Clark, *Domestic Relations*, 1968, p. 231.

Angeles conciliation court, argued that the "contagious disease of divorce" could be stopped by statewide adoption of premarital and predivorce conciliation procedures based on his Los Angeles model.

Divorce lawyers and family court judges really wanted to get the "morality" issue out of divorce. They said their goal was to stop arguments over who is most at fault for the marital breakdown—to reduce the hostility and acrimony in divorce proceedings. Law Professor Herma Hill Kay of the University of California at Berkeley testified that the "divorce procedures themselves add to the bitterness and sense of personal failure . . . by requiring that at least one party be found guilty of marital fault." She urged restructuring the divorce process so that people "who are entitled to divorces can get them with the least possible amount of damage to themselves and to their families." However, Professor Kay did support the establishment of a Family Court that would provide counselors to assist in making arrangements for child custody and a financial settlement in an objective, rational way.

Weitzman reports that a fourth source of pressure for no-fault came from divorced men who charged that "the divorce law and its practitioners were in league with divorced wives to suck the blood, not to mention the money, of former husbands." They contended that the existing law allowed women to "take their husbands to the cleaners" in alimony and property settlements, and they urged that divorce treat men and women "equally."

California Governor Edmund G. Brown in 1966 appointed his own "Commission on the Family," which strongly supported the idea of a Family Court for both liberal and conservative reasons. Conservatives hoped that the Family Court would help save troubled marriages through mandatory counseling, while "liberals hope it would improve the divorce process, structure more equitable financial settlements, and facilitate postdivorce parenting." It was this Commission that drafted the no-fault reforms, and proclaimed that no-fault was a new way to "preserve the family."

In a side note, Weitzman says, "The lack of opposition to the no-fault reform from such likely foes as the Catholic Church may be explained in part by the reform rhetoric of both the Governor and the Commission."

However, feminists, divorce lawyers, and hostile men who wanted reform were a stronger combined force than the conservatives interested in saving the family. The bill that was passed in 1969 was a flat-out liberal bill that amputated the Family Court at the last minute. (The California Bar Association said it opposed having nonlawyers advising clients!) Judges said that a Family Court would be "too intrusive." And the Assembly thought that it would be expensive. What remained was a radical law that:

- Removed the grounds needed for divorce, eliminating the need to prove guilt or fault;

- Permitted one spouse to terminate a marriage against the will of a spouse who wanted to save the marriage;
- Eliminated "fault" as a grounds for divorce, or as a basis for dividing property;
- Set new standards for alimony and property awards that seek to treat men and women equally.

NO-FAULT TURNS MARRIAGE COMMITMENT UPSIDE DOWN

Only now, a quarter of a century later, can we see with clarity how revolutionary the no-fault change was not simply in divorce law but also for marriage itself. It literally eliminated the moral framework undergirding marriage. Lenora Weitzman summarizes it well:

> When the new law abolished the concept of fault, it also eliminated the framework of guilt, innocence, and interpersonal justice that had structured court decisions in divorce cases. With this seemingly simple move, the California legislature not only vanquished the law's moral condemnation of marital misconduct; it also dramatically altered the legal definition of the reciprocal obligations of husbands and wives during marriage.

By wiping out the moral structure supporting marriage in the law, no-fault turned America's very concept of marriage upside down:

- Instead of a lifelong commitment, marriage became a partnership of convenience that either spouse can unilaterally terminate without the consent or agreement of the other spouse.
- Instead of presuming that marriage is a societal strength to be preserved, that can be broken only with sufficient cause, *no* grounds are needed to obtain a no-fault divorce, nor does any fault have to be proven.
- Instead of punishing marital misconduct, such as those who run off with a paramour, by awarding property to the "innocent" spouse— no-fault often *subsidizes* the guilty's exit by forcing the sale of a family home and splitting the assets equally between the guilty and innocent.
- Instead of recognizing that a wife who pours herself into children and home has contributed as much to a marriage as a husband, and meanwhile has lost economic value in the marketplace, and thus needs the continuing support of a husband whose wages are far greater than hers will ever be—no-fault cut the percent of women getting alimony to only 15.5%.
- Instead of awarding alimony till death or remarriage, no-fault gives alimony less often and in declining sums, usually ending after one to four years, to push wives into becoming "self-sufficient even if she has been a homemaker for thirty years."

VOICES OF THE DIVORCED

Marriage Savers is packed with suggestions for what individuals and churches can do to save marriages. Many examples have been offered that demonstrate how to save nine out of ten marriages, but *the United States as a whole will not dramatically reduce its divorce rate without restoring the moral frame-work of marriage by removing the perverse incentives no-fault gives people to walk away from their marriage vows.* Foolish laws of the last generation must be repealed or overhauled by this generation.

To communicate the "unanticipated, unintended and unfortunate consequences" of no-fault, Lenora Weitzman makes the pain clear with dozens of quotes from people hurt by the current system. Any state legislature that holds hearings on no-fault divorce will hear voices such as these:

A divorced woman: "You may want to kill the guy, humiliate him and make him pay through the nose, but go and try to find a lawyer that will help you do it. All they know how to say is, 'It's not relevant. It's not relevant.' I've heard it a hundred times like a broken record. Why isn't it relevant? He sleeps with my best friend and they say, 'You have to learn to forget it. . . .' What did I get? Not one red cent."

Another divorced woman: "This law legitimizes desertion. It says you do something that is wrong, and we won't call it wrong. We'll say it's okay. Well, it's not okay. It is not okay for a man to just walk out on his family when we haven't done anything wrong."

Many divorced men and women are simply stunned that their spouse can get a divorce without their consent. As two men said:

"I really could not believe it! I felt totally powerless. She didn't ask me what I wanted . . . She didn't even tell me she was going to file. . . . One day I got home from work and found the papers in the mail."

"Now, *she* walked out on *me*, and what do *I* get? Nothing. Nothing. And what does *she* get? She gets half my house, half my pension. . . (etc.) For what, I ask you? For running off with a jerk psychologist. That's my reward?"

A divorce lawyer said: "I've seen men get away with the most outrageous conduct and they still get half the property. . . . I've seen instances where women have literally been driven to psychiatrists and psychologists; they are extremely emotionally upset and disturbed by their husbands' wrongful conduct. He flaunts it to her, knowing that it will have no effect upon the required equal division of the community property."

Another attorney: "So often the only asset of any consequence is the family residence. When a couple divorces, it is ordered sold and the children are deprived of their home. . . . There should be a way to keep the home intact for the children."

A woman was unable to refinance the house to pay off her husband. She thought she could use the $600 in support she was promised to pay off the mortgage, but "No bank would give me a loan and no one was willing to accept my spousal support as 'income.' One loan officer said to me, 'Spousal support and child support don't count. Most men stop paying them and we have to repossess the house. Another bank officer said he had seen 'hundreds of women like me.' He was 'sympathetic' but said that I was too poor a risk to get through the loan committee."

According to the Census Bureau, alimony or spousal support was given in only 15.5% of divorces in 1989, and instead of lasting until death or remarriage, it is now typically given for only a year or two. Few women who have devoted their lives to their families, especially if they are over fifty, can get decent-paying jobs. As one victim put it: "An older woman is a pariah. . . . One employer told me I was too old to learn the job. Another assumed to think I'd bankrupt his medical insurance plan. . . ."

More than four-fifths get no alimony. As one woman said bitterly, "He doesn't believe in the alimony laws. I could support myself, that was his feeling—either by work or public assistance. . . . He didn't care. It wasn't his problem."

As I reported earlier, 42% of ten million women raising children alone are not even eligible for child support.[5] Of the 5.7 million who are, only half get full payment; a fourth get partial payments, and 1.25 million receive nothing. A woman with no support says: "My own children, like thousands of others, have been denied their economic birthright by a father who swore he would never pay a dime in child support, and by courts that have failed to enforce their own orders. The truth is that if a father chooses to be uncooperative, there is little a mother can do."

On the other hand, "no-fault divorce has also encouraged opportunistic behavior by faithless wives," says Dr. Bryce Christensen of the Rockford Institute. "Even when the wife has first betrayed her husband and then initiated the divorce, no-fault divorce frequently gives her one-half of the household assets *and* custody of the children." John Ackeret of Topeka, Kansas, wrote me: "Let me start by saying I am a divorced father. I have no children—only divorced mothers have children. This is by decree of the courts. Every time the court makes a decision on custody, they give the children to the mother. In one study we did in Kansas the judges gave the children to a state institution more often than they did to the fathers. . . . I tried for ten years to get some type of shared time with my children. I thought that because I was a good father and an active participant in their lives that this was in the best interest of the children. I was wrong. It was denied repeatedly, and I was punished every time I requested it. I finally got the message: 'All you bastards want is my money.' "

Another father from Scranton, Pennsylvania, said that he pays $285 per

---

[5]"Child Support and Alimony: 1989," Bureau of the Census, September, 1991.

month for one child plus total medical coverage. He, too, had to fight legally to see his daughter. "I have never missed a support payment," he writes. Nevertheless, he had to spend $10,000 in legal fees even to see her. This is clearly unjust. He says plaintively, "You have no idea how it feels to be separated from your child for extended periods of time and then to meet with total frustration in the judicial system that will not give fathers equal time with their children."

Another father in Delano, California, angrily wrote me: "The courts assume that childbirth creates a person who puts the life of the child ahead of all else. I suggest the courts look into the real world. Mothers are using drugs—using child-support money to buy them. Mothers are putting children in danger around boyfriends. . . . Mothers are using children as weapons to get even with perceived wrongs from their ex-spouse—driving great voids between them."

Sociologist Richard Gelles of the University of Rhode Island estimates that there are 313,000 parental kidnappings after a divorce or separation.

Dick Wood, director of a group in Iowa called "Fathers for Equal Rights," provides convincing evidence that the mothers are themselves responsible for much of the lack of child support because many refuse to allow fathers to visit the children. He says, "A Bureau of Census study of September 1991, 'Child Support and Alimony: 1989' reports that a high percentage of fathers with visitation rights—79%—*are* current on child support. But of those without visitation or joint custody, only 44.5% are current on child support." I have confirmed these figures with Census.

Thus, nearly *twice* as many mothers and children could get child support simply by giving the fathers access to their own kids! "The payer (of child support) should have access to the children so they can spend time with their children," says Woods. Of course, he's right.

Clearly, the problem is not just "Deadbeat Dads" but "Mad Mommies"!

Victor Smith, director of "Dads Against Discrimination" in Portland, Oregon, adds: "No-fault has created a lot of irresponsible women. Women are responsible for filing two-thirds of all no-fault divorces." He's close to being correct. The National Center for Health Statistics reported in 1991 that only 32.5% of divorces are initiated by men; 60.7% are begun by women; and 6.8% by both husband and wife. While women are twice as likely to file, often the cause is a man's moving out of the house.

At a deeper level, the problem with no-fault divorce is that it clearly failed to achieve one of its primary goals of reducing hostility and bitterness. Its injustice fosters deep, seething, permanent anger.

CONTRAST WITH THE BRITISH SYSTEM

In sharp contrast to U.S. "no-fault laws," which treat older stay-at-home mothers particularly harshly, British law is astonishingly sympathetic to the plight of older homemakers. Weitzman writes, "The English law seeks to maintain the standard of living that prevailed during the marriage. This standard is based on a conception of marriage as a life-long union in which the husband has an ongoing obligation to 'maintain' his former wife."

For example, in a long-term marriage to an affluent man, earning $72,000 after taxes, English courts awarded a woman the home, financial security, and lifelong support. As one judge makes clear, she had "earned" decent treatment: "She's an older wife, and that has to be considered. He has to protect her—he has to house her and give her a portion of his income and security for the future. She's entitled to the total assets a wife should get: She's been married twenty-seven years and had three children. She's doing everything a wife can do except keep him amused."

JAMES SUNDERLAND TRIES TO SAVE HIS MARRIAGE

An argument can even be made that no-fault divorce in America is unconstitutional at two levels. First, the local court granting a divorce hears only one person alleging that "irreconcilable differences" have led to the "irremediable breakdown of the marriage." If the other spouse says the marriage can be saved, the court ignores that person and thus denies that spouse "due process." Second, The U.S. Constitution, in Article I, Section 10, clearly prohibits any state laws that retroactively take away a contractual right. The exact wording states: "No State shall . . . pass any . . . Law impairing the Obligation of Contracts. . . ."

James and Bronte Sunderland married in 1962, seven years *before* California's 1969 no-fault law was passed. The earlier law required that a person who wanted to leave a marriage had to prove the partner was "at fault" for breaking the contract. Sunderland argued that the state had no right to apply the Family Law Act's no-fault provision retroactively to his marriage. He said that violated Article I of the Constitution, and he took his case all the way to the U.S. Supreme Court in 1992.

In 1988 Bronte Sunderland filed for divorce. James filed a response that contended there was a reasonable possibility of reconciliation. The case went to trial May 18, 1990. Bronte claimed that there were "irreconcilable differences," and that she was unwilling to participate in counseling. Her attorney argued that closed the case.

In the trial, James's attorney disagreed, asserting that the judge had only heard "the petitioner's uncross-examined testimony" in a "unilateral way." The judge interrupted, warning impatiently: "I'm not going to waste very much time on this, because I disagree with that 100 percent. It's virtually a presumption of irreconcilable differences when one of the parties gets up there and says, 'I don't want to live with him anymore.' "

However, he reluctantly allowed a very brief cross-examination and testimony by Mr. Sunderland, who outlined three reasons why he thought that the marriage was salvageable:

- He acknowledged "deep sorrow" for his "failure in the marriage," expressed an "abiding and deep love" for his wife, and made a public commitment to personal growth and change.
- He said, "We are both professing Christians who perceive the Bible as God's Word. By our creed, divorce is not permitted except in extreme circumstances, such as adultery. None of these circumstances exist in our case."
- Finally, he reaffirmed his commitment to the original vows of 1962.

Bronte was asked if James had ever expressed anything but a "sincere and heartfelt and unequivocal desire to reconcile . . ." Although she replied, "He has in (sic) no time indicated other than a desire to reconcile," the divorce was granted.

The California Court of Appeals affirmed the decision, even though it agreed that James "correctly points out that marriage was, by statute, a civil contract" under California law when he married; but it rejected his assertion that the 1969 law violated the Constitution's Contract Clause, which forbids states from applying laws retroactively. But there's not one known case of a contested divorce being denied since no-fault became law.

The California Supreme Court denied review. Therefore, James Sunderland took the case to the U.S. Supreme Court for its 1991–92 session, arguing that it gave the Court "an important opportunity to restore the original understanding of the Contract Clause of the Constitution." As part of his case, Sunderland quoted an extraordinary opinion written in 1819 by the famous early Chief Justice John Marshall that is eerily prescient in foreseeing Sunderland's case:

> When any state legislature shall pass an act annulling all marriage contracts, or allowing either party to annul it without the consent of the other, it will be time enough to inquire whether such an act be constitutional.

"That occasion has now arrived," claimed Sunderland's brief. Regrettably, the Court disagreed, refusing to hear the case, as in 98% of Supreme Court appeals. But California Appeals Court cited an 1888 Supreme Court case, *Maynard versus Hill*, which contains this remarkable endorsement of marriage:

> Marriage, as creating the most important relation in life as having more to do with the morals and civilization of a people than any other institution, has always been subject to the control of the legislature. It is an institution, in the maintenance of which in its purity the public is deeply interested, for it is the foundation of the family and of society, without which there would be neither civilization or progress.

Why isn't *Maynard versus Hill* viewed as a support for marriage? I do not know. I have read the case and do not understand its lack of support.

WHY DID PRO-FAMILY GROUPS SUPPORT SUNDERLAND?

Focus on the Family, the Family Research Council, the Institute in Basic Life Principles, Concerned Women for America, *et al.*, thought the case important enough to file an *"amicus"* brief backing Sunderland. Why?

"The *amici* share a common interest in legal protection of marriage and in the support and encouragement of families of two natural parents and their children as the central unit of human society," it said.

"This brief chronicles the shocking evidence of increased poverty, suicide, illness, school failure, crime, drug abuse, and second-generation divorce produced by no-fault divorce laws. The social costs attendant to divorce are so high, and still rising, as to impeach no-fault as sound law or public policy. The result of no-fault is no less than disastrous. . .

"No-fault laws not only have helped the divorce rates rise by denying non-consenting spouses a right to be heard and encouraging divorce instead of reconciliation efforts, but they send a message that marriage is not legally significant. The state, ignoring marriage as a contract and the parties' contractual obligations, allows divorce for no reason and prefers quick divorce to the difficulty of repairing a damaged marital relationship. . . . No-fault divorce does not require efforts to save marriage. It devalues marriage and defeats the expectations of the nonconsenting spouse, facilitating a family breakup that risks harm to children. No-fault works counterproductively, even nonconstructively, to create alternative family arrangements that society cannot afford. The research studies cited in this brief lead to the conclusion that *any state interest in perpetuating no-fault divorce is indefensible from any reasonable point of view, whether economic or social*" (emphasis added).

WITCHER VERSUS WITCHER

Another legal attempt to overturn no-fault is being pursued by Phyllis Witcher, whose husband, Murray Witcher, filed for divorce under Pennsylvania's no-fault law. Unlike Sunderland, she did not try to save her marriage, but she did feel that, because she had suffered physical abuse while married and he had since abandoned her, he was at fault. He conceded in court that she was a "supportive wife." She argues that his fault should be considered when distributing property. At the time the divorce was filed in 1987, Pennsylvania law permitted consideration of "fault" in the distribution of property.[6] But the law was changed in 1988 to no-fault, and property became a 50-50 split. "How could this be justice," she asks, "if equity in the law is de-

---

[6]Fault can still be a factor in awarding property or alimony in thirty-eight of fifty-three U.S. jurisdictions (states, Washington, D.C., Puerto Rico, etc.).

nied and the innocent spouse is prevented from receiving recovery relative to that innocence but the guilty spouse is allowed to profit from his or her wrongful behavior?" She hoped for a 70-30 split. (To pay her mortgage she has had to rent out rooms to strangers.)

The case has also attracted the support of pro-family groups, such as the Free Congress Foundation, the Family Research Council, and Phyllis Schlafly's Eagle Forum. Why? The Family Research Council says the case "provides a rare and possibly unique opportunity for a constitutional challenge to laws that allow people to violate their wedding vows with impunity, knowing that the laws governing the institution of marriage will enact no penalty for such misbehavior, no matter how grave."

However, the odds are quite small that any legal case will overturn the momentum of twenty-five years of no-fault divorce. "There is a well mobilized constituency in favor of no-fault—the lawyers and feminists," says Michael Schwartz of the Free Congress Foundation. He notes that even Lenora Weitzman, author of *The Divorce Revolution*, is not calling for repeal of no-fault laws but only for changes that "treat women better."

CALIFORNIA FINDS FAULT WITH NO-FAULT DIVORCE

Interestingly, the first state to find fault with no-fault was California— where it all started! And Weitzman's book inspired the change. State Senator Gary Hart (no relation to former U.S. Senator Gary Hart of Colorado) heard Professor Weitzman, then of Stanford University (now Harvard) being interviewed on the radio. He told me in a 1987 interview: "I am not an attorney and have never been divorced, but I was impressed by what Professor Weitzman said. I bought her book during a vacation, read it, and felt it raised very important issues.

"As a result, I took a couple of her ideas and introduced them in legislation. Last year (1986) one was signed into law on child support. When there is a child support order by the court, instead of relying on the father to make the payments on behalf of his ex-wife, what we did was make it automatic" through wage withholding. "The previous law only did a wage assignment if there was a problem. You had to petition the court. A lot of women are too poor to get an attorney. We made it simplified and less costly." This California law became a model for a federal welfare reform act passed in 1988, now beginning to take effect: automatic child-care withholding.

Weitzman reported that 38% of wives do not work outside the home and that those who do, earn only 44% of their husband's income. Only a quarter work full-time, year-round. Why? Their priority is the family—not a career. Yet, as noted above, 85% of divorcing women get no alimony, 42% have no child-support orders, and another 12% get nothing though they have a child-support order.

Senator Hart summarized the impact: "We now see, after the dust is settled, that it (no-fault) is harming women. If you believe Weitzman, and I do, men make out better in divorce. We have created a law that may in fact be *causing* people to split! In California we have the highest number of single-parent families in the nation—900,000 (in 1987) and 505,000 are as a result of divorce. They stand a five times greater chance of being in poverty. I believe these laws are contributing to divorce. I am interested in seeing that these laws are at least neutral."

He created a "Senate Task Force on Family Equity" that included state senators, judges, and divorce attorneys to suggest solutions for the problem.

THE CALIFORNIA NO-FAULT REFORM PACKAGE

After evaluating the faults of no-fault law for nine months, the task force developed what I call a "California No-Fault Reform Package":

- Require the court to consider specified, child-related criteria to determine whether to temporarily defer the sale of the family home, in order to minimize the adverse consequences of divorce on minor children. (It is bad enough for children to lose their dad and his income. To have to also sacrifice home, friends, and school is excessively unfair.)
- Extend the parental duty of child support to age twenty-one unless the child is married, or is in the military.
- Change the primary standard for spousal support awards to the "standard of living" established during the marriage, except in marriages of long duration, where the standard would be equalizing the standards of living between post-divorce households.
- Require payment of retraining expenses by the supporting spouse.
- Require that requests of post-decree disputes over implementation of visitation or custody be given access to mediation within sixty days.

In my August 29, 1987 column, I argued that these proposals, seen together, "would swing the economic incentive away from encouraging divorce—toward encouraging families to stay together." If they became law, the senior demographer on marriage and divorce, Barbara Foley Wilson of the U.S. Center for Health Statistics, predicted in my column that the impact would be to "lower the divorce rate sharply."

At the time I wrote my column, bills to make the suggested changes had passed the state Senate, but all had gone down to defeat in the Assembly.

Virtually none of the state's religious or moral leaders, such as California's Catholic bishops or Protestant leaders, had testified for the legislation. The net result was silence from the strongest possible advocates of change. So I concluded that column:

Major groups concerned with moral values, preservation of the family, and children, have been silent. Only the Lutherans supported the bill. Where were the Catholic bishops? Out to lunch. Ditto for the Jews, all other Protestants, the Moral Majority, concerned Women, the PTAs.

RELIGIOUS LEADERS PUSH THROUGH REFORM BILLS

However, in 1988 two of the key bills *were* passed because religious leaders *did* lobby actively for change:

1. Judges were asked to consider whether it was in the best interest of the children "to temporarily defer the sale of the family home, in order to minimize the adverse consequences of divorces on minor children."
2. Raise the primary standard for spousal support to the "standard of living" established during the marriage, particularly for marriages of more than ten years' duration.

Frances Teller, co-president of the Los Angeles Council for Jewish Women, pulled together a host of women's groups who lobbied state legislators. She told me, "Although the primary wage earner is usually the man, we feel that the wife has had a share in making his income possible." The bills passed. However, they sat on the governor's desk unsigned. He was undecided about whether to sign the spousal support bill. Father William Wood, the Jesuit priest who directs California's Conference of Catholic Bishops, wrote a letter to the governor:

> I am sure you are fully aware of the Catholic Church's teaching on the indissolubility of marriage.... We nonetheless realize that divorce has become an inescapable reality of life for thousands of men, women, and children, subject to the pressures and confusions of life. The aftermath of divorce is generally devastating for all concerned, but because of the inequities in either the law or the process, the cycle of recovery has tended to the advantage of the man, rather than the women and children.
>
> The emotional and financial scars for the mother and children not only tend to last longer, but statistical evidence indicates they grow deeper and more painful as the time passes. The phenomenon of women and children living in poverty is a specter whose shadow grows longer with each passing year.

It was as if leaders of the faithful remembered Malachi 2:16: "For I hate divorce,' says the LORD, God of Israel." Father Woods' eloquent appeal was persuasive. New spousal support became law in 1988, as did the deferral of a sale of the family home.

What has been the impact of the bills on the divorce rate?

Joanne Schulman, an attorney for the Senate Task Force, who has since returned to her Oakland practice, told me in 1991 that "There has been no change in the deferral of the sale of a family home. Courts will not do it. But men now have to pay spousal support until she remarries or dies." And a higher percentage of mothers are getting child support due to wage garnishment.

The encouraging result is that the number of divorces in California has begun to edge down as these numbers suggest:

Divorces in California		*U.S. Divorces*
1987	135,000	1,166,000
1988	131,000	1,167,000
1989	125,000	1,163,000
1990	128,000	1,175,000 (prov.)
1991	*	1,187,000 (prov.)

Thus, California's divorces fell by a significant 5% from 1987, the year before passage of the legislation, through 1990. In these years, the state's population actually grew by 2 million, or 7%.

California's drop in divorces also cannot be attributed to a fall of U.S. divorces. Clearly, they grew by 21,000 in those years (and are the highest rate of any nation in the world). Barbara Foley Wilson, America's top divorce demographer, who predicted this outcome in 1987, says: "The fact that California divorces declined 5% while the population grew 7% following passage of legislation requiring greater fiscal responsibility to dependent family members, appears to have had the effect of giving some people pause in their headstrong pursuit of individual freedom. Perhaps the legislation provided incentives for them to work on positive aspects of what was once a loving and supporting relationship." Had the number of divorces remained constant at 1987's level of 135,000, California would have had 21,000 more divorces through 1990.[7]

A RATIONALE TO REPEAL NO-FAULT

A rationale to *repeal* and not merely *reform* no-fault is growing in the legal community. Judge R. Michael Redman of Twin Falls, Idaho, wrote the lead article, "Coming Down Hard on No-Fault," for a special 1988 issue of *Family Advocate*, a national journal for family-law attorneys. He writes: "The radical increase in the divorce rate coincides nicely with the adoption of *easy* divorce. Although *no-fault* and *easy* theoretically are not the same, in practice they have become identical. . . . No-fault has spawned the popular argument that fault should play no role in property division or alimony . . . even though the supporting arguments are illogical."

His 1987 article outlined an argument that lies behind recent attempts to repeal no-fault by having couples choose a "Marriage of Commitment" or

---

[7]Data for 1991 is unavailable; budget cuts forced a halt in collecting it.

a "Marriage of Compatibility": "The conflict between no-fault divorce and fault-based property division and alimony awards reflects a much broader conflict within society—between those who view marriage as a relationship of convenience and those who view it as the cornerstone of society. . . . As long as that dichotomy exists, one will also exist within the legal system. That dichotomy will disappear only if we redefine marriage to coincide with the marriage of convenience. Since I suspect that will never happen, I suggest instead that we abandon no-fault divorce as inconsistent with the very nature of marriage."

Judge Redman quotes court decisions along this line, such as *Maynard Versus Hill* and *Loving Versus Commonwealth* in which the U.S. Supreme Court said, "Marriage is one of the 'basic civil rights of man' fundamental to our very existence and survival." The Iowa Supreme Court rejected the argument that "cohabitation without marriage is so pervasive in modern society it must be recognized as permanent and the parties logically have the . . . right of married persons" when it stated in *Laws Versus Griep*:

> The policy of this state is that the *de jure* family is the basic unit of the social order. . . . The policy favoring marriage is not rooted only in community mores. It is also rooted in the necessity of providing an institutional basis for defining the fundamental relational rights and responsibilities in organized society. This policy would be subverted if a person could gain marital rights without accepting correlative marital legal responsibilities.

Judge Redman added,

> When the commitment to marriage is conditional, we modify the model so that any citizen can "divorce" himself from society and its laws simply because he or she doesn't like the way things are going. . . . The lifetime bonding of a man and a woman is not only for their mutual benefit but for the benefit of society. The law has fostered this bond and wishes to protect it for its own sake. No-fault divorce helps to destroy the bond, benefits and the institution.

> Certainly there are situations where divorce is justified, and can be granted on fault grounds. . . . The state must decide from which side of its mouth it wishes to speak. The easy divorce *does not* promote the institution of marriage; it belittles and relegates it to a relationship of temporary convenience. It is a cancer that attacks the very fiber of social cohesion. . . . If marriage is the foundation of civilization and if marriage and its longevity are promoted by the state, then divorce is an offense against the state. Divorce indicates a failure to fulfill the most significant of commitments. Therefore, if the destruction of this social unit is substantially the fault of one party, that fact should be considered in court,"

wrote Judge Redman. (See Repeal #4 following.)

A SUMMARY OF THE GAINS AND LOSSES OF NO-FAULT

Dr. Bryce Christensen, editor of a monthly publication, *The Family in America*, published by the Rockford Institute, gave a "hard look at a soft law" in a special issue, "Taking Stock: Assessing Twenty Years of 'No-Fault' Divorce" in September, 1991. He asks whether there have been any gains of no-fault: "Legal scholars have noted a 'dramatic decline in the number of litigious actions' after no-fault swept through the states. But he cites Weitzman's book as evidence that acrimony is not dissipated. And Judith Wallerstein's *Second Chances* reports "a relatively high prevalence of unresolved rage among men and women who had gone through 'no-fault' divorces ten years earlier." My mail from readers confirms the impression.

No-fault added a half million divorces a year but has *not* even reduced the percent of unhappy marriages. Christensen writes, "According to national surveys taken from the early 1970s to the late 1980s, the probability that men and women will report being 'in a poor marriage has *increased*' slightly. At the same time, a decreasing proportion of couples report 'marital happiness,' apparently because of a reluctance by men and women to 'commit fully' to a union they expect may not last." His source is a 1991 article in *Journal of Marriage and the Family* by Norval Glenn.

More important, he says, "No-fault put the state—for the first time—in the absurd position of requiring a license for the pronouncing of public vows which the state subsequently regards with indifference. . . . By making it easy to void a wedding vow without incurring legal guilt, the state discourages self-sacrifice and emotional commitment to the marriage."

Christensen says amen: "Taxpayers who have preserved their own marriages through personal integrity and sacrifice may find it puzzling and offensive that state officials appear so willing to dissolve marriages and to collectivize the costs." Therefore, he concludes, "Legal integrity, social health, and political liberty all require of the nation's lawmakers a critical reassessment of 'no-fault' divorce."

FOUR REPEAL STRATEGIES

I know of four attempts to repeal no-fault divorce by state legislators in recent years. The first three outlined below were introduced in Washington State by Senator Ellen Craswell. None was passed by either house. The fourth was proposed by Oklahoma Representative Ernest Istook and was passed by Oklahoma's House in 1992, but failed in its Senate.

1. *No-fault is replaced with the traditional fault system.* The bill's summary: "Fault-based grounds for divorce are reinstated, eliminating divorce based on 'irretrievably broken' marriages."

2. *Couples have a choice: fault or no-fault.* Instead of the prevailing no-fault system, "parties may enter into a written marriage contract providing

that the marriage may not be dissolved except by mutual consent, or by the fault of one of the parties," says the bill.

3. *Judges may consider fault in deciding property division, alimony, and child support.* No-fault divorce is permitted, but courts can consider "the nature and extent of marital misconduct" in awarding alimony, child support, and property division. A philanderer can divorce but can't expect to get half the value of a home, child custody, and may have to pay alimony.

4. *Judges may deny a divorce involving children for incompatibility.* In any action for divorce when the parties have any minor children of the marriage, the court shall not issue a final order" for divorce for "at least six months," says this bill passed by the Oklahoma House. And if children are involved and the issue is "incompatibility" and "both parties to the action do not consent to the grounds of incompatibility, the court may refuse to grant the divorce on such grounds . . . if the court finds that such divorce would not be in the best interests of the minor children."

Some discussion of each proposed repeal of no-fault is warranted:

Replace No-Fault with a Traditional, Fault-Based System

Senator Ellen Craswell, President Pro Tem of the Washington State Senate, told me, "Ultimately, the ideal solution is to return to fault divorce, which would make marriage like any other legal contract, which cannot be broken by one party acting unilaterally. One party would have to show that the bill, SB 5705, offers a rationale: 'Some studies indicated that in jurisdictions where divorce is more difficult to obtain, or when economic consequences are more equitably distributed, there may be a greater tendency to put additional effort into the quality and viability of the marriage relationship."

The bill would reinstate "Fault-based grounds for divorce" and eliminate no-fault divorce "based upon 'irretrievably broken' marriages." Dissolution would be granted for a wide range of reasons: "consent obtained by force, duress or fraud; marriage under the age of seventeen; adultery; impotence or various sexually transmitted diseases not known at the time of the marriage; 'infection' with a fatal disease; abandonment for one year or more; habitual and ongoing addiction to alcohol or drugs, imprisonment for two years or more; sexual or physical abuse or 'extreme mental cruelty;' legal insanity; or separation for two consecutive years."

The bill had absolutely no support. Not even the Catholic Church testified in favor of it. There were no hearings. And all of the press criticism of Craswell's bills focused on this proposed total overhaul rather than on the compromise bill of giving couples a choice.

With its near-zero chance of success, I believe that reformers should forget about a frontal repeal of no-fault at this time.

Couples Have a Choice: Fault or No-Fault

Senator Craswell said her primary hope was placed "upon a voluntary marriage covenant that allows a couple to enter into a contract that would, in effect, exempt no-fault divorce." This approach would "allow a couple to establish a contract when they first get married, that would not be able to be broken unless fault were shown on the part of the other party, such as adultery, desertion, imprisonment, drug or alcohol abuse." The bill, SB 5707, was passed by one committee in the Senate, but died in another committee.

Actually the bill as introduced would grant those marrying, or those who are *already* married, the opportunity to "enter into a written consent that the marriage may not be dissolved except by mutual consent or by the fault of the other party by a preponderance of the evidence." An already married couple could thus add legal authority to their wedding vows.

However, this return to traditional marital law would be optional. Alternatively, couples applying for a marriage license could get the current version that permits "no-fault" divorce.

Thus, any married couple in the state and every newlywed could make a conscious choice about what kind of marriage they want. That choice could offer a profound educational lesson. This compromise repeal has the greatest chance of success. It does not challenge no-fault directly. Few newlyweds would consciously choose no-fault, so it would be a rolling repeal that would painlessly reverse it over time. Illinois and Florida legislators have proposed creative versions of the repeal outlined below.

Judges Should Consider Fault in Property Distribution

Marital misconduct ought to be a factor in distributing property in child custody disputes and in awarding alimony. As Judge Redman wrote, it is "illogical not to do so." A reader wrote me that she divorced her husband of fifty-two years after repeated drunken attacks on her. He had not worked since 1963, and she paid for their little house. He is now living with another woman, but he got the court to order his ex-wife to pay him $11,000 as his share of the house and $258 per month from her retirement!

Judges need the freedom to consider whether the evidence points to one spouse as primarily responsible for the divorce. If so, that party should not benefit financially from the innocent spouse. No-fault demands that the innocent should subsidize the philandering and/or violent spouse.

Judges May Deny a Divorce Involving Children

Oklahoma Representative Ernest Istook sees another evil of no-fault divorce: "What motivated me was how divorce is devastating the family. It is linked to crime, drug use, teenage pregnancy, decreases in school performance. It becomes a worsening spiral when we have a generation of kids without role models, who don't know how to be parents, who are not encouraged to keep the family together. In a divorce, what is in the best interest of the child? It is an issue that is never taken into account. If a husband and wife have three kids, only two sides are presented in court. The other three interests are not considered.

"This legislation would introduce a new fact—that these children have an interest in the survival of the marriage. If there are no grounds for divorce other than incompatibility, then you have to consider children not just in terms of custody and financial issues—but the basic question of whether a divorce will be granted," said Istook.

MARRIAGE OF COMMITMENT VERSUS MARRIAGE OF COMPATIBILITY

Illinois Representative Bernard Pedersen proposed a similar two-tier compromise bill, but brilliantly labeled the two options. He says, "We would include a section on the marriage license indicating whether the parties have chosen a 'Marriage of Commitment,' or a 'Marriage of Compatibility.'"

What's the difference?

A. *A Marriage of Commitment* reinstitutes the traditional marriage that could "not be dissolved" except by providing evidence of fault. Clearly, couples choosing a "Marriage of Commitment" would be making the most profound choice, *giving legal teeth to the vows* recited in most weddings.

B. *A Marriage of Compatibility* might better be called a "Marriage of Convenience," as Judge Redman labeled it. Of course, it is simply the no-fault divorce now on the books in forty-eight states, allowing either partner to walk away with no questions asked. It is divorce for a disposable society that discards marriage partners as routinely as college students change roommates.

Representative Pedersen, who has been married "forty-two very good years," says "I was brought up to believe marriage is a lifelong commitment. I would tend to favor making divorce harder to do. If a couple has to make a little checkmark on the marriage certificate, choosing between a 'Marriage of Commitment' or a 'Marriage of Compatibility,' it will capture their attention. The guy and the gal might have second thoughts about what they are doing. It is much better to discuss these issues before they are married rather than afterward," said Pedersen.

"However, this is completely voluntary. It is not a mandate."

A state legislator, Representative Daniel Webster, introduced a similar bill in Florida, calling his option, "Covenant Marriage." He explains: "What we took was the law of twenty years ago, and we put it side-by-side next to no-fault. You can choose to get married under a Covenant Marriage or under no-fault. We are trying to get people to think through whether they are making a commitment for life or not." They would have to sign notarized documents that they understand that "a Covenant Marriage may not be dissolved except by reason of adultery," and they "promise to seek counsel in times of trouble."

One important difference in Webster's version is that he requires "presentation of proof that both parties have attended premarital counseling by a clergyman or marriage counselor" so that they fully understand the significance of the choice.

It seems to me that Pedersen's language describing the choice between fault and no-fault ought to be combined with Webster's requirement for premarital counseling before the couple makes the choice.

However, opposition to these bills in Washington, Illinois, and Florida was so intense that as of July, 1992, they had not even been approved by one House. Why? How could anyone object to giving those applying for a marriage license a choice?

OPPONENTS OF GIVING MARITAL OPTIONS

For an answer, the Everett, Washington, *Herald* editorialized:

"The idea of legislating divorce reform carries with it the happy thought that holding bad marriages together would somehow 'be good' for society . . . Unhappily, unworkable marriages are not new. Suffering them needlessly is the stuff of 19th century novels.

"Keeping bad marriages together is no solution. It assumes that Washington residents are too stupid to see the possibilities for improving their marriages unless the state strong-arms them."

But there is a more profound response. No one twists arms of brides and grooms to take a vow to "love and cherish" one another "for better, for worse, in sickness and in health, till death us do part." If they live up to those vows, the marriage *will* last. If couples do not want to make such a commitment, they should not use those words. Indeed some marital vows are ". . . for as long as love shall last." But if couples choose to add legal teeth to underscore their commitment to a lifelong marriage, the state should honor it. Saving marriages is in the interest of the couples involved, their children, and of society as a whole.

On the other hand, most people do not know how to save a bad marriage. One goal of *Marriage Savers* is to provide evidence that even the worst marriages can be saved, if people try, even very belatedly, to live up to their vows. Half the people who go on Retrouvaille weekends are *already* separated or divorced. Yet 80% of those marriages are saved.

Oklahoma Representative Ernest Istook sees another evil of no-fault divorce: "What motivated me was how divorce is devastating the family. It is linked to crime, drug use, teenage pregnancy, decreases in school performance. It becomes a worsening spiral when we have a generation of kids without role models, who don't know how to be parents, who are not encouraged to keep the family together. In a divorce, what is in the best interest of the child? It is an issue that is never taken into account. If a husband and wife have three kids, only two sides are presented in court. The other three interests are not considered.

"This legislation would introduce a new fact—that these children have an interest in the survival of the marriage. If there are no grounds for divorce other than incompatibility, then you have to consider children not just in terms of custody and financial issues—but the basic question of whether a divorce will be granted," said Istook.

His bill is a bold but only partial repeal of no-fault. First, a judge can order a six-month delay when children are involved, with the hope for reconciliation. But a more important provision would allow a judge to "refuse to grant the divorce" in a case involving kids if the issue is only incompatibility. The key sentence: "In any action for divorce on grounds of incompatibility and the parties have any minor children of the marriage, if both parties do not consent to the grounds for incompatibility, the court may refuse to grant the divorce . . . if the court finds that such divorce would not be in the best interests of the minor children of the marriage." (A similar bill was introduced in Iowa by state Senator Bill Dieleman, but it did not get out of committee.)

The impact of divorce on children is always devastating. Research indicates they are much better off living with parents who argue than in *losing* a parent. A divorce does *not* stop arguments, but the loss convinces kids that *they* are not loved by the person who leaves. And they deserve to be given priority when the only cause for the proposed divorce is incompatibility. (If there's physical or sexual abuse, that's different.) Parents can learn to get along with each other for a few years until the children are out of the house. Then their selfishness is not as harmful.

WELFARE REFORM

Another major legal strategy to save marriages is welfare reform. The problem is mammoth—much more vast than can be treated in this book. However, from the perspective of a Marriage Saver, there are two issues:

1. *Illegitimacy Rates Have Soared.* Births out of wedlock have shot up from 5% of all births in 1960 to 27% in 1989. It is two-thirds of blacks, and a fifth of whites.
2. *Divorce Pushes Many into Poverty.* A divorced mother with kids is six times more likely to be poor than a married mom.

And 84% of the 4 million added to poverty rolls in the 1980s are mothers and their kids. Many will end up on welfare, when each single mother gets a "paycheck" of between $8,500 and $15,000, counting the value of various public programs, depending on the state. "She will continue to receive her 'paycheck' as long as she fulfills two conditions:

- She does not work, and
- She does not marry an employed male."

"I call this the incentive system made in hell," says Robert Rector in an article in the Summer 1992 issue of *Policy Review*.[8]

He distinguishes between "material poverty," and "behavioral poverty," defined as "a breakdown in the values and conduct that lead to the formation of healthy families, stable personalities and self-sufficiency." While there is little malnutrition in America, *behavioral poverty is abundant and growing*, such as growing illegitimacy. Every increase in welfare benefits increases behavioral poverty. Women raised in single-parent families are 164% more likely to have children out of wedlock themselves. And if they do marry, their marriages are 92% more likely to end in divorce than women from two-parent homes.

Therefore, Rector, a conservative, makes some radical suggestions:

1. "Require work in return for benefits," at least of mothers whose children are in school. That attaches a cost to welfare and will make a private sector job look attractive.
2. "Reduce benefits," particularly in high-benefit states.
3. "Require responsible behavior." Unmarried minors must live with their moms. Those who have additional babies get no more money.
4. "Establish paternity and enforce child-support payments," reducing the incentives for macho males to sire children.
5. "Increase the rewards to responsible couples who marry," thus encouraging marriage.
6. "Provide tax credits or vouchers for medical coverage to all working families."

Clearly, the agenda Robert Rector has outlined will be costly. And it is only one man's view. But he's right that welfare must be transformed from a reason *not* to marry into an incentive *to marry*. Rector's proposals are the most promising welfare reforms I have seen in twenty-five years of covering welfare.

FOR CHRISTIAN ATTORNEYS

Reforming divorce law is not an issue for laymen. But it is an ideal one for Christian attorneys. Let me speak to you Christian lawyers directly.

Most of you make a good living, but what are *you* doing to serve the Lord? What kind of "pro-bono" work are you doing that could help hold

---

[8]"Requiem for the War on Poverty: Rethinking Welfare After the L.A. Riots."

thousands of families together? Why not be a Marriage Saver? What could be a higher calling? My dream is that you Christian attorneys will take on this mission so effectively that there will not be just one lone legislator in an isolated state making a case to save families—but a phalanx of legislators to be reckoned with in every state legislature. You have the know-how to make the case. How many politicians of both parties in your state now claim to be "pro-family?" Virtually all. Ask them, "What will *you* do to cut the divorce rate in this state?" Then outline alternative answers:

A. *Reform no-fault by making walking away more expensive:*

- Increase fiscal support of children and custodial parents.
- Defer the sale of a family home if children are involved.
- Require mediation to resolve visitation rights (and thus increase the odds of fiscal support and reconciliation).

B. *Repeal different aspects of no-fault:*

- Create a two-tiered marriage license system—a "Marriage of Commitment" for life, or a "Marriage of Compatibility."
- Require consideration of fault in awarding property.
- Allow judges the discretion to deny divorces to couples with children who are claiming only incompatibility.

As you pursue legal reform, remember to *call on religious leaders to testify!*

TWELVE

Community Marriage Policy: How to Cut Your Town's Divorce Rate

Our concern as ministers of the Gospel is to foster lasting marital unions under God and to establish successful spiritual families. Almost 75% of all marriages are performed by pastors, and we are troubled by the more than 50% divorce rate. Our hope is to drastically reduce the divorce rate among those married in area churches.

—Community Marriage Policy, October 1991
(signed by pastors in three Illinois cities:
Peoria, Moline, Quincy)

*"'I hate divorce,' says the L*ORD *God of Israel."*

—Malachi 2:16

AN OBITUARY OF MARRIAGE AS A LIFELONG DREAM

The institution of marriage is dying. Middle-aged readers will remember growing up hearing our parents say that "Marriage is for life." We all aspired to the dream. Now, however, we could write an obituary of the death of that dream of lifelong marriage. Many don't assume that the dream will come true anymore. The notion that marrying is a gamble—often a losing one—has replaced that hope.

Of the three siblings in my family who married, only my own marriage is still intact. I am the "lucky" one. Both my sister and brother are divorced. One marriage lasted ten years; the other, twenty. I helplessly watched the terminal illness of dying commitment but felt powerless to reverse it. Their painful experience inspired me to search for answers. The solutions outlined in *Marriage Savers* come too late to help them. Hopefully, many others will find help in time to save their marriages, or those of family or friends.

An editor of this book attending his 25th high school reunion, was stunned to learn that of forty classmates, only four were still married to an original spouse! Several had married and divorced *twice*. Yet there was no sense of shame or regret. In fact, one former classmate, introducing his girlfriend, gushed, "Divorce was the best thing that ever happened to me."

It wasn't for my sister. After her divorce she became profoundly depressed and a chronic alcoholic unable to hold a job. One morning she was found unconscious, lying on the floor of her apartment. She was revived but suffered irreversible brain damage and has lived in a nursing home for five years. She is only forty-eight.

A George Barna poll found three-fifths of Americans strongly believe that "God intended for people to get married and stay in that relationship for life." However, only 55% of U.S. adults live in a married couple relationship today! That's the lowest percentage in history. Why? Here's the autopsy:

Two powerful forces are killing marriage: divorce and cohabitation.

1. *Divorces* have tripled since 1960. Six out of ten new marriages today are dissolving.

2. *Cohabitation* has risen sixfold and for millions is a substitute for marriage; for others, a precursor of divorce.

Divorce is so commonplace that young people *fear* marriage. In 1991 some 41 million Americans had never married—double the number in 1970!

CHURCHES HAVE IGNORED THE ISSUE

What has been the reaction of America's churches to these trends?

In October 1981, only eight weeks after starting to write my column, "Ethics & Religion," I began one with these words:

> It is time to acknowledge that the American church is partly responsible for the soaring divorce rate. According to one study, 88% of all U.S. marriages are blessed by the church . . .[1]

> However, America's divorce rate is soaring off the charts. In 1960 there were 393,000 divorces. By 1979 that figure had grown to 1,170,000—tripling in less than a generation!

> Yet the United States is the most churchgoing modern nation in the world. According to the Gallup Poll, 40% of Americans say that they attended church or synagogue in the last week—a figure that has remained stable for a decade. (It was 42% in 1991.)

> By contrast, Gallup found that only about 10% of Europeans attended services, and only about 2% of Japanese attend some form of religious service. One would think that with the much weaker role of religion in those countries that their divorce rates would be much higher than in this religious nation.

> But America's divorce rate is twice that of Europe. And it is five times higher than that of Japan, where most people are atheists!

> It is time for America's religious leaders to examine their all-too-casual attitude toward marriage and divorce.

---

[1]The number cited here is a bit high. In 1960, 83% of first marriages were performed in the church. By 1990, it was 74%.

The indictment is as valid today, twelve years later, as when I wrote it. The vast majority of America's 300,000 churches are only "blessing machines," preparing couples for weddings—not *lasting marriages*. Cases in point:

Sermons: Rarely does a weekly churchgoer hear a sermon on marriage or divorce, let alone on the pervasive and destructive pattern of cohabitation. Surely, Scripture is clear on these issues, as is the sociological evidence, but pastors fear offending their congregations and losing members. In their cowardice, pastors fail to minister to the needs of their flock.

Singles: Many churches in America have programs for "singles," but they rarely go beyond social events. Who offers course material for seriously dating couples on how to put Christ at the center of their relationship?

Premarital counseling is being offered more widely now than in 1981, but it is usually so perfunctory that it rarely prompts any couple to break their engagement. With a 60% divorce rate, church-sponsored training for engaged couples should be rigorous enough for couples with weak relationships to discover it themselves *before* the wedding.

Married couples: Certainly the church's greatest oversight is the already married couple. What church has a conscious strategy to strengthen the marriages of its church members? In a dozen years of writing my column, I have come across only one local church that sponsors a retreat like Marriage Encounter to help *every* couple recapture their love. A pastoral mission that should be central to local church life is absent from more than 99% of local churches. Indeed, it is difficult to find any church with a program in place to strengthen existing marriages other than couples' Bible studies. In more than a decade of covering conventions of every major religious denomination, I've heard the words "marriage" or "divorce" only twice. Several parachurch ministries, such as Marriage Encounter and Marriage Enrichment, have sprung up among lay people, and they are quite effective, but national religious leaders turn a blind eye to the issue. They don't feel compelled to help their local churches deal with the destruction of the family. Other than evangelization, however, there *is* no more urgent mission of the church than binding men and women in joyous, lasting marriage.

Troubled marriages: True, most pastors counsel couples whose marriage is disintegrating. Sadly, by then it is often too late. Only Catholic lay people from the Marriage Encounter movement have developed Retrouvaille to intervene with help. Unfortunately, it is only in 58 of 184 dioceses because it is simply not an issue for the hierarchy. There is nothing comparable in any Protestant denomination.

The separated and divorced: An increasing percentage of churches do have an outreach program for this group, but it is primarily social, not religious. It is aimed at helping divorced singles discover each other and remarry. That is compassionate but unbiblical. And it is a monumental failure. Sixty percent of divorced people who remarry—divorce again! Children with stepparents do no better in school, or in picking a mate than do children from what is euphemistically called "single-parent families." (More accurately, in six out of seven cases they are "fatherless families.") At the minimum, churches should sponsor programs to help the separated and divorced to reconcile with their spouses—at least to the level of bringing civility to their relationships for their own sense of peace and for the sake of their children. Remarriage of separated and divorced couples to each other should be the long-term goal. Special classes also should be added for children of the divorced.

MARRIAGE-SAVING COMES FROM THREE BRANCHES OF CHRISTIANITY

Conversely, I have seen a number of churches that are pioneering with creative strategies that could:

- avoid bad marriages before they begin;
- improve 90% of existing marriages;
- save even four-fifths of bad marriages and restore them to health;
- slash the divorce rate itself in any community where churches are cooperating as Marriage Savers.

Over the years, I have written dozens of columns on the most creative innovations by America's religious community in helping to preserve existing marriages and even in saving marriages of the already separated and divorced. What is particularly encouraging is seeing strands of excellence in each of the three broad streams of American Christianity: Roman Catholic churches, evangelical Protestant churches, and mainline Protestant congregations. Some marital pioneering can be seen on a national basis in every community—particularly in the Catholic Church. Other shining examples are the work of a single pastor. But each branch of American Christianity has reason for pride as well as humility. However, I have seen no church implementing more than a handful of strategies with a proven potential to save marriages. A quick review of *Marriage Savers* solutions is in order:

THE CATHOLIC COMMON-MARRIAGE POLICY

No denomination has been more rigorous in demanding preparation of young couples for marriage than the Roman Catholic Church. Its innovations have both breadth and depth. They can be seen in almost every diocese, and they are a multi-pronged effort. I first wrote about Catholic marital pioneering in a 1981 column quoted earlier: "Perhaps it is time for America's Protestant denominations to take a look at what is happening in two-thirds of America's Catholic diocese," that have adopted a "Common Marriage Policy" —"aimed at getting the church out of the marrying mill," says the Reverend Tom Lynch, the former leader of the Family Ministry of U.S. Catholic Bishops. "Our goal is to help couples see if they have the psychological maturity and faith maturity for marriage." How? I explained in that 1981 column: First, most dioceses will no longer automatically marry any teenage couple who walks in the door, unless the young woman is pregnant. The Newark Diocese, for example, requires a six-month waiting period. Only time can test the maturity of the love. . . .

> Second, as part of their Pre-Cana meetings, both the engaged man and woman are asked to sit down separately and fill out a Premarital Inventory, giving quick answers to more than one hundred questions on such sensitive matters as children, finances, religion, communication, and sex. By comparing their answers, a priest can quickly spot key differences and prompt needed and often-painful dialogue by the couple.
>
> "Most couples don't want anything like this," says Lynch."They say, 'Everything is wonderful. Why is the church holding our marriage up?' But for every 100 couples, 8 to 10 engagements are broken or canceled as people realize that they are not ready for marriage."
>
> Bravo! The test of effectiveness of premarital counseling should be how many engagements are broken. Better, broken engagements than broken marriages.

In 1985, Father Joseph Protano, then Director of Marriage Preparation for the diocese of Providence, told me, "The people getting married were simply not prepared for marriage. But the program was very controversial when it started." Why? Engaged couples found that regardless of which priest they went to in Rhode Island, there was a Common Marriage Policy for every Catholic church, that included:

Preparation period. Arrangements for a wedding had to be made six months to a year in advance in order to give the couple "a solid insight into the responsibilities and joys of marriage," said Protano. Of course, many couples find they can't reserve a hall for the reception in less than six months, but most couples, once they have decided to marry, want to do it in much less time. Stretching out the engagement allows time for the church to help the couple deepen their relationship, not plan for the wedding.

Mentor couples, older couples with solid marriages, rather than celibate priests, are trained to do most of the marriage preparation. In Providence, 253 "Coordinating Couples" were told by Protano, "This is your sacrament. We religious learn from you." There is a strength in having male-female teams work with engaged couples to provide a more wholistic view than even a married Protestant pastor can give, as well as more time than he typically can spare. Also, *mentoring is a joyful ministry.*

Premarital inventory. From the beginning, most Catholic preparation programs used some form of a premarital inventory to give the couples an objective view of their agreements and conflicts, strengths, and weaknesses.

The man and woman answer a questionnaire separately, and the results are compared. Ideally, mentor couples use the results to probe those areas of conflict or immaturity (see chapter 6).

Marriage Instruction classes are offered on such substantive subjects as money, communications, children, and religion. Three different forms of instruction are offered to Catholics. From the weakest to the strongest, they are:

1. *Pre-Cana Classes*: usually held in an all-day Saturday session.
2. *Evenings for the Engaged*: They meet usually 3-4 evenings in the home of mentor couples.
3. *Engaged Encounter*: an intensive weekend retreat that helps most couples deepen their skills of listening and sharing. It is so rigorous that a tenth of the attendees decide that they should break their engagement.

Clearly, this is a far more demanding marriage preparation program than is found even in the strongest Protestant churches. Protestant pastors tend to define their marriage preparation in the number of counseling sessions that are required. Many have no requirements at all. On average, a couple will meet with a pastor three times—six at the outside. Typically, there are no "mentor couples," no minimum time requirements, no weekend retreats such as Engaged Encounter to help a couple improve communication skills, no premarital inventory to help a couple assess their maturity, no religious ceremonies other than the wedding, and little or no instruction on substantive issues such as money, or sex.

CATHOLIC LEADERSHIP WITH THE ALREADY MARRIED

The Roman Catholic Church lay leaders also deserve credit for creating two very powerful programs for the already married:

1. *Marriage Encounter,* a weekend retreat led by lay couples, which has involved 1. 5 million American couples since it was introduced to the United States by Catholic priests. More than thirty academic studies confirm that eight or nine of the couples who go, fall back in love with their spouse! This movement is one that has penetrated denominational lines into ten Protestant denominations. But together, Protestants are only about 300,000 of attendees (see chapter 9).

2. *Retrouvaille* (French for *rediscovery*), begun by Marriage Encounter leaders who felt that the Marriage Encounter program was not reaching couples with deeply troubled marriages. It follows a similar weekend retreat format, with the important difference that its leaders are couples who nearly broke up—before they learned to heal their marriages. About half of attendees of Retrouvaille are already separated or divorced, yet about eight out of ten marriages are saved. Unlike Marriage Encounter, which is available in all

parts of America, Retrouvaille was only in a third of the nation's dioceses in 1992 but growing rapidly (see chapter 10).

EVANGELICAL LEADERSHIP IN MARRIAGE PREPARATION

On the other hand, Catholic premarital programs often teach little or nothing about what Scripture says about marriage, divorce, or relationships. The best evangelical Protestant churches excel in preparing young couples with a biblical foundation for marriage. Catholics often sidestep the issue of cohabitation, let alone premarital sex. Again, strong evangelical churches will not knowingly marry any couple who is cohabiting. Many Baptist churches will insist that a cohabiting couple separate and live apart for several months.

Strong evangelical churches also refuse to marry any couple who is either not a member of the church or who has not "accepted Christ as their Savior." They see the marriage preparation period as a time to evangelize young couples.

One problem for Protestants, of course, is that the more demanding of engaged couples a church is, the more likely the couples are to go to another church that is less demanding.

One of the model programs that *Marriage Savers* has spotlighted were created by a single Baptist pastor, Dr. Jim A. Talley. For twenty years he was the "pastor of singles" at the First Baptist church in Modesto, California, where he worked with about 10,000 single people during those years. While serving there, he created a powerful course for the seriously dating couple, called "Relationship Instruction" (chapter 5).

Any couples who take this course must agree in advance and sign a contract that they will:

— Not be sexually active;
— Limit their time together to 140 hours over four months;
— Be mutually exclusive—no outside dating;
— Complete the course even if the relationship breaks up;
— Avoid discussing a possible engagement between themselves.

Slightly more than half of those who take the course do not marry, but of those who do, less than 10% get divorced! There's a real Marriage Saver!

MAINLINE PROTESTANT INNOVATIONS

Mainline Protestant churches make the fewest demands of engaged couples but are the most open to learning from successful innovations by others. For example: Marriage Encounter and Engaged Encounter have penetrated denominations such as the Episcopal Church, United Methodist, Evangelical Lutheran, and Presbyterian Churches. In fact, there is a "United Marriage Encounter" that is ecumenical by design and nondenominational in its structure.

It was an Episcopal priest, Father Dick McGinnis, who created "Marriage Ministry" for seriously troubled marriages in his church, St. David's Episcopal church in Jacksonville (see chapter 10). Seven couples whose marriages had once been on the rocks but healed, developed seventeen "Marriage Ministry" principles common to their recovery, such as:

— Make a decision/commitment to love Christ, mate, self
— Make a decision to stay together
— Accept my mate as he or she is
— Begin to look at myself as needing change, find out how to change, and begin to change.

The seven original couples have now shared their stories with thirty-three other deeply troubled marriages at St. David's. Thus far, *none have divorced* after five years—a remarkable track record of saving marriages!

Also, the most widely used premarital inventory, PREPARE, was developed by a Lutheran psychologist, Dr. David Olson of the University of Minnesota, and was first widely used in Catholic and Lutheran churches. More than 100,000 couples a year now take PREPARE, and 20,000 Catholic pastors, counselors, or mentor couples have been trained to give it. Among the clergy, the vast majority are mainline Protestant pastors. Given to the male and female separately, the 125 questions can predict, with 80% accuracy, which couples will divorce! More important, the couples' responses, when compared on a computer report, clearly provide an X-ray of the strengths and weaknesses of the relationship. However, the results are not handed to the couple but are presented during at least two counseling sessions by a pastor or mentor couple. PREPARE is so effective an instrument that about 10% to 15% of engaged couples break their engagements, and the rest are helped to strengthen their relationships. See chapter 6.

Dr. Olson created a very similar relational instrument called ENRICH, which is designed to help a pastor or counselor assess the strengths and weaknesses of a marriage (see chapter 8). Since about half of newlyweds are horrified at the conflicts that emerge soon after the honeymoon, ENRICH is a valuable diagnostic tool in spotting areas of conflict and helping newlyweds find constructive solutions. About 50,000 couples a year now use ENRICH increasingly—in mainline and Catholic churches.

A COMMUNITY MARRIAGE POLICY

Most of these innovations developed within one part of the Christian world and were virtually unknown across denominational lines. Yet the most creative innovations, such as the Catholic "Common Marriage Policy" is not theologically unique. (Protestant churches are not theologically opposed to a minimum engagement period, the use of mentor couples, and so forth.) Similarly, the teaching of biblical principles of marriage could be picked up from the evangelicals by Catholics and Lutherans. Of course, they all use the same Bible.

Indeed, the potential of the best marital innovations to be adapted across denominational lines is beautifully illustrated by the success of Marriage Encounter and Engaged Encounter moving out from the Catholic Church to the Episcopalians, Presbyterians, and Lutherans, and so on. Similarly, many Catholics now use PREPARE/ENRICH developed by a Lutheran.

Nevertheless, so many churches are doing so little to strengthen marriages that something is needed to jump-start tens of thousands of marriage-saving programs. What could spark that change? The answer to this puzzle was suggested to me a decade ago by the Reverend Bob Hoover, a Presbyterian pastor in Massilon, Ohio: "*All the churches in a community ought to unite in setting some standards of what it means to get married in a church.*"

He gave me the idea of taking the Catholics' "Common Marriage Policy" and attempting to forge in a local area a Catholic/Protestant consensus that might be called a "Community Marriage Policy." My theory was that if every pastor in town *knew* that all other pastors in the area were going to make some minimal demands of engaged couples, all might be emboldened to demand more of them. Therefore, whenever I got a chance to speak to local groups of pastors, I tried out the idea.

SOME FAILED SPEECHES

In 1983, *The Shreveport (LA) Journal* invited me to speak to local clergy, as did newspapers in Long Beach, California, and Biddeford, Maine. That gave me the opportunity to ask pastors explain, for example, the Catholics' "Common Marriage Policy." Then I asked, "Wouldn't it make sense for Protestants to join Catholics in setting some minimal standards of marriage preparation? If Catholics are requiring six months of preparation, could Protestants agree to *any* minimum time period?

The response was polite but cool. Pastors, however, expressed anguish about the wedding business. I took notes. Dr. D. L. Dykes, pastor of the First United Methodist Church, was candid: "Many of the hundred couples who come to us to be married are living together. There is a lack of the unconditional commitment, the unconditional love, in which each person really means to 'take thee to have and to hold, to love and to cherish, till death do us part.' Instead, many individuals believe, 'If you don't meet my needs, it is okay to get out of it.'" But he never refused to marry a couple. Why? "They'll get married anyway."

At the opposite extreme was Reverend Larry Pyle of the First Assembly of God in Long Beach: "I refuse more weddings than I perform. I refuse to contribute to the divorce rate in our society. I require six hours of counseling, because during that time, we've had couples decide not to get married. We give compatibility tests, which can reveal to the couple that they are drastically divided on who is the head of the family, the number of children desired, whether the wife is to work."

A Catholic priest in Biddeford, Father Leo Polselli of the Most Holy Trinity Church, blurted out, "Of the thirty couples that I marry, I enjoy doing only five. I am dismayed by fifteen of them. Do you say, 'No, you can't get married,' and turn them off to the church? I give them the basics and have a sick feeling in the pit of my stomach."

THE *COMMUNITY MARRIAGE POLICY* IDEA

In speeches to the clergy of Columbus, Georgia, and Lakeland, Florida, I sharpened the focus to a "Community Marriage Policy" that would be acceptable to the entire spectrum of local Christian churches: a minimum preparation period for engaged couples of four months (a compromise between the Catholics' six months and the no-minimum period among Protestants); the training of older couples with solid marriages to be "mentor couples" who would meet with the engaged; the requirement of a premarital inventory; attendance at an "Engaged Encounter," or some other retreat for engaged couples; teaching them key biblical doctrines on marriage and divorce; and encouraging all presently married couples to attend "Marriage Encounter, or a "Marriage Enrichment" weekend retreat.

The response was encouraging. More than 100 pastors in Columbus seemed enthusiastic, and Lakeland pastors gave more than perfunctory applause. But I never heard anything further from either group of pastors and doubt that anything lasting occurred. There was something flawed with my approach, but I could not figure out what.

MODESTO'S COMMUNITY MARRIAGE POLICY: THE NATION'S FIRST

Therefore, I was prompted to do something unprecedented when asked by *The Modesto Bee* to speak to the clergy of Modesto, in central California, in September 1985. As the paper's executives looked on, I began with a prayer:

> Lord, you know that I have failed every time I have tried to create a "Community Marriage Policy" in other cities. I ask you to give me your words that would move the hearts of those here. And I ask for ears to hear what you would want these pastors to do to cut the divorce rate in Modesto.

From the corner of my eye I could see my editor and publisher squirming and turning red. But I plunged ahead, trusting the Lord:

"Marriage-saving answers can be seen in Catholic, evangelical, and mainline churches. But they are not learning from each other. Stretching out engagements increases the odds that couples will make mature choices. If Catholics are requiring six months of marriage preparation, can Protestants agree to four months? Catholics are training lay couples as mentors and routinely administer a premarital inventory to help the couple measure compatibility. Don't those steps make sense for your churches too? On the other hand, Jim Talley, from First Baptist in Modesto, created Relationship Instruction for seriously dating couples, which has a divorce rate of *under 5%*! Evangelicals do a better job teaching Scripture than Catholics. Can Catholics learn from evangelicals to teach the engaged, biblical verses on marriage and divorce? Lutherans, Episcopalians, and other mainline churches have adopted Engaged Encounter and Marriage Encounter as ways to bond couples. My wife and I went on an Episcopal Marriage Encounter, and we fell back in love with each other. Shouldn't *every* church encourage *every* couple to go on a weekend?" I asked.

"What I want you to consider is an agreement, a covenant that stretches across denominational lines so that it means more to get married in any Modesto church than it does before a Justice of the Peace. One reason that many Protestant churches don't make many demands is fear that the couple asking you to marry them will go down the street to some "Marrying Sam" with no demands. But what if *all* pastors in Modesto agreed to some minimum standards that are designed to cut the divorce rate?

"First, I think that couples would accept your demands and later, even thank you for them. Second, I think that if churches really cooperated—*you could slash the divorce rate in half in Modesto!* What's needed is a "Community Marriage Policy" that you all agree to that sets minimum standards for anyone who wants to get married in a Modesto church."

I felt odd, preaching to preachers—a reporter with no seminary training. But I pulled out my Bible and read a number of verses from Malachi 2, ending with "'For I hate divorce,' saith the Lord God of Israel." And I added, "I am not an absolutist on divorce. There are times when divorce is warranted—particularly if there is physical abuse. But it seems to me that the church has a responsibility to do all it can to strengthen the odds that any given couple will bond together for life. In particular, there needs to be a willingness to learn from churches outside one's own tradition. And there needs to be an identifiable "Community Marriage Policy" supported by all pastors, whether Catholic or Protestant. For all churches have a common interest in saving marriages."

MODESTO'S PASTORS RESPOND

When I finished, the applause was vigorous. My prayer was answered in a way that only the Lord could devise. One of those seated in the audience was Jim Talley of the First Baptist Church of Modesto, whose marriage-saving pioneering I had praised. He saw the need of a Community Marriage

Policy but also spotted a hole in my concept that should have been obvious to me, a writer. *My idea was not in writing!*

After I left town, Jim was led to do what I should have thought to do—summarize the Community Marriage Policy on one page! He formed a committee of pastors to review and revise it. They approved an eloquent preamble in which pastors, for the first time in any American city, formally expressed anguish over the high divorce rate and set a stirring goal written by Talley: "Our hope is to radically reduce the divorce rate among those married in area churches."

But it was just a draft, signed only by the committee. Therefore Jim and the committee had me cross the country months later in January 1986 to repeat my speech to a wider cross-section of Modesto clergy.

One pastor asked a hard question: "What if the woman is pregnant? Would you still insist on four months of preparation?" I asked a Catholic to respond, since the Catholic Church requires six months. "Our experience is that shotgun weddings don't last. Therefore, we usually say, 'The preparation we are giving will increase the odds that your marriage will make it. We urge you to go through the process even if the baby is born early.' "

An evangelical pastor said, "I won't marry a couple unless both have accepted Christ as their Savior. That goes beyond your standards."

I replied, "I admire your stand, but I don't think that every pastor would be comfortable with it. This is an area of theological difference where churches are not likely to agree. Any pastor who signs the Policy is only agreeing to *minimum* demands. Any pastor can add requirements. Do the rest of you agree that "accepting Christ' should be optional—not a community requirement?" Around the room, pastors nodded.

Another asked, "What should our policy be about couples who are cohabiting? An awful lot of those who now come to me are cohabiting. Their assumption is that "It is better to try on the shoe before wearing it."

I cited data that those who cohabit greatly increase their odds of divorce. Reverend Garth Bolinder, then pastor of Modesto Covenant Church, sighed: "If it's true that couples take a great risk in living together, my failure to insist on biblical principles—*my compassion*—is putting them in jeopardy." Reverend Jim Talley said that he insisted that couples living together separate during marriage preparation, and even offered financial help, if needed, to set up separate housekeeping. Very few ever requested it. But separation prompted many engagements to break before the wedding, thus, pastors saw that such a stand would help avoid future divorce. But the Policy did not become a "Community Marriage Policy" either.

The toughest question came from Reverend Charlie Crane, the pastor of Greater True Light Baptist Church. He noted that "80% of all black families are single-parent families. Our number-one problem is to encourage these guys to get married and face their responsibility. If I waited months, I'd lose half of them. I try to marry them as fast as I can." I had no answer. Nor did anyone else. His case was the best argument against a Community Marriage Policy that I ever heard. Nevertheless, I noticed later that he had signed the covenant, and I asked him why.

"Because it's the right thing to do," he replied. Three years later, I asked Pastor Crane how it had worked out. "It has benefited *me*. Before, I felt I had a sermon with no strings attached, with no real meaning. Now it has very much more meaning. I try to have six sessions over six months. If neither are Christian, I will try to lead them to Christ. If they are living together, I try to separate them. One couple did so and now attends the church regularly."

Talley, who is a Paul Bunyan of a man, standing six feet seven inches, handed out the "Community Marriage Policy" and said, "I think we ought to sign this now before Mike goes home. Whether it was intimidation or inspiration, most did so, forty-four in all, on January 28, 1986. In subsequent weeks, Jim encouraged fifty-one more pastors, priests, and one rabbi to sign the covenant—a total of ninety-five from every major denomination.

The combination of our efforts led sunny Modesto to become America's first city to boast of an aggressive strategy to cut the divorce rate. It was one of the proudest moments of my life. It gave me hope that the demise of marriage in America might be reversed.

Below is what they agreed to, a statement unchanged from Talley's draft. I've never seen such remarkable candor about the failure of a local church to equip people for marriage—nor such an ecumenical determination to do a better job.

MODESTO'S COMMUNITY MARRIAGE POLICY

I. *Concern: Marriage Is Holy*

One concern as ministers of the Gospel is to foster lasting marital unions under God and to establish successful spiritual families. Almost ninety percent of all marriages are performed by pastors, and we are troubled by the nearly fifty percent divorce rate. Our hope is to radically reduce the divorce rate among those married in area churches.

It is the responsibility of pastors to set minimum requirements to raise the quality of the commitment in those we marry. We believe that couples who seriously participate in premarital testing and counseling will have a better understanding of what the marriage commitment involves. As agents of God, acting on His behalf, we feel it is our responsibility to encourage couples to set aside time for marriage preparation instead of concentrating only on wedding plans. We acknowledge that a wedding is but a day; a marriage is for a lifetime.

II. *Scripture: "What God hath joined together, let no man separate"*
(Matt. 19:6).

God has established and sanctified marriage for the welfare and happiness of the human family. For this reason, our Savior has declared that a man shall leave his father and mother and be joined to his wife, and the two shall become one. By His apostles he has instructed those who enter into this relationship to cherish a mutual esteem and love; to share in each other's infirmities and weaknesses; to comfort each other in sickness, trouble, and sorrow; to provide for each other and for their household; to pray for and encourage each other; to live together as heirs of the grace of life; and to raise children, if there are any, in the knowledge and love of the Lord. In Malachi 2:13–16, it says that God hates divorce, and in Ephesians 5, the image of marriage is that of Christ and His church.

III. *Implementation: These are the minimum expectations:*
   A. *Waiting period:* A minimum of four months from the initial marital appointment until the wedding date.
   B. *Premarital Counseling:* A minimum of two sessions that would include a relational instrument, inventory, or test (Meyers/Briggs, or Taylor-Johnson Temperament Analysis) to help the couple evaluate the maturity of their relationship objectively.
   C. *Scripture:* Teach biblical doctrines on morality, marriage, and divorce. Encourage couples to memorize key verses on marriage.
   D. *Engagement Seminar:* Encourage the couple to participate in a concentrated period of joint introspection.
   E. *Helping Couples:* Provide, as needed, a mature married couple to meet with them to assist in the concept of marital "bonding."
   F. *Postmarital:* Commit ourselves to counseling the couple as needed.

IV. *Covenant:*
   A. I covenant to build successful spiritual families.
   B. I covenant to follow Scripture and to implement these minimum preparations for the couples that I marry, to substantially reduce the divorce rate in our area.
   C. I covenant to join with other spiritual leaders to encourage couples to seriously participate in premarital preparation.

_____   _____
Signed   Date

IMPACT OF COMMUNITY MARRIAGE POLICY IN MODESTO

Three years later, in 1989, I visited Modesto to see if there were any signs of the impact of the Community Marriage Policy (CMP). What I sensed was a new feeling of pride and backbone among the clergy. The Reverend Wayne Bridegroom (Isn't that appropriate!) of Central Baptist Church said that the CMP gave him "something to lean on that helped me express my convictions and ammunition to say to couples, 'If all you want to do is get married, go find a Justice of the Peace. If you want to work toward something that is really lasting, you need to do it the way we suggest.' In the past, every couple I agreed to marry without adequate time for premarital work—*every single one of them—is divorced. I refuse to do it anymore.*"

Another result was that pastors who had made no demands in the past began to insist upon them; and those with already solid programs made them stronger. Reverend Prichard Amstutz, who gave no counseling to unchurched couples, "because I did not see the seriousness of it," now has a minimum of two sessions. On the other hand, the Reverend John Blakeley of the large and growing Neighborhood Church, said, "We have gone to a six-month process, broadening the requirements of our premarital counseling to twelve hours of teaching. We show four hours of videos, "Maximum Marriage," and have several assigned books. . . . I have been fortified by the covenant to say to some that "This may not be the best time for you to get married." He noted, "One girl was very insecure and had a poor self-image." With the delay and help, she built new confidence and married a year later.

The story that best symbolizes the change in Modesto came from an American Baptist Church pastor. A couple whom he did not know asked him to marry them. He explained the four-month minimum-preparation period and the six required counseling sessions when the man interrupted: "We don't need that many. We've already had three counseling sessions at First Baptist." The surprised pastor asked, "Then why aren't you getting married over there?" The man sheepishly looked at his shoes and said, "Well, they found out we are living together and told us we have to separate." The pastor replied: "We have the same standard here, but you'd have to start all over. I suggest that you separate and go back to First Baptist." They did so. Thus, even pastors who compete for church members are cooperating.

Through one of my columns this case came to the attention of H. Norman Wright, America's most prolific writer on Christian lifelong marriage, with thirty books to his credit. In his 1992 book, *The Premarital Counseling Handbook,*[2] Wright said that the Modesto couple married at First Baptist now has "a much better chance for success in their marriage."

---

[2] H. Norman Wright, *The Premarital Counseling Handbook*, Moody Press, 1992.

For too many years it has been too easy to get married. Unfortunately, in many cases the church has contributed to the divorce problem of our nation by promoting easy weddings. People have spent more time preparing to obtain their driver's license than in preparing for their marriage. The situation is changing. A growing number of programs are designed to prepare couples for marriage. One with great promise is the "Community Marriage Policy," which originated in the central California community of Modesto, where church pastors adopted a community-wide marriage policy in 1986 to make it tougher to get married. . . . Modesto demonstrates that churches can raise their standards for marriage preparation with a uniform community policy.

DID THE DIVORCE RATE DROP?

I had predicted that the Community Marriage Policy would slash Modesto's divorce rate in half. During my 1989 visit I checked the numbers. Divorces had begun to edge down even though the population was jumping due to the proximity of lower-cost Modesto to San Francisco.

There were 1,923 divorces in 1987. They fell to 1,821 in 1988. In fact, that was slightly below the 1,833 divorces of 1985! Yet, in that time, the population jumped from 133,000 to 145,000. That was a 5% drop of divorces in a time when population grew by 9%. A number of national magazines took note of these facts and pronounced the Community Marriage Policy a success. *Christianity Today* headlined a full-page story on September 8, 1989: CHURCHES UNITE TO TAKE A STAND TO PREVENT DIVORCE. *Charisma and Christian Life* wrote in its April 1990 article: "At a time when the divorce rate remains high across the country, it is falling in Modesto, California. One reason may be that the clergy of this middle-class town in the San Joaquin Valley have taken steps to prevent divorce among couples for whom they conduct wedding ceremonies."

The divorce figure bounced around in subsequent years, dropping as low as 1,566 in 1990—an apparent plunge of 18% since 1987. But the figure for 1991 was 1,985—about where it was in 1987. The population, however, had spurted up to 172,000, 27% ahead of 1985.

I am disappointed that there was not an absolute and major decline of divorces. True, if the divorces had grown with the population, there would have been 350 more divorces in 1991 alone than there were and about 700 more in 1990. But I continue to believe that if *all* churches would sign on to a Community Marriage Policy that a town's divorces would drop by half. One problem is that only a third of Modesto's 300 churches have signed up. Though the largest churches are involved, there are still many "Marrying Sams" around. Of course, the people who are most likely to divorce are those whom the churches never see—the 800 cohabiting couples a year who have "confidential marriages" at City Hall. . . .

268

Norm Wright adds: "There has not been enough time for the Community Marriage Policy to have an effect. The average marriage ending in divorce takes seven years. The better bonding of couples married in 1987 to 1990 should be seen during 1994 to 1997."

COMMUNITY MARRIAGE POLICY SPREADS IN CALIFORNIA

Thrilled by Modesto's success in creating a Community Marriage Policy, I wrote two columns about it in 1986. That sparked invitations to present the idea in other California cities, four of which adopted a CMP.

Fresno, California: Fresno added a fresh element to the core approach in Modesto: pastor training. The first to create a CMP modeled on Modesto's pioneering effort, Fresno, located ninety miles south in the San Joaquin Valley, had 105 pastors sign the covenant in 1987. The Reverend David Bunker, on staff of a ministry called Love in the Name of Christ (Love *INC*), assumed responsibility for organizing seminars to train pastors to do a better job in strengthening marriage. One Saturday seminar focused on different forms of premarital questionnaires that might be given to the engaged. Another grappled with the difficult problems of "blended families," in which the husband or wife (or both) have been previously married. Nearly half of all marriages today involve a formerly married person. For children, this can be as traumatic as divorce itself. Therefore, it is healthy for clergy associations to learn better how to bond couples. Yet I know of no clergy association or council of churches that focuses on marriage and divorce—except those with a Community Marriage Policy.

Tracy, California: Jim Talley was invited by pastors in nearby Turlock and Tracy, California, to explain the Modesto policy that he had drafted. Both towns launched Community Marriage Policies. In 1992 I called Reverend Don Higgins, pastor of Crossroads Christian Church in Tracy and asked about CMP's impact.

Pastor Higgins replied, "Usually a mom calls up and says, 'My daughter is getting married in two weeks, and we need a minister. We want a church wedding.' "What they are saying is that, "We want the church's blessing." They want us to show up and say a few words and leave. When they find out that we have this policy requiring four months' lead time, counseling, and a commitment to remain celibate— time to allow me to share with your daughter the biblical aspects of the marriage, with an emphasis on using premarital inventories to promote a lot of communication—the mom says, "I understand. That's great. I see that you really do care.' They hang up and I never hear from them again! That has happened virtually every time. I could have a wedding every weekend. Instead, I have one about every three to four months."

Vacaville was the fifth city in California to adopt a CMP after I spoke there, but I was unable to sell the clergy of Sacramento or Bakersfield. Why?

Because too few showed up to make a community-wide policy credible to those who did attend. The organizers of clergy participation failed to involve top leaders of the three branches of Christianity—Catholic, Evangelical, and mainline Protestantism.

Fairbanks, Alaska, Pastors Strengthen Policy:

Mrs. Terry Reichardt, director of a ministry called Love *INC*, invited me to Fairbanks in February 1990 (when the temperature is -43 degrees) to speak about CMP. A committee of pastors wanted to modify two of Modesto's requirements. One pastor said, "This is a military area, with personnel coming and going on short notice. We feel that a three-month preparation period is the most we can ask. However, we notice that Modesto requires only two counseling sessions. We think there should be at least six." I replied, "Fine. There is nothing sacred about the elements of the covenant. It has to make sense to you in your area. I particularly like your strengthening Modesto's counseling requirement."

The Fairbanks Daily *News Miner*, which publishes my column, helped underwrite the cost of my 6000-mile trip to the Arctic Circle. Though only seventeen clergy agreed to the Community Marriage Policy, it was front-page news! The story began, "Couples planning a church wedding will have to wait at least three months and undergo religious counseling before saying 'I do,' because of a new policy adopted by some local churches." More important, the paper wrote an editorial, published March 4, 1990, excerpted below:

> Fairbanks has a family problem that needs a solution. The rate at which families disintegrate is greater in our community than it is in the United States at large. . . . Numerous organizations exist to help people pick up the pieces after going through the agony of a broken marriage. Now some local churches are trying to make sure that the vows exchanged at marriage ceremonies are not unceremoniously broken by divorce. . . .

> The high divorce rate is a troubling phenomenon that creates havoc in the lives of adults and children who go through it. Michael McManus, a nationally syndicated columnist whose writing regularly appears in the Fairbanks Daily *News Miner*, recently presented a seminar here on what churches can do to reduce the number of divorces. . . .

> Anyone can walk into the state courthouse and get a marriage license in four days. About 25 to 30 couples say 'I do' at the courthouse every month. It's quick and simple. With such an effective civil system in place, there is no reason for churches to be marriage factories. After all, religious institutions have different responsibilities from those of government agencies. If people want to get married in a church, then it seems appropriate that the churches should do something to increase the odds that those people will stay married. Training and discussion of spiritual principles are vital if the union is to work. . . .

In the interest of stronger marriages and a reduction in the divorce rate, we hope that more of the 100-plus churches in the Fairbanks and North Pole areas embrace this policy.

That editorial had an impact. The number of pastors signing the policy doubled from seventeen to thirty-five, and more pastors are adhering to the CMP but have not signed it. But there are about fifty small, independent Baptist churches who refuse to cooperate with anybody. Many of them are Marrying Sams, but they are "under a lot of pressure to stop doing it," says Mrs. Reichardt.

What's been CMP's impact in Fairbanks? There are *fewer* church weddings! Many pastors are getting angry calls from people who have made the rounds: "What's the matter with you guys in Fairbanks?" said one man who wanted a quickie wedding. "There's not a a pastor in Fairbanks who will marry us. Why don't they marry people anymore?"

One who has received such calls is Pastor Verle Peterson of Fairbanks Covenant Church. "The major thing the Community Marriage Policy has done for us is that it has helped us stand up and say, 'This is not a service we pass out wholesale. There is a meaning to a Christian marriage.' It has also changed the communication between me and the congregation. The congregation has voted to become part of that. In other words, members of the congregation have agreed that their pastor will uphold the standards even if there is pressure by an elder to marry a daughter in less time."

Like Fresno, Fairbanks clergy also put on occasional workshops to help pastors implement the policy. A "Support Couples Seminar" encouraged ministers to find older couples to share experiences with the engaged and newlyweds. A PREPARE/ENRICH Seminar trained pastors in using those instruments to diagnose the strengths and weaknesses of couples. A third seminar on Budget Counseling was offered to both clergy and couples, addressing the fact that there are more arguments over money than about any other issue. Some clergy now ask the budget seminar expert to help train their couples.

MEDIA SUPPORT HELPS SPREAD
COMMUNITY MARRIAGE POLICIES

The above editorial in a daily newspaper should encourage clergy in other communities considering a CMP. It shows that there is media support for their effort to demand more of couples: more time, more preparation, more deliberation—before they can get married in a church. Nor is this unique. Newspapers publishing my column were partners with local clergy in creating nine Community Marriage Policies in addition to Fairbanks: Fresno, Modesto, Vacaville, Kokomo, Indiana; Bethel, Connecticut; Homestead, Florida; and three Illinois cities (Moline-Rock Island, Peoria, Quincy) where the papers also wrote heartening editorials. (Other cities with CMPs are Beaver, Pennsylvania; Cuyahoga Falls, Ohio; Tracy and Turlock, California).

FAILURES AND LESSONS IN LAUNCHING
COMMUNITY MARRIAGE POLICIES

By 1992, Community Marriage Policies had been established in fourteen cities noted above. It was heartening to see CMPs planted in different parts of America. To be candid, however, I failed to persuade the clergy of Seattle and Jacksonville to do so. Why? They are larger metropolitan areas.

And in neither case was a bishop-level executive involved. This leads me to conclude that it is essential to have a Catholic, Lutheran, or Episcopalian bishop or a Baptist Superintendent take the lead in organizing in a larger city—a church leader with enough prestige to convince peers in other denominations to get involved.

I discovered, however, that there is a more difficult problem to overcome even in smaller communities. The three branches of American Christianity—Roman Catholicism, evangelical and mainline Protestantism—simply do not cooperate. Pastors in one of those three worlds know many local clergy within their tradition but not in the other two. Catholic priests rarely participate in anything with Protestants. Evangelicals only talk to each other—certainly not to Episcopalians and Methodists or Catholic priests. Local Councils of Churches invariably have only mainline Protestant participants. The Sacramento Council of Churches helped gather people for my presentation, but it did not get evangelicals or Catholics involved. Without the three legs of the Christian stool cooperating, a Community Marriage Policy will fall over like a two-legged stool.

Frankly, it is not easy to launch a Community Marriage Policy. There are two essential ingredients:

1. Some prestigious local religious leaders must assume leadership. In Modesto the two key people were Jim Talley and his boss, the pastor of First Baptist Church. Love *INC* boards also took a lead.
2. All three branches of Christian churches must be involved at the outset. The absence of any key segment dooms the policy. Too many marriages involve people from different denominations.

EPISCOPAL CHURCH ENDORSES
COMMUNITY MARRIAGE POLICY

A fresh answer surfaced in 1991 when the Episcopal Church became the first national denomination to endorse a Community Marriage Policy. What's more, a resolution passed at the church's triennial General Convention in Phoenix calls upon the bishop of each diocese to take the lead in organizing minimal community requirements for all who want to get married in a local church, including:

> a significant preparation period and a minimum number of premarital counseling sessions; the training of married couples as mentors and role models for engaged couples; teaching of biblical doctrines on morality, marriage, and divorce; encouraging both engaged and married couples to participate in intensive weekend seminars such as Engaged Encounter or Marriage Enrichment; and post-nuptial support for already married couples.

The resolution explained that "No one can deny that marriage, the most precious institution in human civilization, is in crisis." It cited the high divorce rate and added, "We are called as a church to respond. The Episcopal Church could have a significant part in strengthening marriage and reducing the divorce rate. At the parish level, clergy and trained lay leaders could, in their parishes and communities, take the lead in calling together representatives of many denominations in order to create an ecumenical "Community Marriage Policy," in which pastors of congregations join together in covenant to strengthen the marriage vows—following an agreed statement of minimal requirements."

The Episcopal bishop most responsible for the resolution's passage, Rt. Rev. Edward MacBurney, has demonstrated how to implement that resolution. He shows how much one single committed religious leader can do to launch a Community Marriage Policy movement. He planted CMPs in all three cities within his Illinois diocese: Quincy, Moline-Rock Island, and Peoria. More important, thanks to his leadership, the Community Marriage Policy has become as focused on how to *save* existing marriages as it has on preparing young people for marriage.

ILLINOIS CITIES PUT EQUAL EMPHASIS ON POST-WEDDING DEMANDS

When Bishop MacBurney invited me to join him in creating CMPs in Peoria, Quincy, and Moline-Rock Island in October 1991, he wanted to place an equal emphasis on post-wedding strategies to save marriages as well as marriage preparation. He invited Catholic Bishop John Myers and leading Assemblies of God pastor, Reverend Paul Martin, to co-sponsor the Peoria Community Marriage Policy with the Episcopal diocese. Nor was this just a letterhead collaboration. The night before we made the public presentation, Bishop MacBurney invited them and the editor of the Peoria *Journal-Star* to a dinner at his home. There the religious leaders decided to draft a second generation of Community Marriage Policies that built upon Modesto's pioneering. In the version submitted to the clergy the next day were four new elements aimed at revitalizing and saving existing marriages:

273

1. At least one post-marital counseling session with mentor couples.
2. An encouragement for all married couples to attend a couples' retreat such as Marriage Encounter or Marriage Enrichment.
3. Create a Marriage Ministry of mentoring couples whose marriages once nearly failed, to work with troubled marriages.
4. We pastors will cooperate fully to learn more about how to bond couples for life.

The *Journal-Star* reported that at the next day's meeting, "More than 70 religious leaders—Peoria's largest gathering of religious leaders from all denominations since the 1970s—turned out at St. Paul's Episcopal Cathedral." Bishop MacBurney opened by saying: "We are looking at a problem that concerns all of us, the growing incidence of poor marriages and multiplying divorces. Young couples come to us thinking 'wedding.' It is our responsibility to focus them on 'marriage.' "

Peoria area clergy from nineteen denominations not only endorsed the drafted CMP but added to it. First, they decided to require two post-marital counseling sessions, because it is after the wedding that most problems surface. Second, a pastor urged that the policy be taken "back to our churches to be ratified by the appropriate boards" to give it extra weight and to make the policy binding upon that church's future clergy. Another pastor said, "Before we urge others to go on a retreat (such as Marriage Encounter), the clergy should be the first to go." Both policies were added to the Peoria Covenant, and when we took the Peoria version to Moline-Rock Island and to Quincy, dozens of pastors in each city also adopted Peoria's Ten-Step CMP for their own cities, without making any changes.

The Peoria Community Marriage Policy is a national model. First, it endorses strategies with a proven potential to help engaged couples make a wise choice and to prepare for a lifelong marriage. Its wording on the premarital steps is also clearer than that of Modesto. Second, it puts a welcome new emphasis on deepening and refreshing existing marriages and on restoring those that are breaking. Since it is an improvement on the Modesto version and is a better model for other cities, I quote the complete text of the Peoria version:

PEORIA COMMUNITY MARRIAGE POLICY

I. *Concern: Marriage Is Holy*

Our concern as ministers of the Gospel is to foster lasting marital unions under God and to establish successful spiritual families. Almost 75% of all marriages are performed by pastors, and we are troubled by the more than 50% divorce rate. Our concern is to radically reduce the divorce rate among those married in area churches.

It is the responsibility of pastors to set minimal requirements to raise the quality of commitment in those we marry. We believe that couples who seriously participate in premarital testing and counseling will have a better understanding of what the marriage commitment involves. As agents of God, acting on his behalf, we feel it is our responsibility to encourage couples to set aside time for marriage preparation instead of concentrating only on wedding plans. We acknowledge that a wedding is but a day; a marriage is for a lifetime.

Suggested Policy for Peoria by:

The Reverend Paul Martin, Faith Christian Assembly of God Church
The Rt. Reverend Edward MacBurney, Diocese of Quincy (Episcopal)
The Most Reverend John Myers, Diocese of Peoria (Roman Catholic)

1. A minimum of four months' marriage preparation.
2. A minimum of four counseling sessions with one devoted to the use of a premarital test or inventory and one devoted to the biblical understanding of marriage and divorce.
3. Training of leader/mentor couples in each church to work as role models and counselors with engaged couples.
4. Attendance at an '"Engaged Encounter" weekend or seminar for engaged couples to improve communication skills and to establish their marriage with Christ at the center.
5. At least two post-marital counseling sessions with a mentor couple, six months after the wedding and one year after the wedding.
6. Encouragement for all married couples to attend a couples' retreat such as Marriage Encounter or Marriage Enrichment.
7. Create a Marriage Ministry of mentoring couples whose marriages once nearly failed, to work with troubled marriages.
8. We pastors will cooperate fully to learn more about how to bond couples for life.
9. The clergy should be the first to attend a couples' retreat, and many of us will go to a Family Life Ministries' "Weekend to Remember."
10. As pastors we will take this covenant back to our churches to be ratified by the appropriate boards of our churches.

Signed: Pastor _____
Address: _____

IMPACT OF PEORIA'S COMMUNITY MARRIAGE POLICY

Peoria's successful Community Marriage Policy immediately sparked diverse positive spin-offs. The day after thirty-eight clergy in Peoria signed its Community Marriage Policy, a similarly sized group from the Moline-Rock Island, Illinois area adopted the same Policy. Within days, dozens more in Quincy, Illinois, did so, thanks to the organizing effort of Bishop MacBurney. Neither city changed a word of Peoria's text. *The Rock Island Argus* began its page-one story with a quote from me: "The breakdown of the American family is the central domestic problem of our time. The church is part of the problem, and I have real hope that it can be part of the solution."

The Quincy Herald Whig noted that a committee of pastors had organized to follow up, and praised their initiative: "All pastors of all churches have an interest in doing everything possible to help the people they marry stay married. A Community Marriage Policy provides a framework that helps ministers discharge such a responsibility."

But what ultimately matters is what transpires in individual churches. Quite by accident, I learned of a dramatic result in a Peoria congregation, as I was reading the September/October 1992 issue of *The Presbyterian Layman*, a national newspaper with 400,000 circulation. After signing the Peoria CMP, the Reverend Roane Deckert of the Northminster Presbyterian Church has taken his own new initiatives. First, he convinced the church session to endorse the CMP as church policy. Second, he now tells engaged couples, "We want to help you prepare for marriage, not just for the wedding" and outlines what happens in the four months of preparation: meeting with one of five "mentor couples"; the taking of PREPARE to learn "communication and conflict-resolution skills"; and attending an Engaged Encounter weekend, and the need for a "post-wedding check-up" with their mentor couples six months after the wedding.

Finally, Pastor Deckert preached a sermon noting "that many previously launched marriages are in trouble." He asked Northminster couples who have "been to the edge and back" to step forward and meet with him after the worship service, to consider helping "other couples make it through rough water as well." *Fourteen* couples remained afterward. Over time, they identified a list of recurring Marriage Ministry Principles, or "turning points" that helped them weather their difficulties. Now these "M&M" couples, as they are known, volunteer to provide "consultant care" to any couples seeking help. Church literature describes it: "Those who wish to consult in confidence with one of these couples may simply contact one of the pastors. These loving couples will listen with sympathy and understanding and share with you the M&M principles that have worked for them."

Seven years from now, on the two thousandth anniversary of the birth of Our Lord, may your church and 100,000 others be able to report many thrilling *results* of such Marriage Saver efforts!

A FINAL WORD

All of us know marriages that are in trouble. For years I did not know what to say to my brother or sister, for example, but in reporting my column, "Ethics & Religion," I came across so many sources of hope that I decided to write *Marriage Savers* to put the answers down in one place. And I've written this book, packaging the solutions in chapters on a given age or marital status. If your daughter is engaged, she should read chapters 6 and 7. If your brother's marriage is breaking apart, tell him to read chapter 10.

More important, *you* can have the rewarding experience of being a Marriage Saver. There are so many ways to do so. One is simply passing on information. If your son is tempted to be sexually active, you can tell him: "If you remain a virgin 'til you marry, you cut your odds of divorce by 60%!" Or if you know someone who is cohabiting in a "trial marriage," you now know what to say: "Marriage is not something that can be tried on like a pair of shoes. People who live together before marriage increase their odds of divorce by 50%." It takes courage to say such things, but no more than telling a smoking teenager, "You will cut eighteen years off your life if you continue smoking." The job of a parent or an elder in a church is to pass on the wisdom that comes with the gray hair.

If your son just became engaged, give him a present that could help him put God at the center of his relationship—Engaged Encounter. How much more useful is that gift than sterling salad servers? And give him twenty-five dollars for the couple to take PREPARE with a pastor or counselor of their choice.

Jesus said, "What God hath joined together, let man not separate." And what God has joined together, *let other married couples help hold together.* You, too, can begin a mentor couple program in your own church.

If you are really ambitious and want to save not only marriages of family and friends, you could help organize a Community Marriage Policy.

If you are an attorney or a politician, you could be a Marriage Saver by working to reform your state's no-fault divorce laws.

You, too, can be a Marriage Saver. *A Marriage Saver is a Life Saver!*

Of course, you cannot be a Marriage Saver unless your own marriage is strong and vibrant. "Don't permit the *possibility* of divorce to enter your thinking. Even in moments of great conflict and discouragement, divorce is no solution."[3] If your own marriage is sound but lacking in joy, go on a Marriage Encounter with your spouse. You will fall back in love with each other! *Give your relationship that present.* My prayer for every reader is that your marriage will be so full of joy that you will *want* to help save the mar-

---

[3]Dr. James Dobson, *Love for a Lifetime*, Multnomah Press, Portland, Oregon, 1987.

riages of others: those of your children, your friends, and marriages of people you will never meet. For example, if you help your town create a Community Marriage Policy, dozens of churches that you will never set foot in will become Marriage Savers like Northminster Presbyterian Church in Peoria! The Lord can multiply the effort of any of us who are yielded to him.

May the Lord bless your efforts as *Marriage Savers*.

Appendix

Marriage Savers reports on many different ministries whose long-term goal is to help bond couples in life-long marriages. This Appendix is a quick reference guide to the most effective ministries reported on, divided by age and marital status, like the book itself. I have made a few comments to summarize each ministry. If none of the ministries below seem targeted at a reader's need, the best single source on all matters on the family is Focus on the Family (Colorado Springs, CO 80995). It answers 10,000 letters per day, yet all get a personal reply.

A. *For Teenagers:* The primary goal of these ministries is to help teens develop self-discipline and a commitment to chastity (chapter 4):

Courses taught in public schools:

SEX RESPECT
Respect Incorporated
P.O. Box 349
Bradley, IL 60915
815-932-8389

Teen Aid, Inc.
1330 N. Kalispel
Spokane, WA 99201
509-328-2080

Postponing Sexual Involvement
Teen Services Program
Grady Memorial Hospital
P.O. Box 26158
Atlanta, GA 30335-3801

For a church youth group (a program used by 60,000 churches so far):

Josh McDowell
Why Wait?
P.O. Box 1000
Dallas, TX 75221
214-907-1000

B. *For Seriously Dating Couples* (Relationship Instruction, a four-month course, described in Chapter 5.)

> Dr. Jim Talley
> Relationship Instruction
> 4216 N. Portland Ave.
> Oklahoma City, OK 73112
> 405-949-2227

C. *For Engaged Couples*

1. PREPARE is a Premarital Inventory to help a couple assess the strengths and areas for growth in their relationship. Described in Chapter 6, it is normally administered by a counselor or pastor, 20,000 of whom have been trained to give it in many denominations. For a list of those trained in your area in your denomination to offer PREPARE—or for a schedule of future training sessions, write:

> PREPARE/ENRICH
> P.O. Box 190
> Minneapolis, MN 55440-0190

2. Engaged Encounter is an intensive weekend retreat attended by 30,000 engaged couples in 1991. It is *the* best teacher of communication skills in America. The weekends are organized by lay Catholics, Methodists, Presbyterians, Lutherans, Episcopalians and Reformed. Write:

> Dave and Millie Florijan
> Engaged Encounter
> 5 Tara Drive
> Pittsburgh, PA 15209
> 412-487-5116

3. Growing Together is a small group program for premarital couples and/or newlyweds that builds on the PREPARE/ENRICH inventories, focusing on such issues as families-of-origin, communications, sexuality, conflict resolution, finances, and planning for growth. See address above.

D. *Newlyweds* are rarely thought of as needing help, but half of couples are horrified by unexpected conflict. For an objective analysis of their difficulties, Chapter 8 recommends couples take ENRICH, a marital inventory similar to PREPARE, but aimed at the already married couple. The address and phone are listed above for both those qualified to administer the questionnaire, and for dates to train pastors/counselors. Newlyweds should also attend weekend retreats listed below for married couples.

E. *Married Couples* can strengthen their marriages by going to Marriage Encounter, attended by 1.5 million couples to date. Chapter 9 reports that nine out of ten couples fall back in love with their spouse, at a deeper level.

A call to the 800 phone of Worldwide Marriage Encounter can put you in touch with someone in your area in one of 10 denominations that organizes ME weekend retreats. Two other groups organize ME weekends: National Marriage Encounter in which there is a mix of Christian traditions at each weekend, and United Marriage Encounter that is mainline Protestant in orientation. An evangelical version of a weekend designed to refresh a marriage is organized by Family Life Conferences of Campus Crusade for Christ, attended by 22,300 couples—both married and engaged. Finally, Marriage Enrichment offers retreats and support groups that reach 18,000 couples a year. The retreats do offer dialogue between couples attending, while the other versions make the experience private, with dialogue only between husband and wife.

Worldwide Marriage Encounter
1908 E. Highland #A
San Bernadino, CA 92404
800-795-LOVE

National Marriage Encounter
4704 Jamerson Pl.
Orlando, FL 32807
800-828-3351

United Marriage Encounter
P.O. Box 209
Muscatine, Iowa 52761
800-334-8920

Family Life Ministries
P.O. Box 23840
Little Rock, Ark. 72221-3840
501-223-8663

Marriage Enrichment
P.O. Box 10596
Winston Salem, N.C. 27108
800-634-8325

F. *The seriously troubled marriage* can be saved! Chapter 10 puts a spotlight on two approaches: Marriage Ministry, developed by a local church listed below, has equipped seven couples whose marriages once nearly failed to help 33 others now in trouble, none of whom have divorced. Send $5 for information since this is not a national ministry. Retrouvaille ("Rediscovery") is a Catholic, lay-led movement similar to Marriage Encounter, which is in 58 larger Catholic dioceses. Protestants may attend. Half of the 2,400 couples who participated in 1992 were separated or divorced, but 80% are rebuilding their marriages.

Marriage Ministry
St. David's Episcopal Church
12355 Fort Caroline Rd.
Jacksonville, Florida 32225
904-641-8177

Retrouvaille
209 Fanning Dr.
Hurst, Tex. 76053
817-284-7078

G. *Community Marriage Policy* is a movement Mike McManus has launched in more than a dozen cities. Up to 105 pastors of all major denominations in a community have agreed to minimal standards of marriage preparation and support for existing marriages. As Chapter 12 explains, anyone getting married in a Peoria Church, for example, must take four months of marriage preparation that includes PREPARE, four counseling sessions before the wedding and two afterward with a mentor couple, attending Engaged Encounter, and study of Scripture. Married couples are all urged to attend a marriage enrichment weekend, and pastors have agreed to create Marriage Ministries to save marriages in serious crisis or to refer them to Retrouvaille. For further information contact the author:

Michael J. McManus
Community Marriage Policy
9500 Michael's Court
Bethesda, Maryland 20817
301-469-5870 (nights only)

The author is grateful to the following authors and publishers for permission to quote from the following works:

Miriam Arond and Samuel L. Pauker, M. D., *The First Year of Marriage*, by Warner Books, copyright © 1987. Professor Larry Bumpass, Center for Demography and Ecology at the University of Wisconsin, *National Survey of Families and Households* Working Papers #2 and #5, 1989. Dr. James C. Dobson, *Love Must Be Tough*, copyright 1983 by Word, Inc., and *Love for a Lifetime*, copyright 1987, published by Questar Publishers; Multnomah Press. All rights reserved. Used with permission. Julia Duin, *Purity Makes the Heart Grow Stronger*, Servant Publications, 1988. George Gallup, Jr., for Gallup Poll surveys conducted in 1989. Andrew M. Greeley for quotes from *Faithful Attraction*, published by Tom Doherty Associates, Inc., 1991. Marion Howard, Ph.D., for quotes from her course, *Postponing Sexual Involvement* and *How to Help Your Teenager Postpone Sexual Involvement*, by Continuum Publishing Co., 1988. Dr. David B. Larson and his wife, Susan, who wrote "Divorce: A Hazard to Your Health" in *Physician* magazine, 1991. Kathryn A. London, Ph.D. and Joan R. Kahn, Ph.D., for their article, "Premarital Sex and the Risk of Divorce," in *Journal of Marriage and the Family*, November, 1991. Coleen Kelly Mast, for her course, *SEX RESPECT: The Option of True Sexual Freedom*, copyright 1986, Respect, Inc. Josh McDowell, for his course, *"Why Wait?"* by Thomas Nelson Publishers, 1987. Episcopal Bishop John Shelby Spong, for *Living in Sin? A Bishop Rethinks Human Sexuality*, by Harper & Row, 1988. Jim A. Talley, Ph. D. and Bobbie Reed, for *Too Close Too Soon*, by Thomas Nelson Publishers, 1982. And Stan E. Weed, Ph. D., for his 1992 study, *Family Accountability Communicating Teen Sexuality (FACTS)*. Copyright © 1992, from "Bridal Magazines Find Cupid Is Recession-Proof," by Deirdre Carmody, March 9, 1992, by the New York Times Company. Reprinted by permission. Bernie Siegel, M.D., *Love, Medicine, & Miracles*, HarperCollins, 1990. Arthur J. Norton and Paul Glick: "One-Parent Families: A Social and Economic Profile," published in *Family Relations*, January 1986. Judith Wallerstein and Sandra Blakeslee, *Second Chances: Men, Women, and Children a Decade After Divorce*. Ticknor & Fields, New York, 1989. *Divorce Busting*, by Michele Weiner-Davis, copyright © by Michele Weiner-Davis, MSW, CSW. Reprinted by permission of Summit Books, a division of Simon & Schuster, Inc. *THE DIVORCE REVOLUTION: The Unexpected Social and Economic Consequences for Women and Children in America*, by Lenora J. Weitzman, copyright © 1985 by Lenora J. Weitzman.